THE LIBERAL PARTY

Triumph and Disintegration, 1886–1929

G. R. SEARLE

M
MACMILLAN

First published 1992 by
THE MACMILLAN PRESS LTD
Houndmills, Basingstoke, Hampshire RG21 2XS
and London
Companies and representatives throughout the world

ISBN 0–333–55915–0 hardcover
ISBN 0–333–55916–9 paperback

A catalogue record for this book is available
from the British Library

Typeset by Footnote Graphics,
Warminster, Wiltshire
Printed in Hong Kong

THE LIBERAL PARTY

Triumph and Disintegration
1886--1929

British History in Perspective
General Editor: Jeremy Black

CONTENTS

ACKNOWLEDGEMENTS

I would like to thank Dr John Charmley, Dr Brian Hill, Dr Roger Virgoe and Dr Terry Jenkins for their advice and encouragement.

1

INTRODUCTION

Major political parties seldom disintegrate; at least that has been the experience of Britain over the last 200 years or more. They may go through a period of prolonged electoral unpopularity, as the Conservative Party did after the schism over the Repeal of the Corn Laws in 1846, or as Labour has done during the 1950s and 1980s. But parties of government, though sometimes written off, have usually bounced back again. The case of the Liberal Party is different. On the eve of the First World War it was enjoying its ninth successive year in office. But in the course of the War it underwent a fatal split and, despite spluttering attempts at revival in the 1920s, soon found itself on the fringes of national political life. By the mid-1930s the Liberals had dwindled to a rump of a mere twenty-one MPs. Only in the collapse of the Irish National Party and its replacement by Sinn Fein between 1917 and 1919 do we have anything remotely like this swift descent from glory to impotence.

But the collapse of the Liberal Party was not only unusual, it also had momentous consequences, since it heralded the arrival of the party duopoly which has survived to the present day: a party alignment with deep roots in social class. Quite simply, the replacement of the Liberals by Labour as the only serious alternative party to the Conservatives is the most important single development in early twentieth-century political life. No wonder that posterity has been preoccupied with the issue.

Unfortunately, so obsessive has been the search for the 'origins'

1

of the Liberal disintegration that it has distorted our understanding of the late Victorian and Edwardian Liberal Party. As
Trevor Wilson observed in a pioneering study first published a
quarter of a century ago, some have traced the start of the
process back to the 'Great Labour Unrest' of the pre-First World
War period; some to the foundation of the Labour Party at the
start of the century; and some to the split in the Party over Irish
Home Rule in 1886; 'to satisfy every view about when and why
the Liberal party met its doom', he comments, 'one might as well
go back to the time when there was a party bearing the name
Liberal at all'.[1] Wisdom of hindsight can so dominate our
thoughts that we are tempted to assume the imminent 'death' of
the Liberal Party almost before it had been born!

This distortion of vision has particularly affected the reading
of the electoral data. Obviously no party can expect an uninter-
rupted tenure of power. Even the most successful of parties loses
a general election from time to time. A single electoral reverse, or
even a sequence of reverses, does not usually signal the start of
an irreversible decline. But because we know the decline of the
Liberal Party to be just around the corner, the difference between losing an election and sliding into insignificance can easily
be overlooked.

For example, in the years immediately preceding the Great
War, the Liberal Ministry headed by Asquith ran into a patch of
deep electoral unpopularity. Irish Home Rule was on balance a
vote-loser, and many voters were displeased by having money
deducted from their wages to finance the recent National Insurance Act. Between 1911 and 1914 the Liberals lost no fewer than
fourteen seats to the Opposition in by-elections, in some of them
on swings to the Opposition that were very high by the standards of the day (10.8 in South Manchester in March 1912, for
example). Historians disagree over whether the government
would have been able to repair its fortunes in time for the general
election which, had war not broken out, would have been held
by December 1915 at the latest. The omens were not entirely
favourable. On the other hand, the Liberals had earlier recovered from a somewhat similar trough of mid-term unpopularity to win a qualified victory in the general election of January

1910.[2] In any case, even if the probability is that the Liberals' long run in office was indeed about to end in August 1914, that by itself does not necessarily tell us much about the reasons for the Party's subsequent decline.

Moreover, there is something very unsatisfactory about applying to the Liberal Party 'performance tests' that no sane person would apply to the Conservative or to the Labour Party, simply because we know that the latter 'survived', whereas the Liberals did not. Yet it would be easy to demonstrate that the Conservatives were themselves in deep crisis during the Edwardian decade, with weak leaders, serious policy divisions and a sad record of electoral failure (in 1914 they had lost three elections in a row). The Labour Party on the eve of the war faced an even more problematic future. All of its MPs owed their seats to the operation of an electoral pact with the Liberals, to whom they stood very much in the role of junior partners. True, in the immediate pre-war by-elections many Labour candidates took their courage in their hands and ran independently of the two major parties, but they all, without exception, came bottom of the poll. On the basis of evidence like this, one might be tempted to trace the origins of the Labour Party's inevitable decline back to the Edwardian years – except that, knowing what the future had in store, no-one would embark on so foolish an enterprise.[3]

Another aspect of Liberalism can easily be distorted by wisdom of hindsight. The Conservatives tend to subscribe to values of hierarchy, tradition and deference, and Labour rests on notion of class solidarity. The old Liberal Party, by contrast, was a party of ideas and ideals, much given to discussion and argument. This often made it appear fractious and quarrelsome. As we shall see, some of the Liberals' policy divisions were indeed damaging, especially when they led to personal rancour among the leadership (one thinks of the feud between Rosebery and Harcourt in the mid-1890s, or the later estrangement between Asquith and Lloyd George). But in many ways the debate about policy priorities could be seen as a sign of health, not of sickness. Walter Bagehot thought that the glory of the British political system resided in the fact that it involved 'government by discussion', and the Liberals were perhaps simply honouring the spirit

3

of that system when they engaged in open public debate – amongst one another, as well as with their political opponents. Nor should deep significance be read into all the leadership clashes. As A. B. Cooke and John Vincent pertinently observe:

> It is naive to think that the Liberals were bound to split because they were always quarrelling. Commentators who themselves lead the lives of church mice, note and are shocked by cabinet dissensions and tend to magnify the normal hurly-burly of politics as the end of the world. In fact, quarrelling was one of the party's greatest strengths, and the Tories' refusal to argue with each other led to an unenviable torpor.[4]

To conclude these preliminary observations, the larger question of when the Liberal Party went into irreversible decline is not being prejudged at this stage. It is important, however, to keep an open mind on the subject and not to forget that in the late Victorian and Edwardian years Liberalism was in many ways a vibrant and successful political movement, with major achievements and triumphs to its credit.

The Marxist Account

But there may be reasons for believing in the 'inevitability' of Liberal decline, quite other than a lazy assumption that what in fact happened was destined to happen. For the collapse of the Liberal Party in Britain was not an isolated occurrence. Liberal parties in other European countries suffered a similar fate at approximately the same time. So there is some plausibility in the contention that the fate of British Liberalism formed a part of some wider social and political development affecting all industrialised societies. And the most commonly accepted explanation of what underlay this world-wide 'crisis of Liberalism' is the one put forward by Marxists, though in its broad outlines it has also been followed by many historians who are not socialists of any kind.

This interpretation can be summarised as follows.[5] Liberalism was the ideology of the new entrepreneurial middle class thrown up by industrialisation, the Liberal Party serving as its principal

4

political agency. Liberalism expressed the hostility of businessmen towards the world of aristocratic and landed privilege. The
main objective of this creed was 'free trade', in its widest sense,
that is to say, a liberation of commercial and industrial life from
all trammels and interference, whether customary or legislative,
so as to maximise production and to secure optimum conditions
for economic growth. True, resentment against old monopolies
and privileges was usually expressed in a 'universalistic'
language. Liberals, with perfect sincerity, claimed to be furthering the interests of 'the People': they spoke, not of the needs of
capital, but of individual rights and of citizenship. Indeed, many
members of the lower orders (manual workers included) joined
energetically in the assault on the old 'feudal' order. But the
'freedoms' and liberties which Liberals espoused were all, in
essence, class-specific, rooted in the economic needs of the
bourgeoisie.

But Liberalism, Marxists claim, could only flourish in the
early, pioneering, optimistic phase of capitalist development. By
the last quarter of the nineteenth century social and economic
circumstances were no longer so favourable to the Liberal cause.
Joint stock company legalisation and amalgamations had led to
the replacement of the individual entrepreneur (the owner-
manager characteristic of the early industrial revolution) by the
large impersonal corporation. As the size of the average business
unit increased, so the gap between employers and their workforce
grew too large for the successful display of employer paternal-
ism. Paralleling these developments was growing social segrega-
tion in the big cities, as the middle classes withdrew to the outer
suburbs, leaving behind them working-class areas over which
they could exercise little direct influence. Moreover, sharpening
the social tensions generated by these changes in the last quarter
of the century was the onset of a world-wide industrial depression (more prolonged, if less acute, than the cyclical slumps
which had marked the early and mid-Victorian years), resulting
in reduced profits, intensified competition (as more and more
countries underwent their own industrial revolutions), and high
unemployment.

According to the Marxist account, the former buoyant confidence in the future of manufacturing industry collapsed under these pressures, as the commercial and industrial classes found themselves driven into adopting increasingly defensive strategies in the face of the twin threats of working-class unrest at home and foreign competition abroad.

Middle-class Liberals had long agonised over whether manual workers should be brought within the pale of the constitution and be given the vote, so signalling their acceptance into the community of free citizens. Was it wise to confer political rights on 'uneducated' men who patently did not understand the teachings of political economy – in other words, was capitalism compatible with democracy?

By the last quarter of the nineteenth century this issue had effectively been resolved. In nearly all industrial countries the working classes possessed the vote, either on the basis of universal male suffrage, as in the post-1870 German Reich, or in a gradual and partial manner, as had happened in Britain. The problem was, how long would the newly-enfranchised masses be content to vote for representatives of the older political parties, including the Liberal Party, which claimed to have the working man's interests particularly at heart? Sooner or later, Marxists argue, an appreciation of the divergent interests of employee and employer was bound to weaken the popular base of the Liberal Party, as working men sought to create new forms of political organisation which would reflect their own class needs. The forming of 'independent' Labour parties would thus necessarily be followed by a widespread acceptance within working class communities of the socialist creed, which laid bare the realities of capitalist exploitation and offered its victims a practical means of redress.

Central to the Marxist interpretation is the claim that these changed economic and political circumstances faced Liberal parties everywhere with an intolerable dilemma. They could seek to hold on to their traditional working-class support by a concessionary policy of social reform. But though this might delay, it could not decisively halt the efforts of class-conscious manual workers to break free from the political control of their superiors. Furthermore, it is said, the very attempt to 'woo' them in this way carried with it the risk of alienating the more timid members of the middle class, who began to drift in increasing numbers out of the Liberal Party into the security offered by Conservatism. In consequence, the Conservatives, no longer so heavily dependent upon the agricultural interest and upon 'pre-industrial' social groupings, were able to broaden their electoral appeal, until eventually they came to be looked upon as the 'natural' defenders of all forms of property, landed, commercial and industrial.

But, paradoxically, the Conservatives and their allies the length and breadth of Europe were simultaneously able to attract significant support from the working classes (over and above the 'deference voters' to whom they had always made an appeal). For at a time of mounting international tension and economic stress, nationalism and imperialism held a great attraction to people from all walks of life, and both these creeds became appropriated by the parties of the 'right'. In particular, Conservatives began to associate themselves with protectionism, which enjoyed a revival, as manufacturers sought to counter foreign penetration of their markets. To the Conservatives, this brought obvious advantages. The employer's loss of profits and the working man's loss of wages and employment could both be blamed upon 'the foreigner', from which the moral was drawn that all social classes should subordinate their short-term interests to the campaign to overcome this common enemy. Fears of foreign invasion also contributed to the new mood of nationalist hysteria, in which Conservatives presented themselves as custodians of the 'national interest'. Needless to say, it was a conception of the 'national interest' which very largely rested upon middle-class premises.

In short, so runs the Marxist interpretation, in the last quarter of the nineteenth century economic and social developments were splitting the populations of the advanced industrial countries into two antagonistic camps: a working-class camp, represented by the Labour/Socialist parties, and the camp of those who, fearing a working-class political ascendancy, had rallied behind the modernised parties of the right. This polarisation left the Liberal Party high and dry. Its individualistic ideology now

7

seemed archaic, while its programme of 'peace, retrenchment and reform' was ill-suited to an 'Age of Imperialism'. And so Liberalism, a bankrupt creed, went into decline as its social base atrophied. The pace of Liberal disintegration may have differed from country to country, but the social and economic forces producing this disintegration were everywhere the same, being ultimately located within the dynamic of capitalism itself.

The 'Revisionist' Case

The Marxist interpretation is bold and in many ways appealing. But is it true? Only at the end of the entire book will any attempt be made to answer this question. From the very start, though, a number of cautionary points need to be made.

Firstly, even if this interpretation is broadly correct, it still leaves unresolved the issue of how and when the Liberal collapse occurred. Historians (unlike social scientists, perhaps) are concerned with the specific form which events take. They are less interested, for example, in the general circumstances which produced the economic and political emancipation of women in mature industrial societies than in precisely how and why this happened in particular countries. Similarly with the downfall of the British Liberal Party. The exact chronology of events is particularly important. Thus, the later course of British political life was materially affected by the fact that the Liberals were strong enough in the early twentieth century to form a stable and long-lived ministry and did not disappear as a potential party of government until the mid-1920s. Had the collapse occurred earlier, both the Labour and the Conservative parties would almost certainly have developed in different ways. In untangling these difficulties, the general explanations furnished by the Marxists offer only limited help.

Secondly, the Marxist account has never held the field unchallenged, in large part because no steady decline in Liberal fortunes in fact took place in the later nineteenth century. On the contrary, not only did the Liberals enjoy a period of almost unparalleled electoral success between 1906 and 1914, but the legislative achievements of the Campbell-Bannerman and Asquith ministries during these years (most obviously in the field of social policy) probably eclipsed those of Gladstone's last three governments. Indeed, during the 1970s a 'revisionist' school of historians emerged which argued that the Liberal Party had successfully adapted itself to the requirements of class politics during the Edwardian years before unexpectedly falling victim to the First World War.[6] This 'revisionist' case needs to be examined very seriously.

Thirdly, there are many historians who have been struck by the way in which the Liberal Party was damaged, not so much by the operation of deep impersonal forces, but rather by 'bad luck', misunderstandings and such like 'contingencies'. True, those who place most emphasis upon these 'accidents' tend to be historians deeply sympathetic to the Liberal Party.[7] But that does not mean that their work can simply be dismissed as 'special pleading'.

To take but two instances where 'accidents' seem to have played a large role (and both will be dealt with more carefully later in the book). It does seem as though Asquith and Lloyd George were tantalisingly close to agreement over the composition and functions of a re-modelled War Committee in December 1916 before a chapter of misunderstandings brought about the breach between them that eventually split Liberalism into two distinct parties, each with its own leader – a disaster from which the Liberals never fully recovered.[8]

An even more telling example of an unanticipated happening wrenching history away from what had seemed to be its natural course of development was the very narrow failure of Parliament to end the 'first-past-the-post' system of voting in 1918; it would be hard to show that this was in any way 'pre-determined'.[9] But its outcome was momentous since, arguably, it brought about the stark class-based duopoly which reduced the Liberals to their later peripheral role in British politics.

Finally, is it reasonable to follow the cruder sort of Marxist in linking together so closely the fate of 'Liberalism' as an ideology and of the Liberal Party as an electoral machine? Employing, for once, a bit of 'wisdom of hindsight' ourselves, we can clearly see that the disappearance of the Liberal Party as a major force at Westminster did not mean the 'death of Liberalism' in any simple sense. On the contrary, many of the values and beliefs of the old Liberal Party were carried over into a succeeding period by the Labour Party, while others found a central place in the political thinking of Stanley Baldwin, the highly successful leader of the Conservative Party between 1923 and 1937. Moreover, many of the tenets of the 'Manchester School' Liberals of the early nineteenth century have recently been revived (albeit in new forms and in a quite different context) by the Conservatives close to Mrs Thatcher. Symbolically, even the arguments for Free Trade (once dismissed as an early and mid-Victorian period-piece) now enjoy widespread credibility. Liberalism has proved to be surprisingly resilient as a political and economic creed, and, despite the failure of the 'Alliance' to achieve the breakthrough which once seemed possible in the early and mid 1980s, it looks quite likely to outlive the 'hard' Marxist theories predicting its inevitable supersession. Can we, then, be quite so sure that there was no place in mid-twentieth century British political life for some kind of modernised Liberal Party?

These are issues which will be explored in subsequent chapters before some tentative answers are put forward in the Conclusion. But perhaps enough has already been said to indicate that an understanding of what befell the Liberal Party between 1886 and 1929 is both important and difficult. The purpose of this book is to provide a map for helping readers find their way around the many different explanations which historians have produced.[10]

2
THE RISE OF THE LIBERAL PARTY

The Liberal Party came into existence in the nineteenth century because the country's political system so obviously lagged behind its industrial development. True, following the Municipal Reform Act of 1835, rival middle-class groups vied for control in the major urban centres, but in the counties local government remained largely in the hands of the landed interest. At national level the predominance of the aristocracy was equally apparent. It had become customary to entrust offices like the Presidency of the Board of Trade to men of commercial backgrounds and experience, but the prestigious Secretaryships of State were, almost invariably, given to members of one of the great aristocratic families. In Parliament, too, the landed interest was predominant. The House of Lords could almost be seen as its institutional embodiment; only after 1885 did middle-class men become ennobled in any significant numbers and it would take decades before this significantly affected the composition of the Chamber as a whole. As for the Commons, here landowners and their dependents never comprised less than one half of the membership of the House. A traditional 'ruling class', it seemed, controlled political life, an elite all the stronger in that it was connected with other bastions of state power, like the diplomatic service, the court, the armed services, and the Church of England.[1]

As the century proceeded, many of these 'anomalies' were

removed or mitigated. The 1832 Reform Act, in addition to extending the franchise, took away 143 seats from the 'rotten' boroughs, allowing extra representation to be given to the populous counties and to new manufacturing towns like Birmingham and Manchester. The landed property qualifications was abolished in 1858. Further Reform Acts in 1867 and 1884–5 gave recognition to the importance of the manufacturing districts and London. Yet political reform in all these matters was slow in coming, often encountered considerable resistance, and, even by 1885, was far from complete.

Moreover, two aspects of British public life continued to reflect the survival of the old pre-industrial order. First, there was what some contemporaries called 'the land monopoly'. Not only did land provide the basis of the political system, it also enjoyed special legal privileges and immunities. For example, land did not pay its fair share of probate duty. And finally the system of primogeniture and entail meant that large concentrations of land remained in the hands of the great aristocrats – protected from the laws of supply and demand which regulated the accumulation and distribution of other forms of wealth.

Secondly, there was the privileged position occupied by the Church of England. The 1851 religious census revealed that Anglican worshippers had already been overtaken in numbers by Dissenters. This was particularly true of Wales, where Anglicanism was a creed confined to a small 'alien' class, but it was only slightly less true of some of the new manufacturing districts; for example, in Rochdale and Bradford, Nonconformity supplied over 68 per cent of those attending a place of Christian worship.[2] Yet the Church of England still functioned as the 'national' church, being associated with all the rituals of state. It also enjoyed a clear advantage over the other religious sects in the provision of education, and it long monopolised the prestigious ancient universities of Oxford and Cambridge.

To protest at these 'anomalies' was the mission of the 'Radicals', the 'advanced guard' of the Victorian Liberal Party. It is important to remember that in the years before 1885 the Radicals formed a minority group (often a small minority) within the 'Whig-Liberal' alliance. Yet it was these men, of whom Richard Cobden and John Bright were the most prominent, who gave Liberalism its cutting edge and distinctiveness and who frequently set the agenda for political change. For what groups in the community did the Radicals speak?

The Nonconformists were closely associated with Radicalism from the inception of the movement, since they saw it as an agency through which the disabilities laid on them by law might be removed. In this they had some success. Compulsory payment of Church Rates ended in 1868, the following decade saw the repeal of the Test Acts which had previously closed Oxford and Cambridge to non-Anglicans, and an Act of 1880 at last permitted Dissenters to be buried in consecrated ground near to their chapels. But to the more intransigent Dissenters this was not enough. Through the Liberation Society, founded in 1853, many of them pressed for genuine religious equality, which they thought necessitated the abolition of the Established Church. In 1869 the Church of Ireland was eventually disestablished and disendowed, but the claims of the Welsh and Scots (whose own established church was Presbyterian), to say nothing of the English, to a similar measure still remained unsatisfied. Moreover, as we shall see, the grievances of the Nonconformists in the sphere of elementary education actually intensified, rather than disappeared, in the later decades of the century.[3]

But perhaps the very heart of Victorian Radicalism lay in its attacks on the 'land monopoly'. Land, claimed the Radicals, differed from other kinds of wealth in that it constituted a 'natural monopoly'. Whereas industrial enterprise could be expanded indefinitely by hard work and entrepreneurial acumen, land was (by and large) fixed in extent. Yet since land was as necessary to life as oxygen, those fortunate enough to have inherited it were able to exploit the rest of the community. In T. H. Green's words, the real enemy of the working classes was therefore not the capitalist but the landlord, because 'the capital gained by one is not taken from another, but one man cannot acquire more land without others having less'.[4] Such a message appealed to many middle-class groups otherwise solicitous of the rights of property, including many of the great capitalists (Cobden and Bright were themselves 'cotton lords').

Once again, changes in the landed system took place in the course of the century. Most noticeably, the repeal of the Corn Laws in 1846 removed the special protection afforded to agriculture – a symbolic, as well as a practical, triumph for the manufacturing centres. Moreover, the Settled Land Act of 1882 and the Conveyancing Act (prepared by the previous Tory administration) removed some of the more anomalous and indefensible aspects of the land market, thereby taking the steam out of the land reformers' campaign. Finally, the Game Laws, seen by the Radicals as a symbol of the way in which landowners used their position in Parliament to safeguard their own interests, also underwent successive reform. But the fundamental grievances remained barely touched. The outworks, it seemed, had been ceded, but not the citadel.

Because of the close links between landed society and the army officer corps, Radicals naturally moved on from attacking the 'land monopoly' to attacking the armed services. In their eyes, the landed aristocracy was an 'atavism', an anachronistic survival from an earlier era when societies were organised for warfare, but out of place in the modern industrial world. At times of emotional excitement (as in the early 1840s), some Radicals even managed to convince themselves that the big landed families were the descendants of the conquering Normans, a military caste quartered upon the peace-loving industrial population. It was poor history, but made for potent propaganda.

Distrust of the army made Radicals keen to curb what they called 'bloated armaments'. But Radicals also disliked the Foreign Office and the diplomatic service, those other aristocratic strongholds, and this gave rise to a tradition of opposition to the 'official' conduct of foreign affairs. The 'Trouble Makers', as A. J. P. Taylor has called them, tended to view diplomacy as a mischievous pastime carried out by a landed elite for its own advantage and gratification. However, as to what should take its place, there tended to be two broad schools of thought. Firstly, there were those who espoused a policy of 'non-intervention', believing that contacts between peoples should be confined to the civilising influences of trade and that the less foreign policy there was the better. The second approach (confusingly, the same Radicals often switched from the one to the other) was to insist that the British government abandon its preoccupation with 'immoral' concepts like the balance of power and commit itself to an active policy designed to help oppressed nationalities rightly struggling to be free: Italians, Poles, Bulgars, Armenians and so on, depending on the circumstances of time and place.[5]

Underlying all these specific campaigns was the Radical mission to put an end to what Cobden, the greatest of the Radical leaders, called 'feudalism'. In Cobden's view the country was in the grip of a sinister aristocratic system, its constitution being 'a thing of monopolies, and Church-craft, and sinecures, armorial hocus-pocus, primogeniture, and pageantry!'.[6] Like other Radicals, he wanted the country's political institutions and practices to be brought into harmony with its economic base, so that the importance of manufacturing and trading would be fully recognised. In modern parlance, he was self-consciously concerned with institutional 'modernisation'. The Radicalism he propagated was, in many ways, the ideology of the 'excluded' middle class.

Of course, this Radicalism did not find expression in modern class language at all. As Green's remark reveals, Radicals believed that 'the industrious classes', both employers and employee, were the common victims of an aristocratic conspiracy. But more common still was the Radical claim that they were advancing the interests of 'the people' against the forces of 'monopoly' and 'privilege'. Theirs was a secular creed of 'progress' which celebrated the great achievements of industrial capitalism but which spoke less of the growth of trade and prosperity (important though both these things were) than of an enlargement of 'liberty'. Trade was to be freed from all trammels; so was land, which, it was hoped, would in future be a commodity that could be as easily bought and sold as a bale of merchandise. Finally, there was to be 'religious equality', on the American model, with no one sect enjoying a preferential advantage, as well as freedom of speech and assembly.

This, then, was the gist of Radicalism, the creed of the 'advanced' wing of the Liberal Party. Its salient outlines did not fundamentally change from the 1830s through to the outbreak of the Great War. Indeed, Joe Chamberlain in the early 1880s and, a quarter of a century later, David Lloyd George, often echoed the phraseology of Cobden and John Bright, whose lineal descendants they were in many ways.[7]

These Radical beliefs also helped to determine the country's electoral geography right into the twentieth century. Although, as we shall later see, the Irish crisis in 1886 somewhat complicated matters, the Liberal Party continued to be the dominant force in the manufacturing districts, leaving the Conservatives in control of many rural constituencies, as well as of the suburbs, seaside resorts and cathedral cities of southern England. In addition, Liberalism was strongly correlated with Nonconformity, Conservatism with Anglicanism. Finally, on the 'Celtic Fringe' in Scotland and Wales, the Liberals were able to harness the forces of nationalism against a Conservative Party which seemed, through its close association with the Church of England, to be the instrument of an alien nation as well as the custodian of an alien creed.

Yet during the mid-Victorian years the 'advanced Radicals', for all their achievements, never proved capable of forming their 'own' party. In part, this was because, from the very start, the Radicals had difficulty in agreeing upon priorities. For example, those who felt strongly about religious grievances often lacked militancy on the land question.[8] Conversely, there were entrepreneurial Radicals, like the Anglican Cobden, who sympathised with Nonconformist grievances but were hostile to manifestations of Dissenting bigotry – which anyhow threatened the political unity of the industrial middle class. Moreover, the Radicals divided into two main groups. There were the 'Philosophic Radicals', who drew their inspiration from the writing of the Utilitarians, Bentham and the two Mills, a group which judged all institutions and practices by the criterion of whether or not they conduced to the 'greatest happiness of the greatest number'; this group tended to come from the professional (and even from the landed classes) and was London-oriented. Secondly, there were the 'entrepreneurial Radicals', mostly capitalists from the big manufacturing cities, whose prime concern was to emancipate commerce and industry: the latter group tended to look for leadership to Cobden, at least initially.

But there were also two important 'external' reasons for Radical ineffectuality. Firstly, landed society possessed enormous social prestige, in the face of which many industrialists and Dissenters experienced a certain loss of self-confidence. Those anxious for social advancement were tempted to exchange the chapel for the Church of England, a transition which was often a prelude to a rapprochement with the Conservative Party. As Michael Hurst argues, right-wing Liberal defections to the Conservative Party 'began almost as soon as a full-blown Liberal party' emerged.[9] And although few wealthy businessmen chose to accept the responsibilities that went with ownership of a landed estate, the lure of a country house, with its accompanying lifestyle, also did much to blunt the militancy of many whose class needs Radicalism claimed to represent.

In addition, the great public schools, with their classics-dominated syllabus and emphasis on the 'gentlemanly' qualities of honour and service, may have deadened the entrepreneurial appetites of those who received their education at these establishments – nearly all of them Anglican. The quest for places, titles and honorific offices, like seats on the county bench or deputy lord lieutenancies, may have had similar consequences. True, historians disagree over whether such activities should be seen as an aping of aristocratic values or as a healthy assertion by the urban middle class of the social position to which its wealth entitled it.[10] But, in either case, such emulation did little to foster the kind of 'class pride' which had meant so much to Cobden and Bright.

But, secondly, the very discriminations against which Radicals protested made it difficult for them to organise themselves politically in such a way as to 'capture' the institutions of the state. For example, the under-representation of the northern industrial centres (if measured by population or wealth) meant that there were insufficient safe seats to provide them with a base upon which a parliamentary majority could be constructed. The Radicals could form highly efficient pressure groups and run influential campaigns on specific issues; the most famous of these was obviously the Anti-Corn Law League. They were particularly good at mobilising opinion through the press; the provincial newspapers which were so important in the mid- and late Victorian period had often been founded by Radical businessmen: the *Leeds Mercury*, the *Bradford Observer*, the *Manchester Guardian* and the *Eastern Daily Press* all exemplify this trend. But, at the level of national politics, the Radicals constituted only a small coterie. And brief experiments at independence in the late 1840s and 1850s soon convinced them that they were unable to 'go it alone' and that their only hope of influencing events lay through association with one of the two major parties of government.

When the Conservative Party became a protectionist party in 1846, after its leader, Sir Robert Peel, had been expelled for repealing the Corn Laws, the Radicals had little option but to link up with the Whigs. Since the Whig leadership comprised great aristocratic landowners, like the Russells, the Spencers and the Wodehouses, the situation was not lacking in piquancy.

Yet an alliance between Radicals and Whigs had much to recommend it. Firstly, the 'principles of 1688' had bequeathed to the Whigs a strong commitment to 'constitutional liberty', a mistrust of the power of the executive, and a view of Parliament as custodian of the rights of the wider community. These 'principles' were capable of extension to meet new social and political needs. Then, too, the patrician Whig landowners had always prided themselves on playing a skilful mediatory role between crown and 'people', and the social unrest produced by population growth and industrialisation gave them plentiful scope for exercising these particular talents.

Secondly, Whigs were open to modernising influences. The very fact that they tended to come from the great aristocratic families, with a metropolitan outlook and a wide spread of interests, meant that, unlike the Tories, who (especially after 1846) functioned as the 'country party', they were able to see the political problems of their day with a certain detachment, often rising above the immediate interests of their local and class interests. Quite apart from anything else, it required little statesmanship to see that the survival of the Whigs' position as a kind of hereditary governing class required them to show some sensitivity to the wishes and needs of the manufacturing centres.

There were many ways in which such a transmission of ideas occurred. Some landowners held urban and industrial land and so were directly implicated in the expanding capitalist economy. Others had houses or represented constituencies which brought them into contact with the manufacturing districts. Many, too, had studied the social and economic problems of their day with some diligence, reading the political economists, attending discussion groups like the Political Economy Club, and generally keeping abreast of the times. Indeed, the great Whig political leaders, from Earl Grey, through Lord John Russell and Lord Palmerston and beyond, had all acquired a fluent mastery of the idiom of 'progress' which cannot simply be explained in terms of expediency. Even when dealing with the 1870s or 1880s, it would be a mistake to dismiss as an anachronism doomed to disappear a social grouping which not only dominated Cabinet discussions but which also showed an aptitude for new methods of political organisation and propaganda.[11]

Yet Whiggery, even in its most progressive manifestations, was unlikely to satisfy the advanced Radicals' claims. The Whigs were men who had been brought up from birth with the notion that 'duty' might require them to govern their country just as they would have to administer their estates and supervise local affairs. Hence, they brought to political life an administrative ethic, a pragmatic temper. They lacked 'warmth' as reformers and were temperamentally suspicious of 'enthusiasm' in others.

Moreover, there were limits which these great landowners were unlikely to transgress in their measured pursuit of progress. True, a generous conception of the national interest had reconciled them to the abolition of the Corn Laws in the 1840s and with it the notion that agriculture should play a central role in national life. Some were even willing to recognise the imperfections of the land system in Ireland, where many possessed estates of their own, and were ready to sponsor bold remedies for these ills. But the Whigs were essentially 'repenters', not rebels. It was certainly inconceivable that they would deliberately undermine the landed system which provided them with both their wealth and their power. (There were, of course, a few genuinely Radical landowners, like Sir Wilfrid Lawson, just as the twentieth century has seen a few millionaire socialists, but these cannot be taken as representative types.) Similarly with religious grievances: although the Whig leaders often acted as 'friends' of the Catholics and Dissenters, nearly all of them were Anglicans, and very few, except in the special circumstances of Ireland and Wales, showed any disposition to embrace the disestablishment and disendowment of the Established Church, even as a long-term objective.[12]

It may be significant that, whilst the Radical leaders were nearly all manufacturers (for example, Cobden, Bright, Forster, Mundella, Chamberlain), Radicalism in the mid-Victorian period enjoyed its most loyal electoral support from artisans and shopkeepers, not from the more well-to-do members of the middle classes, who, given the option, tended to vote for 'moderate' Liberal and even Whig candidates.[13] Even some businessmen, fierce Radicals when they had first entered politics, later came to find this 'moderate' approach acceptable, and willingly participated in a Whig-dominated Party.

But, in addition, Radicalism and Whiggery were beginning to converge as the century progressed. Significantly, the very term 'Whig' very quickly came to acquire new meanings. It no longer denoted simply a small powerful circle of inter-related landowning families, but was often applied to all cautious, moderate and pragmatic Liberals – regardless of their social backgrounds. The fact that this could happen indicates that the old class divisions between landowners and businessmen were losing their former asperity – though important status distinctions remained.[14] Moreover, from the 1830s onwards, and especially after 1846, a significant number of Radicals and Whigs started to refer to themselves publicly as 'Liberals'.[15] Nor were political roles

20

determined simply by social position. Even in the 1840s some of the Anti-Corn Law League leaders, like Milner Gibson, had been drawn from the ranks of the landowners, while prosperous businessmen quickly gained an entrée into Whig society. By the 1890s the Radicals were being led by William Vernon Harcourt, who had Plantagenet blood in his veins! Another cause of division disappeared when authentic urban Radicals – Forster in 1865, Bright in 1868, Mundella and Chamberlain in 1880 – were given high office, a change in their circumstances which to some degree modified their political perspectives.

Yet it is possible to exaggerate the extent to which the various groups within the Liberal Party had coalesced even by the early 1880s. To the more doctrinaire of the Radicals, Whiggery (however defined) would never provide satisfaction. Apart from anything else, urban Radicals thought it a mattter of shame and humiliation that people of their 'order' could not manage their own affairs but had to 'delegate' the conduct of public business to others, or to occupy a subordinate position to the landowners who continued to dominate government. Walter Bagehot, writing about Bright and his capitalist friends in 1867, well understood this particular mentality: 'They cannot endure – they ought not to endure – that a rich, able manufacturer should be a less man than a small stupid squire'.[16]

The bond between Radicals and Whiggery was, therefore, often fragile. It might not have survived as long as it did, but for the role of William Ewart Gladstone, the effective creator of the British Liberal Party, into which both Whiggery and Radicalism became subsumed. Gladstone had entered politics as a Conservative, before his support for Corn Law repeal drove him, like his hero, Peel, into a more than ten years' sojourn in a political 'no man's land', prior to his eventual emergence as the Liberal leader. Gladstone's peculiar fitness to perform this particular role owed much to his family circumstances and personality. As the son of a Liverpudlian merchant prince, Gladstone enjoyed family ties with the great business centres, and, from the time of his 1853 Budget onwards, the public saw him as the prominent statesman who best understood the needs of the manufacturing and commercial world. As one historian has put it, 'his policies were those which the middle class would have pursued for themselves if they could have found in their midst a leader as appealing and representative'.[17]

Yet Gladstone, though on certain issues he could sound like a Radical, was not really a Radical at all. His experiences at Eton and later at Christ Church, Oxford, his strong High Church beliefs (with which he had replaced his family's Evangelicalism) and his marriage into a minor landed family had all brought Gladstone into an aristocratic world which, as an outsider, he tended to idealise. Far from sharing the Radicals' contempt for the values of landed society, Gladstone, throughout his life, held a high regard for the disinterested public service which he thought to be the hallmark of this class.[18] And far from seeking the overthrow of 'feudalism', Gladstone saw his role as one of class mediator and reconciler. This, along with remarkable abilities and charismatic qualities, enabled him, as the leader of the Liberals, to hold together his motley followers, who, however exasperated they might often be with him, realised his indispensability. Even putting it at its lowest, the Radicals could welcome Gladstone as an ally against Whig inertia, while the Whigs saw his usefulness as a barrier against Radical 'extremism'.

Yet by the early 1880s, not even Gladstone, who had emerged from retirement to impose himself on the Queen in the aftermath of the Liberals' 1880 electoral victory, could damp down the ill-will between the Radical and Whig elements among his followers. Some of the friction was generated by events in Ireland, where Parnell, Davitt and the Land League had succeeded in unleashing the 'Land War'. This also polarised opinion on mainland Britain, since many Radicals viewed with some satisfaction the collapse of landlord power in Ireland – the weak link in the chain of landlordism – and wanted to help it on its way with timely legislative interventions, while Whig politicians took the very opposite view. In fact, the government's 1880 Compensation for Disturbances Bill provoked sixty Whig peers to revolt; twenty of these men were Irish landlords, eleven of whom held estates of over 20,000 acres each.[19] Lansdowne, one of the largest of them, resigned from the government. The following year saw the departure of the Duke of Argyll, who joined the peers on the cross-benches in protest at what he considered to be an attack on the rights of ownership.[20]

The worry was that the curtailment of the rights of landed property in Ireland might constitute a precedent and serve as the prelude to an assault on landlordism on the other side of the Channel. The recent return to Parliament as Liberal MPs of a number of aggressive land reformers, including representatives of the tenant farmers, meant that this was no empty fear. In Scotland the struggle of the crofters for greater legal rights was also proving very disruptive to the unity of the Liberal Party.[21] Against a background of acute agricultural depression, many landowners trembled for the security of their estates.

But these problems were superimposed upon others. During the Liberals' previous administration, an Education Act had been passed (the Forster Education Act of 1870) which wounded the consciences of the Party's Nonconformist supporters by integrating Anglican schools into the new 'national' system.[22] In protest, a pressure group had been formed by a number of Birmingham businessmen (among them the up-and-coming star of Radicalism, Joe Chamberlain), which soon transmuted itself into the National Education League, which campaigned for a secular system of public education. This body, in turn, evolved in 1877 into the National Liberal Federation (NLF). Through control of a new mass organisation in the country, Chamberlain and his friends sought to mobilise the opinion of rank-and-file activists against the 'notables' who dominated the Party at Westminster. How much of a threat this represented to the old political order became apparent when Chamberlain and his friends launched their 'Unauthorised Programme' prior to the 1885 election – a clear attempt to impose militant Radicalism upon a reluctant party leadership. When in June 1885 Gladstone's second administration disintegrated and Lord Salisbury became Conservative Prime Minister, the world was entertained to the spectacle of a political duel between Chamberlain and Lord Hartington, the Whig leader.

What gave this contest its importance was the fact that Gladstone had been indicating ever since his re-emergence from retirement in 1880 that his resignation was imminent. Moreover, with Parliament having agreed to franchise extension and a major Redistribution Bill in 1884–5, the two parties would also have to face a new electorate when the next general election was called, and this added to the uncertainty. At stake, therefore, was not just the leadership of the Liberal Party, but also its future political trajectory.

The likelihood was that Hartington would take Gladstone's place, if only as a stop-gap leader. But how long would it be before the Radicals attempted to seize control of the party, which they had never in the past been powerful enough to do, preparatory to pushing forward with their own militant programme? Or, to put it another way, how much time would elapse before the more timorous Whigs parted company with the Liberal Party altogether and sought some sort of a rapprochement with the Conservatives? Chamberlain may not have been that keen on driving the Whigs out of the party into the arms of the Conservatives, as some of his followers wanted him to do. But the logic of the situation pointed to the possibility of some major party realignment in the not so distant future.[23]

Yet the division within the Liberal Party cannot just be reduced to one between landowning Whigs and urban Radicals. Indeed, Chamberlain was in some respects not really a conventional Radical, in the great tradition of Cobden and Bright, at all. For the 'Unauthorised Programme' aimed at more than simply curtailing the privileges of the Church of England and of ending the 'land monopoly'. Chamberlain and his friends were also offering inducements (opponents called them bribes) to the poor. The most successful of these, judging by the election returns in 1885, was the proposal (emanating from Chamberlain's friend, Jesse Collings) that local authorities be empowered to acquire land for leasing as allotments or small-holdings, colloquially known as 'Three Acres and a Cow'. The Unauthorised Programme also contained policies for free education, for improving working-class housing and the suggestion of a progressive income tax. All of this stemmed from Chamberlain's belief that only a 'constructive' social programme would bind the property-less masses to the established political system and prevent a disastrous drift into class politics – with its accompanying clash between capital and labour.[24]

Now, to understand why Chamberlain was advocating these reforms one must first examine the social issues which were forcing themselves upon public attention in the early 1880s. The problems of the big cities, particularly London, had become a major talking-point following the publication of a series of exposures of what life meant for the 'people of the abyss'. Sensationalist pamphlets like Andrew Mearns' *The Bitter Cry of Outcast London* (1883) aroused feelings both of pity and of fear.[25] The element of fear perhaps predominated in 1885–6, when a business recession pushed up unemployment to the point where, in towns all over the country, riots and popular demonstrations were taking place. This seemed all the more alarming since Britain's first Marxist party, the recently formed Social Democratic Federation (SDF), was helping to organise these protests. Although the threat of revolutionary socialism was as yet very small, these events did raise the spectre of class conflict and made many commentators worry about whether popular forces might not succeed, before too long, in producing major changes in the structure and contents of political life.[26] After all, such developments had already occurred in the German Empire and other Continental countries, where Marxists had made heavy inroads at the expense of the older parties – and particularly at the expense of the Liberals.

Chamberlain's interest in new kinds of social legislation becomes intelligible against this background. But, to some extent, his new policies meant a sharp break with the mainstream Radical tradition. John Bright, for example, had earlier opposed the Factory Acts with great vehemence, believing that state intervention in industrial and commercial life would prove either futile or damaging. True, during the late 1850s and 1860s the dogmatic belief in *laissez-faire* had already begun to subside.

25

Some younger business Radicals, among them men like W. E. Forster and A. J. Mundella, actually wanted to *extend* the Factory Acts.[27] Even so, there remained considerable nervousness among all Liberals (not least the businessmen) about moves in this direction. Indeed, one reason why so many Liberals (notably Robert Lowe) had opposed suffrage extension in 1866–7 was their fear that this would mean the enfranchisement of uneducated labourers who, not understanding the precepts of political economy, would try and use their new-found political power to force through ill-conceived schemes of social reconstruction.

By the 1880s, and with much greater reason, similar anxieties were being expressed by the likes of the City banker, George Joachim Goschen. Goschen had first been elected in a by-election in 1863 on a conventionally Radical platform, although he very soon dissociated himself from Bright's extremism. As a minister in Gladstone's first administration (1868–74) Goschen had demonstrated his loyalty to the principles of political economy. But he had subsequently refused to take office in Gladstone's second ministry, because he disapproved of the party's commitment to the equalisation of the franchise – that is to say, extending the household suffrage from the boroughs to the counties. The Unauthorised Programme filled Goschen with horror.[28] Nor was he alone, since many of the conservative members of the Liberal intelligentsia were becoming similarly worried over the direction of Liberal politics, grumbling that 'sentiment' was replacing 'science' as a guide to public action.[29]

Thus, long before the Home Rule schism of 1885–6, Chamberlain's activities were having a disturbing impact on party unity and alienating, not only many of the big landed families, but also segments of the more socially conservative members of the middle class. Some businessmen even began to have their doubts about land reform, fearing that the Radicals' reckless presentation of its merits might weaken respect for all property.[30] But they also disliked Chamberlain's doctrine of 'ransom' (that is, that owners of *all* kinds of property should pay high taxes as a form of protection money), his wooing of manual workers and farm labourers, and his identification of social progress with an expansion of the role of the public authorities, necessitating in-creased taxation, the burden of which would fall on the wealthy. As Professor Southgate says, 'The governing class was now subjected to a renewal of the sort of attack in which Cobden and Bright had specialised, but with the object of reversing Cobdenite principles of public expenditure'.[31]

Yet, provided that no panic exodus took place, there was no reason why Chamberlain should regret the loss to Liberalism of some timid supporters from the urban middle class. On the contrary, in the summer of 1885, with Gladstone's long career of public service seemingly drawing to its close, the Radicals were able to view the future with optimism. For a reconstruction of the Liberal Party under their own leadership seemed only a matter of time.

Yet things did not work out like this at all. In the winter of 1885–6 Gladstone changed the political agenda by announcing his conversion to a policy of Irish Home Rule, that is to say, giving Ireland a subordinate Parliament for the determination of its own affairs, subject to ultimate Westminster control. The full significance of this decision will be discussed at some length in the next two chapters. But before analysing the Home Rule crisis, it may be helpful to outline, in bald detail, what actually happened.

Gladstone's dramatic initiative quickly won the backing of the majority of his followers, but it alienated many of the Whigs, including Hartington, as well as Goschen and prominent Liberal intellectuals who feared that Home Rule would usher in a period of democratic chaos and Imperial disintegration.[32] But, surprisingly, after a period of hesitation, Chamberlain and some of the Radicals also joined in the denunciation of Home Rule. The outcome was a serious party schism. When Gladstone, back in office, introduced his Home Rule Bill in the summer of 1886, nearly one-third of Liberal MPs voted against it, so securing its defeat and the fall of the government.[33]

At the ensuing general election, the dissident Liberal MPs and peers, who had created a new party of their own, the Liberal Unionist Party (so called because they were Liberals who wanted to maintain the Union with Ireland), formed an electoral pact with the Conservatives. The result was a new Conservative administration, headed by Lord Salisbury, supported by the Liberal Unionists, who held the balance of seats in the Commons. (Following Lord Randolph Churchill's resignation as Chancellor of the Exchequer, Goschen was brought in as his successor in January 1887, the first Liberal Unionist to serve under Salisbury.) After hopes of Liberal reunion had been dashed with the breakdown of the Round Table Conference in 1887, the working alliance between Liberal Unionists and Conservatives (collectively known as the 'Unionists') grew tighter. When the short-lived Liberal administration of 1892–5 collapsed, Salisbury, back in 10 Downing Street for a third time, decided to give office to leading Liberal Unionists, among them Chamberlain, who became Colonial Secretary, and Hartington (now the 8th Duke of Devonshire), who served as Lord President of the Council. The two Unionist parties finally fused in 1912.

On the surface, then, it would seem that, by making the Irish Question the central issue in British politics, Gladstone had thoroughly muddied the waters. People who could agree upon little else now found themselves co-operating together in the Gladstonian Liberal Party (as 'Home Rulers'), while an even more heterogeneous collection of politicians were running the Unionist Alliance. But did the Home Rule crisis really obliterate the social and economic issues which had been agitating the political world over the preceding five years? And what sort of Liberal Party was it that came into existence as a result of Gladstone's extraordinary *démarche*?

3

THE ASSAULT ON FEUDALISM, 1886–1905

On the surface, the Home Rule schism of 1885–6 would seem to have brought the Radical assault on landed privilege to a decisive end, as perhaps Gladstone himself had intended. The extraordinary union between Hartington and Chamberlain, joint leaders of the new Liberal Unionist Party, was proof of how the violent passions raised by the Irish issue had succeeded in making friends out of old adversaries and adversaries out of old friends. For about twenty years the main dividing line between parties was that between 'Home Rulers' (the Liberals and their Irish Nationalist allies) and 'Unionists' (the Conservatives and Liberal Unionists).

The defection of Chamberlain and his drift into Unionism meant that the forces of Radicalism were divided. In Scotland, in particular, leading land reformers, temperance advocates and proponents of disestablishment now sat on the Unionist side of the House.[1] But, equally important, the schism robbed the Radicals of their only credible national leader. This had been seen with piercing clarity by several of Chamberlain's Radical friends on the eve of the great schism. Henry Labouchere ('Labby', as he was familiarly known) wrote an impassioned plea to Chamberlain in mid-April 1886, urging him to swallow his reservations about Home Rule and stay with the Liberal Party, the leadership of which must shortly drop into his lap:

> Your coming over [to the Home Rule party] would ensure the passing of the Irish Government Bill; it would go to the Lords. Then Queen, Lords and Whigs would be on one side, and the Radicals on the other. Mr Gladstone must soon come to an end. You would be our leader. The Whigs would be hopelessly bogged. Radicalism would be triumphant. Does not this tempt you?[2]

In ignoring this advice, Chamberlain seems to have been influenced, not just by his own genuine antipathy to Home Rule, but also by the belief that his separation from the mainstream of the Liberal Party would only be temporary: that Gladstone would shortly retire in triumph or disgrace but that in either case he himself would be welcomed back into the party as its saviour.[3]

It was to be a fateful miscalculation. The weakness of the Radicals had always been that they formed a loose federation of cliques and factions, each peddling its own favourite panacea (land reform, temperance reform, disestablishment, Home Rule for Wales and so on). It needed a politician of rare forcefulness and intelligence to draw these factions together and impose upon them a coherent programme. Lloyd George was to emerge to play this role twenty years later. But meanwhile the Radicals had to put up with the likes of the petulant John Morley and 'Labby', a lightweight figure who inspired considerable mistrust even within the Radical ranks. It was easy for opponents to ridicule Radicalism as an utterly negative creed, a patchwork of fads and crotchets.[4]

Radicalism was also weakened for a somewhat different reason. The Liberal Party's commitment to Irish Home Rule necessitated an alliance with the Irish Nationalist Party, without the support of which they could seldom expect to acquire a parliamentary majority. Only between 1906 and 1910 did the Liberals have an overall majority of seats in the Commons. Between 1892 and 1895 and again between 1910 and 1915 their continuance in office depended on the support of Irish MPs. In addition, although some contemporaries undoubtedly exaggerated its importance, the Irish vote (organised by the United Irish League) was an important asset in many English, Welsh and Scottish urban constituencies.[5]

Yet the social base of Irish Nationalism was formed by tenant farmers, shopkeepers and publicans, who were overwhelmingly Roman Catholic, and this made them uncongenial allies for the Liberals.[6] True, Dissenters and Roman Catholics could join hands without embarrassment when it came to attacking the Anglican monopoly; for example, both groups had approved, though for slightly different reasons, of the 1869 Act disestablishing and disendowing the Church of Ireland. But many prominent English Dissenters abandoned the Liberal Party entirely in 1886 rather than hand over Irish Protestants to 'priestly rule'; included in their number was the ex-Quaker, John Bright, author of the slogan that 'Home Rule Means Rome Rule'. Chamberlain himself was also a Dissenter (a Unitarian). 'I feel the wrong proposed to be done to our Ulster brethren', said the great Baptist preacher, C. H. Spurgeon: 'What have they done to be thus cast off?'[7] Such sentiments were particularly prevalent in Scotland, where Presbyterianism linked the population to the Ulster Protestants.[8]

In time most Dissenters overcame their doubts and, mesmerised by Gladstone, rallied behind the Liberal Party, particularly in 1887–8 when the Unionist Government's Crime Bill provided them with just the kind of 'moral' issue with which they felt most at home. The Wesleyan leader, Hugh Price Hughes, opined that Home Rule was 'simply applied Christianity'.[9] But events like those which followed the scandalous divorce case involving the Irish leader, Parnell, in 1890–1, when the Roman Catholic Church had thrown its weight into the electoral scales on the side of Parnell's Nationalist opponents, re-awakened all the old ancestral suspicions of 'priestly interference' and 'Popery'.

This tension was most acute in the field of education, where the Liberal preference for undenominational or secular schooling ran counter to the Irish Catholics' determination to maintain institutions which would disseminate the distinctive tenets of their own creed. True, Ireland had an entirely separate educational system from that of mainland Britain, so theoretically the two countries could have peacefully co-existed. However, there were large Irish settlements in the big cities of England and Scotland, on whose behalf the Irish Nationalist Leaders felt obliged to intervene. As a result, whenever the prospect of Irish Home Rule seemed remote, there was the danger that the Irish in England, Scotland and Wales would desert the Liberals and join forces with the Conservative Party in defence of church schools and of the general principle of a denominational education. This certainly affected the pattern of voting in western Scotland in the 1900 general election. More seriously, Liberal MPs were aghast at the support given by Irish Nationalists to the Unionist Government's 1896 Bill, which aimed to help the voluntary schools. Hughes now declared that 'Gladstonian Home Rule was dead'.[10] This was a dress-rehearsal for the later quarrel over the 1902 Education Act.

Such problems plagued the Liberal Party for as long as Home Rule figured prominently on the political agenda, just as they constituted a dilemma for Irish Nationalists, many of whom were torn between their political and their religious loyalties. Indeed, the irony is that, if Ireland's national claims could have been amicably settled, the Irish Nationalist Party might have found its natural ally in the Conservative Party, with which it was in general agreement on social policy as well as on education.

Some of these events lay in the future. But, in the short term, Gladstone's placing of Home Rule at the very centre of the Liberal programme in 1886 damaged the cause of Radicalism in yet another way. For, as Gladstone and his friend, John Morley (who twice served as Irish Secretary), openly admitted, it meant that all other reforms would have to wait until the Irish 'obstruction' had been removed.[11] True, after the Parnell scandal and when the disappointing 1892 election results came in, even Gladstone wavered in his faith. But Morley was still defiantly proclaiming: 'I cruise under the green flag – come what will',[12] and Home Rule soon resumed its centrality.

Many Radicals were pleased to follow such a strategy. Apart from a widespread inclination to trust Gladstone's judgement, Radicals could see advantages in revolutionising Ireland's entire political system, since Ireland was viewed as the part of the United Kingdom where the most pernicious manifestations of 'feudalism' were to be found. The cry of 'justice for Ireland' also appealed to many Radicals who instinctively sympathised with small oppressed peoples rightly struggling to be free. 'The men who defeated Home Rule were hereditary enemies', the advanced Radical, Channing, told his constituents in 1886.[13]

On the other hand, there was also resentment in some Radical quarters over the way in which Ireland was crowding all other issues off the Liberal agenda. For example, the ministry of Gladstone and Rosebery (1892–5) gave over the lion's share of its legislative time to pressing on with the Second Home Rule Bill, in the teeth of fierce resistance from the Unionist opposition. No wonder the legislative record of this government proved to be so barren. What made the situation even more frustrating was the fact that the sacrifice was seemingly all in vain, with the House of Lords predictably rejecting the Home Rule Bill. This, in turn, should have served as an occasion for an appeal to the electorate to give the party a mandate for curbing the powers of an undemocratic assembly. Yet this did not happen either. Liberals, at all levels of the party, fulminated against the peers (in the process confirming their reputation as dangerous demagogues), but the Cabinet refrained from dissolving Parliament, since it feared that this was not an issue which commanded sufficient electoral support. (Oddly enough, it was the Whig Rosebery who later tried to lead the party into a crusade on the issue of the Lords, while Morley and Harcourt held back.) The deadlock left the Liberals with no other strategy than that of 'filling the cup', in other words, pressing forward with legislation which the Upper House was likely to reject until such time as a constitutional crisis was provoked.

This, indeed, remained a continuing difficulty for the post-1886 Party. One reason for Chamberlain's refusal to go along with Home Rule had been his sense that public opinion in the big cities of England did not favour this measure. And in this respect Chamberlain's judgement was almost certainly sound. In the absence of opinion polls, one can only hazard a guess, but it is clear that defence of the Union brought the Conservatives and Liberal Unionists support from sections of the electorate which could not otherwise have been tapped, particularly in areas where Irish immigrants were believed to be responsible for unemployment and low wages. Birmingham, a city which had returned Liberals for all seven constituencies in the 1885 General Election, never returned a Liberal again until the Ladywood by-election in 1969! The Liberals also suffered in areas where Wesleyans were thick on the ground; between 1885 and 1892 there was a well-above average swing against the 'official' Liberal Party in Lincolnshire and in the West Country.[14] Admittedly, Herbert Gladstone (the Party's Chief Whip and Gladstone's son) believed that eighty-one of the seats won by the Liberals in 1892 were dominated by the Irish vote,[15] but this was almost certainly a wild exaggeration, and, on balance, the Irish issue was undoubtedly a vote loser.

No wonder, then, that, following Gladstone's retirement in 1894 and the Liberal Party's crushing defeat at the general election of the following year, many Liberals started looking for ways to extricate themselves from the Irish entanglement. Surprisingly perhaps, the Radicals did not take the lead in this campaign. Instead, it was the so-called 'Liberal Imperialists' (Asquith, Grey, Haldane – and, loosely attached to them, Lord Rosebery) who called for a rethink on Irish policy, although the group's effectiveness was marred by a division of opinion between those who advocated delay and those who wanted Home Rule completely abandoned.[16] But perversely or bravely, depending upon one's point of view, most Radicals, inside Parliament as well as the rank-and-file activists, fought to retain Home Rule, believing that to do otherwise would denote an abandonment of principle in the search for electoral popularity.

In late 1905, after years of wrangling, an adroit compromise was found, acceptable to all parties, even to the reluctant Irish Nationalist Leaders: there would be a 'step-by-step' approach to Home Rule. In the forthcoming general election the Liberals would promise that, if they won a majority, they would not introduce another Home Rule Bill in the lifetime of the new Parliament, though they would feel free to introduce more modest measures which were compatible with Home Rule and which might eventually lead up to it. The outcome brought considerable relief to the Radicals. At last the Gladstonian 'obstruction' had been removed, and a further assault on 'feudalism' could, at least in theory, be resumed with some prospect of success. It made for a welcome contrast to the sterile 1890s when so little that they valued had been achieved.

Yet, from the Radical viewpoint, the events of 1885–6 brought gains as well as losses. This was because so many of the Whigs had defected from the Liberal Party. The extent to which this had happened was partly camouflaged by the fact that many of the most famous Whig politicians stayed loyal to official Liberalism in 1886, some out of loyalty to Gladstone, others out of respect for the wishes of Lord Spencer, the former Lord Lieutenant of Ireland, whose experience in that office had converted him to the view that, without Home Rule, Ireland would be ungovernable. In Gladstone's last ministry there were no fewer than five major landowning peers (and several squires), which gave the impression that 'High Politics' had in no way changed. Moreover, when Gladstone finally gave up the premiership in 1894, his personal choice of a successor (the Queen, however, did not ask him for his opinion) was Lord Spencer. In the event the succession went to another Whig, Lord Rosebery – to the indignation of many Radicals.[17]

But these appearances were deceptive. Most Whigs, convinced that Home Rule meant the destruction of the Ascendancy in Ireland, left the Liberal Party in disgust in 1886, never to return. True, Gladstone himself seems to have believed that, under Home Rule, the Protestant landlords of Ireland would rise to their new responsibilities and emerge as 'natural' leaders of the people, as had happened in the late eighteenth century when the Irish possessed a Parliament of their own.[18] But this prospect seemed remote even to most of the friends of Home Rule, and was unlikely to appeal to those who stood to lose so much from the transfer of power to the forces of Irish Nationalism. This had an immediate impact on the balance of social forces within the British Liberal Party. Historians are divided over whether the division lists on the First Home Rule Bill can be explained in terms of MPs' social backgrounds. But, despite elaborate attempts to prove the contrary, it does seem as if former Liberal MPs from landed backgrounds were proportionately more inclined to rebel than were Liberal MPs as a whole.[19] Northamptonshire was typical; despite having Spencer as its premier landlord, 'Home Rule turned the drift to the right . . . into a landslide'.[20] Gladstone was therefore only exaggerating slightly when he said, 'We have say one-twelfth of the House of Lords, one twenty-fourth of the Squires, . . . perhaps one acre in fifty of the Soil'.[21]

In the House of Lords the 'flight of the Whigs' was certainly even more apparent. For much of the century the Conservatives had been in a majority in the Upper House. After 1886 the Liberals were reduced to a tiny rump. When the Second Home Rule Bill squeezed through the Commons in 1893, the Lords destroyed it by 419 votes to forty-one. It has been estimated that between 1886 and 1893 there were 356 Conservative peers, 115 Liberal Unionists, but only eighty-four Liberals. On non-Irish issues, it is true, the Liberal Unionist peers often sided, initially at least, with their former Liberal colleagues. But this, too, changed after 1891 with the appearance of the 'Newcastle Programme' (see below).[22] The fact that Liberalism was so weak in the Upper House had further consequences, in that it gave the party as a whole an incentive to curb the powers of that Chamber or change its composition. This in turn made the Liberal Party seem a more dangerously 'radical' organisation than it really was. The loss of so many great magnates also meant that after 1886 the overwhelming majority of Lord Lieutenants were Unionists – which led to a grave party imbalance on the county benches, since Lord Lieutenants were responsible for forwarding the names of suitable JPs to the Lord Chancellor's Office. This constituted another bitter Liberal grievance.[23]

But the converse to these landowning defections was an upsurge in the importance of 'advanced Radicalism', to which Gladstone found himself under a deep obligation. These groups were even more in the ascendant in the mass organisation of the Party, the National Liberal Federation, which had broken with Chamberlain and stayed loyal to Gladstone and to official Liberalism in 1886. Their importance can be measured from Gladstone's guarded acceptance of a far-ranging Radical programme passed by the NLF meeting at Newcastle in 1891. Included in the 'Newcastle Programme' were Welsh and Scottish disestablishment, local government reform, temperance, land reform, amendment to the Employers Liability Act and Home Rule. It has also been argued that Gladstone himself in his old age was becoming far more of a Radical than he had ever been in the past – though the evidence for this is far from conclusive.[24]

The outcome was a renewed burst of activity in the sphere of land reform. High in the priorities of the Liberal Party was the attempt to win back voters in the agricultural constituencies who had supported Liberalism so well in the 1885 election, only to desert them a year later. In 1890–1 the red vans of the 'Single Taxers' and the yellow vans of the 'Land Nationalisers' took eager 'missionaries' into the country villages to preach the gospel.[25] To raise the social and economic condition of 'Hodge', as the farm labourer was patronisingly called, particularly appealed to the Radical mind. Here, it seemed, was a class of downtrodden men, tyrannised over by their social superiors, who, lacking authentic spokesmen of their own (Joseph Arch, the union leader, had turned out to be a parliamentary failure), would respond to the lead given them by their middle-class friends. Despite all the difficulties they encountered, nothing could dampen the zeal of the reformers, and a commitment to some kind of land reform played a large part in the addresses of Liberal candidates right up until the Great War. In the 1906 election 68 per cent of Liberal election addresses in England mentioned the issue.[26]

But this emphasis on land reform understandably made landlords look with even greater suspicion on the Liberal Party.[27] As a result, by 1906 the social balance within the party had been permanently changed. When in 1905 Campbell-Bannerman formed his government, landed gentlemen (Sir Edward Grey) and traditional Whig aristocrats (Lords Carrington, Tweedmouth, Crewe, Ripon etc.) still received high office, but the majority of the Cabinet was (arguably for the first time!) unequivocally middle-class. In the parliamentary party as a whole, the shift in Liberalism's social base was even more pronounced.

The upper-class groups had fallen by 1914 to a mere 15 per cent (6 per cent landowners, 9 per cent official services) of Liberal MPs, as compared with 45 per cent of their Unionist counterparts (23 per cent and 22 per cent).[28] In the House of Lords the Liberal peers in 1908 numbered only 102 (out of a total of 615), and many of these were recently promoted businessmen or professional men, or else former MPs who had been given office and sent to the other place to ensure that there was *someone* to speak authoritatively on the government's behalf. The Radicals who thirsted for a showdown with the forces of 'feudalism' were therefore in an infinitely stronger position than at any previous time, now that they no longer had to contend with a significant landed element within the Party's own ranks urging caution and offering obstructions.

Nonconformity, too, emerged strengthened from the Home Rule crisis, despite the alienation of many Dissenters over the Irish issue. True, there is also some evidence that material prosperity was weakening the links between Dissent and Liberalism in certain areas. A voluntary poll of Wesleyan Conference delegates (that is to say, leading laymen) in 1887 revealed that perhaps 30 per cent of them were Unionists. And as many as 35 per cent of Congregationalist deacons in London were Unionists, according to a survey taken seven years later. However, since most deacons would have been of higher social status than ordinary chapelgoers, and since London was an area where a pronounced drift away from Liberalism had occurred, the proportion amongst lay Congregationalists as a whole was almost certainly lower.[29] It therefore seems reasonable to conclude that all the Dissenting sects, even the Wesleyans, continued to enjoy close links with the Liberal Party.

Moreover, the sectarian balance within the Parliamentary Liberal Party seems to have remained unaltered. The departure of Radical Unionists in the Birmingham area may have been a blow, but it was accompanied by the exodus of the Whigs, nearly all of whom were Anglicans. After the 1892 election there were as many as 177 Nonconformists sitting in the House, mostly as Liberals, and during the Edwardian period they constituted well over one-third of all Liberal MPs,[30] whereas amongst Unionists (if one leaves aside the Ulster Unionists) they numbered a mere handful – in the December 1910 election only seven, according to Koss.[31] Similarly within the constituencies. In many parts of the country the local activists, who tended to be Nonconformists (the Baptists were the most militant, the Congregationalists the most numerous), worked hard to keep the old sectarian issues at the forefront of the Liberal programme. The same story is told by the electoral geography of Britain. With some notable exceptions, those areas in which Dissenters outnumbered Anglicans were the areas where the Liberal Party regularly returned more members to the Commons than did its Unionist opponents. Wales, the West Riding of Yorkshire, the north-east, the south-west peninsula, and certain areas of East Anglia, for example, long remained Liberal strongholds. Except in the immediate aftermath of the Irish disruption, an overwhelming majority of the MPs which Scotland sent to Westminster also sat on the Liberal benches.[32]

Moreover, in the mid-1890s a new attempt was made to unify the main Dissenting communities and to mobilise them for political action – in practice, in the Liberal interest – with the foundation in 1896 of the National Council of Evangelical Free Churches, to which nearly all the Nonconformist sects (except the Salvation Army, the Unitarians, and the Plymouth Brethren) were affiliated.[33] Thomas Law, a minister from the United Methodist Free Churches, served as its vigorous organising secretary. Thus, even before the 1902 Education Act drove Nonconformists into an all-out attack on the Unionist government, there were signs of revived militancy in the Nonconformist world. The Education Act (which infuriated Dissenters by providing rate aid to church schools) undoubtedly led to thousands of Dissenters who had abandoned Gladstonian Liberalism over Home Rule returning to the fold, especially in the West Midlands – as Chamberlain had warned would happen.[34]

In addition, the bitter disputes in the Commons over the Education Act provided an important milestone in the career of

David Lloyd George, who acted as the principal spokesman at Westminster of the angry Welsh Dissenters – from whose ranks he himself came. Lloyd George's own biographers are divided about his motives. Lloyd George had lost his belief in the tenets of Christianity, it seems, some time in his adolescence. But, as in present-day Northern Ireland, sectarian allegiance involved much more than a set of theological beliefs; it also denoted membership of a distinct community. And Lloyd George, growing up as a boy in the rural area around Criccieth, identified himself passionately with the social and national feelings of the Welsh Dissenters, whose dislike of 'alien' Anglicanism he sincerely shared.[35] It is also significant that the debate over the Education Act coincided in Wales with a great evangelical crusade which swept the Principality, led by an ex-miner, Evan Roberts, in which thousands of hardened sinners publicly repented and the chapels increased their membership by some 82,000. In such ways did religious feeling and political behaviour mutually reinforce one another.[36]

It was, in fact, in Wales that opposition to the Education Act was most fiercely expressed. The Welsh County Councils found a legal loophole which enabled them to refuse rate-aid to voluntary schools, and the government had to pass a special measure giving the Board of Education powers to override the local authorities.[37] The Education Act did not apply to Scotland or Ireland, but in England, as in Wales, thousands of Dissenters refused on principle to pay their rates. This passive resistance movement was organised by the Norwich shoe manufacturer, George White, Liberal MP for North-West Norfolk. The Wesleyans refused to participate, but by 1906 there had been over 70,000 summonses, 2,568 auctions had taken place, and 176 Nonconformists had been sent to gaol.[38] Isolated pockets of resistance still existed on the eve of the Great War.

Anger over the Education Act carried over into opposition to the 1904 Licensing Act, which provided generous financial compensation for those publicans whose licenses had been removed. The Unionist Party saw this as a due regard for the rights of property, but Dissenters, most of whom were strong temperance advocates, were outraged by the state's subsidising of the hated drink trade. Temperance continued, in fact, to provide an important link between the world of the chapel and the secular activities of the Liberal Party.

The celebrated 'Nonconformist Conscience', which decreed that moral and religious convictions were the only worthy guides to political action, also drove the Liberal Party into taking a strong stand on the 'Chinese Slavery' issue.[39] Many Dissenters saw Liberalism as the only guarantor of public righteousness in a wicked world and would have agreed with the blunt verdict of one Congregationalist pastor: 'Toryism is wickedness'.[40]

Such feelings explain why so many Dissenting ministers enthusiastically threw themselves into the electoral campaigns of the Liberal Party just prior to and during the 1906 general election. When the Congregationalists were holding their annual convention at Leeds in October 1905, many delegates took time off to help the Liberal candidate in the important by-election in neighbouring Barkston Ash. And when polling opened in the 1906 general election, it was found that many Liberal candidates had had their nomination papers signed by Nonconformist pastors, who also in many places actually appeared by their side at public meetings. Leading divines went on motorised canvasses of the country. Whitefield's Tabernacle in London, the celebrated Congregationalist Chapel, became virtually a Liberal committee room for the South St Pancras constituency.[41] In the run-up to the 1906 election the Council of Free Churches also supplied twenty-five parliamentary candidates, although the Chief Whip, Herbert Gladstone, drove a very hard bargain at their expense.[42] Well might Conservatives complain that many Nonconformist preachers had abused the privileges of the pulpit in the recklessness of their party zeal.

What, in conclusion, can be said about the way in which traditional Radicalism affected the survival chances of the Liberal Party after 1886? Even at the time there were those who derided traditional Radicals for living in the past. Around the turn of the century there was something of a reaction against what was

41

misleadingly called 'Gladstonianism'. Revisionist groups in the Party, notably the Liberal Imperialists, called not only for the demotion of Irish Home Rule but also for the discarding of the Newcastle Programme and its replacement by a 'twentieth-century' approach which put greater stress on ameliorating the social conditions of the urban poor and improving the efficiency of the economy.[43] In retrospect, this seems like plain common sense.

There were certainly ways in which the Nonconformists acted as a drag on Liberal fortunes. Many of the issues which they forced the Party to prioritise, like Welsh Disestablishment and Local Option (that is, empowering local authorities to restrict the issue of liquor licences), lacked wider electoral appeal. As for Scottish Disestablishment, this was thought by Liberal organisers to be unpopular even in Scotland.[44] Yet such was the strength of the Nonconformist Committee within the House of Commons and so insistent the pressure from constituency activists that the leadership of the party often found itself saddled with commitments that were politically difficult to discard.

The various Nonconformist 'crusades' were perhaps better suited to Liberal spells in opposition than to their periods in power. The 'politics of indignation', in which Nonconformists specialised, led to the moralisation of politics and to a black-and-white approach to complex issues (like the relationship between schooling and the churches), together with a disposition to reject compromise as a temporising with evil. This reinforced the tendency of the Liberal Party to be a party of protest – and assisted the popularity within Liberal ranks of a Leader like Harcourt, who was patently at his happiest when attacking Unionist governments.

Unfortunately, such an approach to politics was often productive of strain between the Nonconformists and the secular intelligentsia (some of them freethinkers like Morley) who had traditionally been drawn to the Liberal Party. Both groups, admittedly, could unite behind the slogan of 'religious equality'. But whereas most intellectuals believed, as Mill had done, in toleration as a supreme virtue, to most Dissenters 'religious equality' merely denoted a wish to establish their own civic equality with Anglicans. Indeed, as self-appointed custodians of 'national righteousness', the Dissenters saw it as their mission to wage war against 'sin', in all its guises; the result was a series of attacks on Roman Catholicism, ritualism, gambling, and fornication in a spirit that brooked no compromise.

The Liberal Party itself became associated with this sort of narrow censoriousness. As one historian has put it, Liberalism gave many outsiders the impression during the 1890s of being 'a Crotchet Castle, from which dreary teetotaling Dissenters launched raids on pubs, music halls, and politicians cited in divorce cases'.[45] The pressure put on Gladstone and Morley to disown Parnell in 1890, even before his fellow Irish Nationalists had had time to discuss his suitability as a political leader, is an example of the way in which the puritanical fervour of the Dissenters could sometimes get in the way of what would have been a more expedient course of political action. The narrow zeal of many Dissenters could also damage Liberal leaders in other ways. Many backbench MPs who objected to Rosebery's emergence as Gladstone's successor in 1894, for example, did so on the ground that he owned a racing stud! Such protests sprang from the Dissenters' conviction that 'immorality' disqualified a man from political leadership.

Asquith, with his smart, society-loving wife, Margot, later fell foul of the same prejudices. His private secretary, Edwin Montagu, felt obliged to warn his 'Chief' in 1908 that the presence at a Prime Ministerial garden party of the '*risqué*' dancer, Maud Allan, had occasioned much dissatisfaction, although, as Montagu noted, it was 'characteristic of our Party that so many Members who object to meeting the lady were able apparently to recognise her'. 'There is no getting away from the fact that ours is a Nonconformist Party, with Nonconformist susceptibilities and Nonconformist prejudices', Asquith was told.[46] It was a warning that no Liberal leader could afford to ignore. How Lloyd George's adulteries did not bring him down is something of a mystery; probably many of his Dissenting admirers simply refused to give credence to the rumours of their hero's peccadilloes.

Was it wise for the Liberal Party to have allowed itself to be so closely tied to Nonconformity? Certainly there are signs from the late 1880s onwards that within large metropolitan areas like

London a growing secularisation was depriving the old sectarian issues of their former importance. Even in Wales the evangelical fervour of the early years of the century soon spent itself, and by 1914 the chapels were reporting a steady stream of defections. In South Wales young working men were prone to desert the chapel for trade unionism and the socialist societies, leaving the older generation of Welsh Liberal politicians looking decidedly old-fashioned. Even where socialism was not making progress, the growth of a new commercial entertainments industry was depriving the chapel of its social and cultural importance in the lives of those who had traditionally been most loyal to the Liberal Party. Most of the Nonconformist sects reached a peak of membership around the years 1905–8 and then declined.[47]

On the other hand, it is easy to exaggerate the speed with which these developments were undermining the traditional political culture. London, for example, was not typical of urban Britain – still less of the country as a whole.[48] The election as Liberal MP for Ipswich in January 1910 of the famous Congregationalist divine, the Reverend Silvester Horne, marked a high point in the political enthusiasm of Dissent. And in Norwich the old chapel networks retained their social and political vitality until well into the 1920s. Neither, as D. W. Bebbington has argued, should all Nonconformist 'desertions' from the Liberal Party be seen as symptoms of creeping secularisation, since this development was caused, not just by religious indifference, but also, in some cases, by a re-awakening of an older set of feelings, those centring around anti-Catholicism. Religion had as yet by no means lost its capacity to shape political allegiance.[49]

It may well be the case that the Nonconformists damaged *themselves* by getting too involved in the early twentieth century with the secular work of the Liberal Party. Ministers who cancelled their religious services in order to speak at Liberal rallies were behaving in a way that was likely, sooner or later, to provoke a strong reaction. Indeed, by 1910 'political Dissent' had reached something of an impasse. Its metropolitan leaders, through close association with the Liberal leaders, were beginning to drift apart from the laity. The Conservative-minded resented the way in which the chapel was being committed to party politics of the most partisan kind, while, paradoxically, rank-and-file militants tended to reject the compromises, like those on the education problem, into which their leaders were necessarily drawn. The suicide of Thomas Law in 1910 (he drowned himself at Brighton, after being seen to wander listlessly about the seafront, his breath smelling of spirits) ushered in a more politically quiescent phase in the work of the Free Church Council.[50]

But for the Liberal Party itself the relationship with Non-conformity brought many benefits. Firstly, it kept many of its traditional supporters loyal to Liberalism. It was essential for Liberals to devise a balanced programme which would retain middle-class enthusiasm (and money), while also appealing to the material self-interest of the poorer sectors of the electorate.[51] A single-minded concentration on social policy, to the exclusion of older concerns, would have narrowed the party's social base and weakened its electoral appeal.[52]

Nonconformity was also an asset in giving the party a sense of moral purpose. To quote a phrase usually applied to the Labour Party, it was widely believed that the Liberal Party was a moral crusade or it was nothing. In protesting against injustice in Ireland, denouncing the evils of Chinese Labour, and pressing for reforms in the conduct of licensed premises, Liberals believed that they had God on their side: that they were engaged in a campaign against class selfishness, materialism, and evil. Finally, at the local level the Dissenters often provided the bulk of the party activists, the local officers and the Liberal representatives on elected bodies.[53] In short, Nonconformity was probably an overall asset to the Liberal cause.

Land reform was also a powerful generator of Liberal energy. But here perhaps the balance-sheet was less favourable. For, despite their enthusiasm, Liberal land reformers were divided over exactly what they wanted to achieve. True, all could agree on removing the fiscal privileges enjoyed by landowners – something partly effected in Harcourt's 1894 Budget, which imposed graduated taxes on all estates, real as well as personal. A common commitment to site value rating (and its prerequisite, land valuation) also drew the various groups of reformers together.

But there agreement ended. Some Radicals subscribed to the nostrum of the American, Henry George, and wanted a 'single tax' to be imposed on land; others favoured land nationalisation. Some wanted to give power to local authorities to purchase land which could be leased in the form of allotments and small holdings; others (joined by many Conservatives) favoured a system of State-aided land purchase, as in Ireland, to create a class of peasant *proprietors*. In other words, there was a primary division between those who wanted to diffuse land ownership and those who wanted to abolish it (or subject it to stringent public controls). In addition, whereas some Radicals saw 'land colonisation' as a remedy for specific *urban* problems like unemployment and overcrowding, others were interested in the regeneration of rural life for its own sake.[54]

Moreover, as Chamberlain and Collings had found in 1885, help for the farm labourer risked estranging the farmers, whom the Liberals were also trying to attract with promises of a measure to strengthen tenant right. Here was a dilemma which was to reappear in Lloyd George's Land Campaign of 1912–14 and again in the mid 1920s. The Radical 'solution', of course, was to unite farmer and labourer in an assault on the privileges of the landowners, but this task was not easily accomplished except in areas like rural Wales where the social and economic ties between farmers and labourers were close and both felt alienated from an 'Anglican' landed elite. Over much of England farmers tended to gravitate towards the Conservative Party.[55] Ironically, it needed one of the declining group of big landowners still loyal to the Liberal Party, Lord Carrington, to convert land reform into a practical programme after 1906, and even then little was done to satisfy the somewhat utopian expectations that had been previously raised.[56]

Yet, when all is said and done, sectarian politics, land reform and similar attempts to prise the government of the country out of the grasp of the landed classes had not lost their relevance. It is tempting to contrast the Liberal Party, rooted in the issues of the past, with the socialist societies and the Labour Movement which represented the 'future'. Yet most socialists and trade unionists strongly backed these traditional Radical causes. For example, nearly all Labour MPs favoured land nationalisation (as did many Liberals). Leading socialists, like Keir Hardie and Philip Snowden, and pillars of trade unionism, like Arthur Henderson, were zealous temperance reformers.[57] And Nonconformity accounted for an even higher percentage of Labour than it did of Liberal MPs.[58] Moreover, the entire Labour Movement could join the Radicals in calling for House of Lords reform, the only difference between the two groups being that Labour tended to favour the abolition of the Upper House, not just the replacement of its 'absolute' by a 'temporary' veto. As for the moralising strains in militant Nonconformity, have not similar traits been observable in the twentieth-century Labour Party?

In short, even in the Edwardian period there was still much work to be done in dismantling the 'aristocratic state', and the Radical-Liberals cannot be accused of living in the past when they reminded the country of its necessity. These preoccupations would only have been damaging had they led the Liberals into a total disregard of other social problems – problems to which traditional Radicalism had given insufficient weight. It remains to be seen whether anything of that kind did, in fact, occur.

Perhaps the greatest danger to the Liberal Party was that it might degenerate, under Radical pressure, into a mere party of protest. In the 1890s, when the Liberals spent most of their time on the Opposition Benches, unsympathetic critics claimed that Liberalism was becoming a bundle of fads and crotchets and a congenial home for an assorted band of 'Antis'.[59] The Party gave many the impression of being the vehicle through which social outsiders expressed their hostility towards the 'Establishment', the peripheries (including the 'Celtic Fringe') protested against control by the Metropolis, and 'Little Englanders' inveighed against the Empire. The utterly negative Harcourt, who behaved like an Opposition politician even when he was Chancellor of the Exchequer ('I am not a supporter of the present Government', he said in 1894![60]), was perhaps an appropriate leader of such an organisation.

Doomed to spend a long period in opposition, the Liberal Party frittered away much of its energy in the 1890s and during the opening years of the new century on internecine strife.

Gladstone's deliberate failure to groom a successor landed the Liberals in a leadership struggle which debilitated the party for the best part of a decade. Thus Lord Rosebery, who eventually filled that post, was never able to impose his will on MPs, and his ministry ended after only a year when it was brought down by a revolt of its own Welsh supporters. The next leader, Harcourt, lasted little longer, just over two years, before the amiable but ineffectual Campbell-Bannerman took over – soon to be disowned by the Liberal Imperialist wing of the party. Foreign affairs provided the basis for most of these squabbles, but they were sharpened by personal animosities. Yet at a deeper level they also reflected the problems which the Liberals were having in developing a set of coherent and *constructive* social policies. What were the factors that had contributed to this particular situation?

4

THE 'PROBLEM OF LABOUR', 1886–1905

The New Electoral System

There was a particular reason why the Liberals should take social politics seriously. For in 1884 Parliament had passed the Third Reform Act, which for the first time gave Britain a popular, though not a democratic, electoral system. By extending the household franchise from the boroughs to the counties, it meant that, probably, some 76 per cent of the adult male population would be able to vote in parliamentary elections.

Accompanying the Third Reform Act was a measure of seat redistribution which also threatened to have a large impact on the older parties. In a way it turned out to be the more important of the two measures. By this Act the single-member constituency for the first time became the norm, both in counties and in boroughs. Whereas before 1885 the large industrial cities constituted two-member, or in the case of the metropolitan boroughs (Manchester, Birmingham, Leeds, etc.) three-member constituencies, they were now divided up into single-member constituencies of *approximately* equal size along lines which recognised the social and economic characteristics of specific urban areas. Thus, Manchester now had as many as six parliamentary constituencies, some of them 'mixed' in class terms, but some of them overwhelmingly middle-class or working-class. Instead of representing, say, Manchester as a whole, an MP might find himself returned for a wealthy residential area of Manchester which made him identify not with other parts of his own city but with similar districts in other big cities. This process seemed likely to encourage the development of a class-based electoral system very different from the one in which the old Liberal Party had been accustomed to operate.[1]

But contemporaries seem to have been more interested at the time in the implications of the franchise extension. Historians once believed that the 'democratic' potential of the Third Reform Act had been much exaggerated. Even after 1884, they argued, the electoral system continued to discriminate against the poorer members of society: while many of the well-to-do benefited from the survival of plural voting, certain categories of working-class people were excluded entirely, among them paupers, domestic servants, and soldiers living in barracks. A lodger vote did exist, but few were able to meet its complex requirements, as a result of which (to take one example) many unmarried men, living in the parental home, were not allowed to vote in parliamentary or municipal elections, even though they might well be politically conscious trade unionists. It has been argued that Labour's inability to make its own way before 1918 owed much to the class bias in the franchise.[2]

However, more recent work has shaken this interpretation. It has been shown that the main 'class bias' in the electoral system was provided by plural voting. But those who were denied the vote hardly formed a separate 'class', since most of them were the sons of existing voters. In fact, the defective lodger vote had the effect of discriminating against the young and the mobile. Far from being predominantly working-class, such groups, mainly unmarried men living in lodgings or in the parental home, came from all social backgrounds.[3] In short, contemporaries were right in their assessment. A 'mass' electorate existed, in which the traditional parties who ignored the wishes of manual workers would do so at their peril.

How did the Liberals react to this changed situation? Some remained unconvinced of the need to make any drastic innovations aimed at wooing the new voters. Even greater anxieties, they remembered, had been stirred up during the Reform Crisis of 1866–7 which had preceded Disraeli's famous 'leap in the dark' – anxieties which in retrospect looked groundless. Sporadic attempts to create independent working-class organisations during succeeding decades had led to nothing. Between 1867 and 1885 'Labour' consisted of little more than one of many pressure groups within the larger Liberal Party.[4] Why should the equalisation of the suffrage (between borough and county) revolutionise the political system in any way?

Yet not all Liberals were this complacent. True, some traditional Radicals continued to argue that both employer and employee had a common interest in breaking the landed monopoly and in extending the realm of 'freedom', and that class attacks from working men against 'capitalists' proceeded from a kind of 'false consciousness'. But such an approach was discredited by the fact that the two decades following the passing of the Third Reform Act were periods of electoral failure for their party – certainly by comparison with the preceding half century, when the Liberals had been the 'natural' party of government. In the 1885 election, held just before Gladstone's 'conversion' to Home Rule, the Liberals had secured a majority of eighty-six over the Conservatives – which was exactly the number of Irish Nationalist MPs, who thus held the balance of seats in the Commons. But that was the best the Liberal Party could do until the landslide victory of 1906. In 1892 they won forty-one fewer seats than the combined Unionist Parties – which again left them dependent on the good offices of the Irish when forming their 'minority' administration. As for the general elections of 1886, 1895 and 1900, these all resulted in resounding Liberal defeats.

By and large the damage to the Liberals was not inflicted by socialist or independent Labour candidates. In some industrial parts of the country, particularly the West Riding, the newly founded Independent Labour Party (ILP) was winning seats on local authorities in the 1890s – often after bitter clashes with the established employer-dominated local elites. But in the 1895 election every ILP candidate came bottom of the poll. The Liberals' discomfiture was the result, rather, of *Unionist* success.

The reasons for this state of affairs are complex. All that need be noted, at this stage, is that it was in the big cities, the working-class constituencies included, where the Liberal performance was most disappointing. In the seven major cities of London, Glasgow, Birmingham, Manchester, Liverpool, Leeds and Sheffield, for example, the Unionists won no fewer than eighty-one of the available ninety-eight seats in the 1895 election and still more (eighty-five), in 1900 (all the rest in both elections returned Liberals, bar the Scotland division of Liverpool, which returned an Irish Nationalist). This reflected the weakness of Liberal organisation, itself partly the result of financial difficulties following the defections of 1886, but it also suggested that the Liberal Party lacked popular appeal. Although, with some notable exceptions (for example, Birmingham and Liverpool), working-class areas tended to support the Liberals and middle-class areas the Unionists, the Unionists were considerably more successful in attracting their 'natural' constituents than were the Liberals.[5] What was to be done? Two obvious remedies suggested themselves: first, a change in policy and, secondly, a determined effort to field more working-class candidates. Let us take these issues one by one.

Liberalism and Social Policy

The party schism over Home Rule prevented Chamberlain from developing the ideas which he had outlined in the Unauthorised Programme from within the ambit of the Liberal Party, but it did not shake his conviction that it was imprudent to ignore the 'social question'. Soon he was trying to persuade his new allies in the Conservative Party that they should identify themselves with these issues. And, as Colonial Secretary in Salisbury's last administration, he was able to put some of his principles into practice when he steered through the Commons an important measure on workman's compensation – provision for which had already been established in Germany, whose social insurance schemes aroused the keen interest of Chamberlain, as well as of many others. It was also significant that Chamberlain had been the first politician of importance to come out (in April 1891) in favour of state-organised old age pensions. This, too, he was working hard to get the Unionist administration to adopt. Indeed, it was not entirely out of the question that Chamberlain would succeed in his ambition of converting 'Unionism' from a narrowly defensive creed, centred on Ireland, into a heady concoction which combined social reform at home with imperialism abroad. This certainly had many demagogic possibilities.[6] Why, then, was the Liberal Party so slow to see the dangers of Chamberlain making all the running as a social reformer?

To be fair to the Liberals, there was a group of younger MPs who accepted the case for Irish Home Rule but were worried about the party's lack of a domestic programme and anxious to provide it with a more constructive, 'governmental' ethos than was likely to emanate from the old-style Radicals. Between 1886 and 1892 this group was organised around the so-called 'Thirty-Nine Articles Club'. One of its most active members, R. B. Haldane, a friend of Sidney Webb, provided a line of communication with the Fabian Society, and some hard thinking on social policy resulted. In 1892 two of the leaders of the coterie forced their way through sheer ability into the Cabinet: Asquith as Home Secretary and Acland as Vice-President of the Council, with responsibility for education. Unfortunately, these young MPs lacked support at the highest levels of the party. John Morley encouraged them in private and disowned them in public. Their later liaison with Rosebery was to be only slightly more fruitful.[7]

In the early and mid-1890s it was the obsession with Home Rule which proved the major obstacle. Not that Gladstone's fourth ministry did nothing in the field of social legislation: Asquith, the Home Secretary, devoted much time to an Employers Liability Bill, which eventually came to grief in the Lords. And in the President of the Board of Trade, A. J. Mundella, the Liberals had one of their few senior politicians with a proven track record as a social reformer. Under his auspices a Labour Department was set up and the groundwork laid for what eventually became the 1896 Conciliation Act. Certain categories of workers also benefited from the period of Liberal rule. Employees in the royal ordnance factories and the dockyards were promised trade union wage rates and granted an eight-hour day, and in the railway industry the workforce was brought under the protection of the 1893 Railway Servants (Hours of Labour) Act (though this piece of legislation was primarily intended to safeguard the travelling public). All these innovations suggested that the Liberal Party was beginning to develop a new set of policy interests.[8] All the same, to make an electoral impact, social reform needed to be placed towards the top of the legislative agenda and vigorously promoted, which was never going to happen as long as Gladstone controlled the party.

But Gladstone's retirement in 1894 and the temporary eclipse of the Irish Question did little to improve the situation. We have already seen how the resulting leadership squabbles sharpened differences amongst the Liberal front bench over foreign and imperial policy, but they also had the effect of inhibiting the party from developing a positive domestic programme. Two examples of how this happened must suffice.

In 1894 Harcourt produced an innovative Budget which sharply increased the incidence of death duties on larger estates. Though this measure was welcomed by many traditional Radicals as a long overdue assault on landed privilege, it also has the appearance, particularly in retrospect, of an important step towards a more 'progressive' fiscal system, i.e. one in which wealth was deliberately redistributed by Treasury policy from the richer to the poorer members of society (the earlier system tended to do the reverse). Yet, although the Budget duly reached the statute book, this was only after bitter protests from Rosebery. This, on the surface, was surprising, since Rosebery had acted as Chairman of the London County Council since 1889, where he had come into contact with 'Progressive Councillors', some of them Fabians; indeed, Rosebery seemed to be making a conscious effort to identify himself with those groups in the Liberal Party to whom a bold policy of social reform deeply mattered. It may, of coure, be that Rosebery's professions of concern for social questions amounted to little more than empty rhetoric. But it is also likely that his reactions to the 1894 Budget were coloured by deep personal antipathy to its author.[9] However, Harcourt's own behaviour was only slightly less perverse. Having pointed the Liberal Party in a promising new direction, he then failed to follow up his success. In 1895 he based his own election campaign on the promise of Local Option, and was defeated by his Derby constituents for his pains![10]

Personal rivalries also damaged the attempts of the Liberal Imperialists to say something fresh and challenging about urban problems. When this group created the Liberal League in January 1902, sympathisers, like the Fabian, Sidney Webb, were attached to the cause. In the interests of 'National Efficiency', attempts were made to develop a range of social policies. But, again, this part of their campaign quickly petered out. Some of the Liberal MPs involved in the group clearly did not believe seriously in social reform at all, their main concern being to testify to their 'responsible' attitude to Empire and national defence and to put distance between themselves and Home Rule. And some, like Robert Perks, came from that wing of the party to which redress of Nonconformist grievances was the only kind of reform that mattered. Contempt for Campbell-Bannerman and a hope that he might be replaced eclipsed serious thinking about housing, unemployment and the like.[11]

But it may well be that the Liberal Party's domestic problems should be ascribed, not simply to the distractions from which it suffered, but also to the kind of party that it was. Here we come to a major source of disagreement amongst historians. At one extreme, there are those who believe that the Home Rule schism alienated from Liberalism most of its wealthy business supporters (as well as most landlords), leaving it a much more 'democratic organisation'. The starting-point of such interpretations is a famous utterance made by Gladstone to his Midlothian electors in 1886: 'On the side adverse to the Government are found . . . in profuse abundance station, title, wealth, social influence, the professions, or a majority of them – in a word, the spirit and power of Class'. Faced by problems of fund-raising, the Whips in the 1890s were talking in a very similar way.[12] The Home Rule schism certainly meant the defection from official Liberalism of the big railway interests, though the origins of this development can be traced back well before 1886.[13] But the corollary of this, some historians argue, was the Liberals' growing dependence upon the working-class elements in the electorate.

In total contrast is the interpretation offered by Professor Lubenow, who insists that the crisis of 1886 'created a polarization of the political nation along ideological, rather than social, lines'.[14] After all, business families, like the Quaker Peases of Darlington, were split, some members following Gladstone, others becoming Unionists. Moreover, the voting on the Home Rule Bill, Lubenow shows, divided Liberal business MPs in almost exactly the same proportion as it did the Liberal parliamentary party as a whole (about sixty-three to thirty-seven).

Yet this study, for all its valuable insights, goes too far in playing down the role of social and class factors in determining attitudes towards Home Rule. Significantly, as Lubenow's own statistics show, the percentage of Gladstonian MPs re-elected in 1886 who were to the right of the median of his scale of ideological position fell to 21 per cent, compared with 8 per cent before the 'Great Separation' – which surely suggests that Liberalism had indeed been 'radicalised' by the Irish issue.[15]

The truth undoubtedly lies between these two extreme positions. Certainly, if we move outside the confines of the House of Commons and look at the behaviour of the *electorate*, strong evidence exists that the events of 1886 stimulated a drift out of the Liberal Party amongst prosperous middle-class voters – although this probably accelerated a trend that had already become established. Professor Blewett, for example, has convincingly argued that the importance of Liberal Unionism was that it offered a stepping-stone to the right amongst wealthy men who still thought of themselves as being anti-Conservative but had, over many years, been losing confidence in Gladstonian Liberalism. These defections, he points out, occurred in particularly large numbers in London and the Home Counties. In such areas voting was heavily class-based from 1886 onwards, perhaps earlier.[16]

Why 'villa Toryism' should have been so strong in southern England has been partly explained by W. D. Rubinstein. The divisions within the middle class over Irish Home Rule, he contends, were by no means arbitrary. Rather, they reflected a deep fissure within the middle class between commercial and financial centres, on the one hand (such as Greater London and Merseyside) and the industrial/manufacturing cities, on the other. Bankers and the larger merchants, he suggests, had always been closer, economically and culturally, to the world of the landed estate than had northern industrialists (many of whom were Dissenters), and it is therefore not surprising that the former should have aligned themselves with the Conservative Party during the decade after 1886, unlike the latter group which did not move decisively in this direction until the 1920s.[17] This, in turn, explains the existence of a pronounced North/ South political divide, with the Liberal Party's centre of gravity lying north of a line stretching from the Bristol Channel to the Humber.[18]

Rubinstein's thesis needs to be qualified and refined. For example, two of the areas which broke most decisively with Gladstonian Liberalism in 1886 were the West Midlands (Chamberlain's fiefdom) and, obviously, the Belfast region (where Home Rule polarised the population between Irish Nationalism and Unionism), both manufacturing districts. Nevertheless, when all necessary qualifications have been made, it remains broadly true that in *most* manufacturing districts, like the West Riding, the north-east and south Wales, business Liberalism retained its strength until 1908 and perhaps later still. Even middle-class constituencies in these areas tended to stay loyal to the Liberal Party.[19]

Businessmen, particularly in the coalfields and the heavy industrial areas, continued, therefore, to play a crucial role in Liberal politics throughout the 1890s. They dominated the party organisation: the powerful President of the NLF after 1886 was James Kitson, the great Leeds railway engineer. They supplied Liberalism with many of its local councillors: over 40 per cent of Liberal councillors and executive members in Leeds, Leicester and Norwich were businessmen, mainly manufacturers, to say nothing of the large shopkeeping element.[20] Liberal 'millocrats' were especially prominent in the towns of the West Riding.[21] At

Westminster, too, the Liberal benches contained large numbers of 'captains of industry', in particular textile manufacturers and coalowners. And finally, the Liberal Party had come by the early twentieth century to depend for its central funding on a mere twenty-seven men, eighteen of whom were businessmen, mostly big Scottish and Northern industrialists.[22]

Now, it was amongst these key supporters that opposition to legislation which raised taxation and interfered with 'industrial freedom' tended to be particularly fierce. Thus, in the early 1890s the Whips were worrying lest employers' liability legislation would 'cripple, if not destroy' the staple industries of the country, as their business supporters were predicting, and thus alienate from the party much-needed financial backing. Similarly on the eve of the Newcastle Conference, Liberal MPs were hearing sentiments about 'the relation of capital and labour analogous to the sentiments of Tory squires on the relation of squire and labourer', as one of them put it.[23] One of these reactionary capitalists, Alfred Illingworth of Bradford, actually announced his retirement from Parliament in protest at the government's sympathy for a Miners' Eight-Hour Day Bill.[24] Liberal MPs who were also major employers of labour involved in bitter industrial disputes, such as C. H. Wilson, the Hull shipowner, were particularly averse to any 'concessions' to Labour. Indeed, so long as these powerful businessmen remained within the Liberal Party, relations with the trade union movement were likely to be tense. Significantly, the one industrial dispute of this period in which prominent Liberals came unequivocally to the support of strikers was the Penrhyn slate workers' dispute at Bethesda in North Wales, where the employer was a landowning Conservative peer.[25] More typical was the West Riding, where working men active in the Labour and socialist movement not infrequently found themselves victimised by their 'Liberal' employers.[26] Thus, business Liberalism was by no means destroyed by the great schism of 1886. Indeed, after 1903 it actually enjoyed a new lease of life in reaction to Joseph Chamberlain's ill-fated Tariff Reform campaign.

The purpose of Tariff Reform was threefold: to bind the self-governing countries of the Empire more closely together through a system of 'Imperial Preferences': to protect native industry against 'unfair' foreign competition: and to broaden the basis of taxation in order to meet growing demands for public expenditure, both for defence and for the provision of social services. But the very suggestion of tampering with Free Trade, the central component of the Liberal creed ever since the 1840s, was bound to galvanise the Liberal Party. Its working-class followers were alarmed at the prospect of dearer bread ('The Little Loaf'), following the imposition of a corn duty. At the same time many businessmen were also dismayed at the probable consequences of any return to Protection. A trade war, they feared, might be sparked off which would threaten their sources of supply (e.g. raw cotton for the textile industry) or their foreign markets (which were considerably larger than the Empire markets, upon which the Tariff Reformers pinned their hopes). Moreover, wage increases resulting from food price rises might well have blunted the competitive edge of British manufacturers in world markets. The industries that were coping most successfully in the export market had a rational economic case for favouring the fiscal *status quo*, and hence working for the return of a Liberal government.

Tariff Reform, then, helped to revive what some historians have called 'economic liberalism',[27] strengthening many businessmen in their allegiance to the Liberal Party. Free Trade also won back some of the faint hearts who had deserted it in the depressing 1890s. This particularly happened in Scotland, where the *Glasgow Herald*, organ of the business community, was staunchly free trade. Two Scottish Unionist MPs, both businessmen, crossed the floor of the House in protest at Chamberlain's *démarche*.[28] As a result, in 1906, even more than in 1886, the Liberal Party was a party in which, especially at parliamentary level, the role of great capitalists was strongly visible. This, in itself, put a break on any attempt to create an advanced programme of social reform.

But Tariff Reform hindered the social reformers in another sense. Already by 1903 party unity had been largely restored.

The divisive war in South Africa formally ended in the summer of 1902. The Balfour Education Bill then drove nearly all Liberals together in opposition to this affront to their principles. Finally, confronted by Tariff Reform, Liberals of all shapes and sizes could unite in defence of Free Trade, secure in the knowledge that they now had an issue ('cheap bread') on which, barring accidents, they would sooner or later be swept back into office.

This meant, however, that a social programme was no longer so necessary. It is even doubtful whether the Liberals would have agreed to the Lib-Lab Pact (discussed below) but for the fact that the negotiations with Labour had acquired an unstoppable momentum by the time that the significance of Chamberlain's activities had been fully appreciated. As the increasingly accident-prone Balfour ministry stumbled to inevitable defeat, what little thinking that had been going on amongst senior Liberals on the social question also came to a halt. Why make rash promises when all that needed to be done was to hold tight and wait for one's opponents to commit suicide?

What this led to in practice is illustrated by a telling vignette. In the autumn of 1904, with the economy in recession once more, Herbert Gladstone produced a memorandum on the unemployment problem, designed to provoke his colleagues into doing more than attack Chamberlain, but the discussion soon petered out.[29] On the eve of the formation of his ministry, Campbell-Bannerman reported his discovery from meetings which he had addressed in Glasgow that 'much mischief was being done by the notion that we had little or nothing to say about the unemployed. So I risked one foot upon that ice, but was very guarded and only spoke of enquiry and experiment'.[30] By the time that the general election of 1906 took place, little serious thinking on social policy had taken place. On the surface it seemed as though the previous twenty years had been utterly wasted, as far as this area of public policy was concerned.

But surface appearances were somewhat deceptive. Away from the world of 'High Politics' Liberalism was changing. This came about in part because interest in the plight of the 'people of the abyss' had never entirely disappeared, even after the economic and social crisis which had originally brought it to prominence had somewhat abated. Throughout the 1880s and early 1890s a motley crowd of middle-class investigators and philanthropists descended on the slum areas of the great cities, in particular the East End of London, to study the problems of social deprivation, to demonstrate their 'neighbourliness' with their poorer fellow-citizens and to search for remedies for the ills which they had uncovered. Most were young men (but young women, too, were caught up in these activities), often graduates from Oxford and Cambridge Universities. Their conscience aroused by having had their attention drawn to the gap between their own living conditions and those that prevailed in all the big cities, these middle class 'do-gooders' were activated by a mixture of feelings, in which guilt, curiosity and fear all played a part. Toynbee Hall and other 'Settlements' acted as magnets for these young social explorers and investigators; in time they also served as bases from which serious social 'field work' could be organised.

Not all of those caught up in the Settlement Movement and similar activities were Liberals. Indeed, in the early 1890s a commitment to the serious study of social problems was widely thought to be something quite apart from 'politics' – an indication of how little these concerns had as yet impinged on Westminster and Whitehall. But perhaps a majority of such people felt a vague sympathy with the Liberal Party, if only because Liberalism seemed to be the creed of those with a belief in the possibility of achieving social progress through the exercise of benevolence and the application of rationality. In any case, the Liberal Party had always been a rather loose-jointed party, through which a variety of reforming pressure groups had tried to exert influence.

A good example of a person involving himself in Liberal politics in this way is Charles Masterman.[31] On graduating from Cambridge, where he had been deeply influenced by Canon Scott Holland of the Christian Social Union, a High Church pressure group interested in social reform, Masterman took up residence, not, it is true, in a settlement, but in working-class lodgings in Camberwell. Soon he was using his personal knowledge of the London poor in contributions to the Radical newspapers and in his books (of which the most famous, *The Condition of England*, was to be published in 1909). When in 1906 Masterman was first elected to Parliament, it was the start of an important political career. But other like-minded young men were following a similar path. The 1906 election saw the return to Parliament on the Liberal side of the House of several former residents of the Settlements Movement, men who could speak with authority about urban problems in a way which, say, the leading Liberal Imperialist politicians could never possibly do. As the most talented of these young MPs began to establish their Commons reputations, the agenda of Liberal politics was likely to change.

What these social investigators learned through their encounters with urban poverty succeeded, in time, in modifying what Liberalism meant. But before this could happen, more was needed than a growth of empirical social knowledge and understanding. For Liberals also had to reassure themselves (as a prelude to reassuring others) that social reform did not mean an abandonment of the principles which their party had traditionally followed. It was not just inertia and distraction from other issues which had made the Liberal Parliamentary Party hesitant to embrace new proposals, like old age pensions; there were also formidable ideological obstacles that first had to be surmounted.

Traditionally most Liberals had started off with a presumption that state intervention in the working of the market was both futile and wrong. This particularly applied to projects of social reform which would involve public expenditure. Gladstone had believed that money was best left to 'fructify' in the pockets of the taxpayer. To overcome this inherited prejudice would not be easy. It was all the more difficult in that, particularly in the municipal arena, Liberal councillors were often closely allied with – or even coterminous with – ratepayer protection groups.

But there was also a more general suspicion of state activities. Nothing should be done that would interfere with the operation of the market, damage work incentives or weaken contractual obligations. By the 1880s many exceptions had been made to these general rules, but usually in the interests of those who were unable to look after their own interests or make binding con-

tracts (like children, minors, and – though this was more controversial – women). Liberal political thought was essentially
individualistic, concerned with the protection of citizen's rights
and the removal of 'trammels' on individual freedom. Before it
was possible to add to the attainment of individual rights the
securing of social justice, which is what most social reformers
wanted, Liberals would have to demonstrate that the new departure was really a logical development of their principles, not
an abandonment of them.

The trouble with much of the pioneering work of Radical
social reformers was that, not being couched in a Liberal idiom,
it was prone to be rejected as a deviation from the true faith.
That was even true of the youthful Joe Chamberlain and his
friends in the early 1880s. The doctrine of 'ransom', constant
invocations of the will of the majority, and talk of the need to
pursue the 'greatest happiness of the greatest number' set many
Liberals' teeth on edge. Chamberlain seemed to be a dangerous
'Jacobin', a latter-day disciple of Jean-Jacques Rousseau. This
revolutionary French approach was not something with which
mainstream British Radicals felt comfortable.[32]

A similar difficulty faced the 'Thirty-Nine Articles' group,
who seemed too closely tied to the Fabian Socialists for most
Liberals' liking. Later in the 1890s the attempt by the Liberal
Imperialists to float a social policy on the back of ideas of
'National Efficiency' also faltered, in part because the rhetoric of
efficiency had no recognised place in Liberal ideology. Even
when being relatively unprovocative, the 'efficiency group' gave
the impression of being motivated by little else than a desire to
occupy the 'centre ground' of politics. On other occasions, they
displayed a certain authoritarian temper, pouring scorn on party
and advocating a 'Germanic' kind of bureaucratic centralism,
totally foreign to the Liberal tradition. This made it easy for
their enemies within the party to castigate them as heretics.[33]

All of this was important. A party easily loses electoral credibility if it gives the impression that, in its eagerness to win
power, it is prepared to jettison all that it supposedly stands for.
Moreover, late Victorian Liberalism assigned primary importance to ideas – which were thought to provide the basis upon

which policy could later be erected. John Stuart Mill was typical of Liberals in his insistence that 'ideas' were primary, 'interest' secondary. Could Liberalism, then, be 'modernised' so as to encompass issues of social policy without the whole ideological tradition being called into question? In particular, what answer could be given to the two Radical MPs for Northampton, Labouchere and Bradlaugh, who opposed social legislation as 'immoral' because it 'would strike a blow at the self-reliance of the individual'?[34]

Many leading Nonconformists, from John Clifford to Hugh Price Hughes, attempted to rise to the challenge. Like leading churchmen of other denominations, they became involved in a discussion of the 'social question', took part in the 'exploration' of 'unknown London', and ran settlement houses in the city slums. In particular, the Congregationalists' Browning Hall Settlement played a notable part in the later old age pensions campaign.

But, left to their own devices, few Dissenters would have made much progress in the field of social reform. For a start, they were less shocked by poverty as such than by the existence of the kind of destitution likely to lead to 'sin'. For example, overcrowding, as revealed by Mearns (himself a Congregationalist minister) arrested their attention because of the links that were shown to exist between it and incest. But few Dissenters (again, Mearns well illustrates the thesis) had either the time or the knowledge to devote themselves to the elucidation of difficult social problems. Hence, with a few notable exceptions, Dissenters (their Anglican counterparts were usually no better) often drifted off into innocuous platitudes, speaking of the desirability of arbitration and urging the need to see that women and children did not suffer during strikes. Alternatively, they simplified complex issues, as when they attributed a range of social evils to a single moral failing, for example, drunkenness or gambling. Finally, like the Radical businessmen (they were often the same people, of course), most Dissenters were nervous of doing anything that would undermine family obligation or the individual's sense of responsibility. Finally, even the most advanced 'social reformers' among the Dissenters tended to attach less significance to these issues than they did to the old sectarian causes.[35]

It therefore needed the secular intelligentsia to work out a considered rationale for social reform. This was the task tackled by the group who have come to be known as the 'New Liberals'.[36] The two most important figures in this movement were L. T. Hobhouse, sociologist and leader writer for the *Manchester Guardian*, and J. A. Hobson, the heterodox economist. The 'two Hobs' did much to convince influential Liberals that their creed was a living, not a static, thing. Their views were disseminated, not just through their books, but also through a variety of newspapers, both national (the *Daily News*) and provincial (the *Manchester Guardian*), as well as through small-circulation but prestigious periodicals, like the weekly *Nation*, whose editor H. W. Massingham played a key role in the development of the New Liberalism. Significantly almost the entire *Daily News* team entered the Commons in 1906, strengthening the social reform elements on the Liberal benches.[37]

In setting out to revise the Liberal ideology, the 'reformers' found that the 'Manchester School' Liberalism of Cobden and Bright, still a source of inspiration to many traditional Radicals, was worse than useless. They were able to make much greater use of the writings of John Stuart Mill, whose linkage of 'liberty' with the idea of the 'realisation of personality' was capable of drastic extensions. These it received, particularly at the hands of Hobhouse, who added elements from the German 'Idealists' (filtered through the writings of T. H. Green) and from the conception of society as an 'organism', popularised by the Social Darwinists. New Liberalism was necessarily an eclectic affair. Its advocates even exchanged ideas with the more congenial socialists, both Fabians and ILPers, like Ramsay MacDonald, through such organisations as the 'Rainbow Circle', a dining club which was founded in 1894 and carried on until the late 1920s. (Ten of the twenty-five members of the Circle were elected to Parliament in 1906.)[38] But the Liberal intellectuals almost certainly had a very much greater influence on these socialists than *vice-versa*, and New Liberalism, despite the fact that it amounted, in Peter Clarke's view, to a kind of 'social democracy',[39] remained an authentically 'liberal' ideology, not a raid on other political traditions.

What the New Liberals were in fact doing was mounting a persuasive case for the view that the all-important concept of freedom had to be defined in more sophisticated ways. It was too simple to contrast 'freedom' and 'coercion'. What mattered was to draw a distinction between the freedom which stimulated and the freedom which cramped the development of personality. New Liberals also contended that (in Hobhouse's famous words) 'liberty without equality is a name of noble sound and squalid result'.[40] Freedom of contract, in other words, was not freedom at all if one side to the bargain was constrained by poverty or in some other way impeded from a rational prosecution of his own best interests. New Liberals also insisted that since property rights had a 'social' as well as an 'individual' dimension, there would be situations in which the community was entitled to intervene: property rights, in other words, should not be treated as absolute.

It was equally necessary to develop an entirely new fiscal strategy. The Liberals had inherited from Gladstone a strong commitment to 'economy' as a good in itself and to the view that taxation should be 'proportionate', i.e. that it should not be graduated in order to benefit any particular class. It took bitter experience to convince Liberals that 'economy' was simply not reconcilable with many of the other objectives they had started to set themselves. But the move away from 'proportionality' (which had been strongly endorsed by Mill) required something of an intellectual revolution. However, from the 1890s onwards, the notion of 'social value' helped the Liberals to escape from the straitjacket of orthodox economic theory and to give priority to social goals. Initially, the emphasis was on ways in which social spending could raise production by stimulating effective demand (Hobson's theory of underconsumption was important here); only later was redistribution of wealth seen as important in its own right. But the important point is that from the 1890s onwards Liberals began to accept the idea that the Budget could be made an instrument of social policy, and this represented an important break with the past.[41]

Now, even this bald summary of the New Liberal creed should be sufficient to demonstrate that a theoretical justification was being advanced of quite far-reaching interferences in the market and that these principles could be invoked, not just in support of all the welfare initiatives which the Liberals were to take in the Edwardian years, but to justify policies which have been too radical for any government that has yet been formed in this country: for example, Hobhouse and others were prepared to countenance minimum wage legislation – as a necessary condition for the realisation of their particular concept of 'freedom'.

Nevertheless, there were also important limitations in the New Liberalism, which also characterised Liberalism as a whole. The purpose of progress was adjudged to be the attainment of 'social harmony' through a collective exercise of rationality. In consequence, Hobhouse specifically rejected the idea that a just society could only come into existence by a process of class conflict. The people he labels the 'mechanical socialists' (i.e. the Marxists) receive very rough treatment. 'Class', indeed, was a phenomenon which could find no legitimate place in this style of political philosophy. Social reform was seen as an enlightened stratagem for promoting the 'common interest', not as a way of carrying out the will of the majority, still less as a way of advancing a sectional interest.

This made even the most advanced of Liberal thinkers view trade unionism with considerable suspicion. As mechanisms for helping the poor and disadvantaged to assert their true needs, trade unions had a useful role to play; as agencies for schooling their members in the duties of citizenship they were wholly admirable. But there was horror at the thought that they might also develop into 'armies' that could wage war on employers or on capitalism itself. Indeed, the New Liberals actually took the side of the employers in the party, in the sense that they too tended to emphasise the interdependence of the interests of capital and labour.

Moreover, although the willing co-operation of the working class was necessary to the achievement of 'social harmony', the New Liberals, by implication at least, assigned the key role of defining the 'common good' to the Liberal intelligentsia – to men like the two 'Hobs'. As one historian has put it, 'the New Liberals were so intent on preserving their policies from the "taint of sectionalism" that they failed to see that it was as a sectional interest that Labour felt most threatened'.[42] Nor, arguably, did Labour *want* 'collectivism', if this meant, for example, the regulation of industrial relations. As Chiozza Money argued in 1906, there may well have been more 'collectivists' amongst the Liberals than in the Labour Party.[43] But this merely indicates that the New Liberals were anxious to 'do things for' the working class, while the Labour Movement was seeking to control its own destiny. This was to be the source of much misunderstanding in the future.

We will return in a later chapter to the vexed question of what contribution, if any, was made by the New Liberalism to the social legislation which the Liberal governments enacted between 1908 and 1914. But three questions can immediately be posed. How successfully did the New Liberalism harmonise old philosophical traditions with new social needs? In other words, was this ideology coherent and persuasive? Secondly, how widely did these ideas circulate? Did they make a significant impression on the Liberal politicians who held power at central and local levels, or were they ingenious intellectual constructions which largely ministered to the amusement of the 'chattering classes' of Hampstead and the leafy suburbs of Manchester, the natural habitat of the Liberal intelligentsia?[44] And thirdly, would this particular concept of social reform be acceptable to politically conscious working men and women, or would it be seen (if encountered at all) as paternalistic or patronising? Here much would depend on what Liberals were doing to increase working-class representation on elective bodies.

Working Class Representation

In fact, one of the Liberals' greatest failures was to match their solicitude over obtaining working-class votes with a willingness to sponsor working-class candidates. There was no shortage of influential voices urging local constituency parties to adopt manual workers. For example, the Secretary of the NLF, Schnadhorst, sent out a warning letter to this effect in 1890;[45] other party leaders echoed his advice. Yet little was done. Only in some coal-mining districts, where so high a proportion of the electorate consisted of miners that the local lodges could impose their own favoured candidates upon the middle-class Liberals in their locality, were these difficulties overcome. These were the so-called 'Lib-Lab' MPs, numbering about a dozen during the 1890s, of whom half were miners: most were trade unionists who consulted the interest of their union in industrial matters but were otherwise happy to take the Liberal Whip.[46] In addition, in Battersea the former SDF leader, John Burns, an engineer by trade, managed to create his own 'Labour' organisation with the help of which he was able to win and retain this poor working-class seat.[47]

But where Liberalism was already well organised, the local managers were usually loath to put up working men for winnable constituencies, and, since the local parties enjoyed autonomy in the matter of candidate selection, there was little that party headquarters could do about it. Perhaps nothing did more to alienate politically ambitious working men from the Liberal Party. Many of Labour's pioneers had only come to the conclusion that a new working-class party was necessary after they had suffered personal rebuffs at Liberal hands. To take a famous example, Keir Hardie was turned down by the Mid-Lanarkshire Association in 1888 (he eventually stood as an Independent Labour candidate and came a humiliating bottom of the poll). A similar fate befell Ramsay MacDonald in Southampton six years later.[48] And although the future careers of these two politicians perhaps suggests that the local Liberal organisers, from their own viewpoint, had judged wisely, it was quite otherwise when many Liberal trade unionists found themselves balked at the last moment of a prize to which they felt that their services to the party entitled them. Arthur Henderson (the later Labour leader), for example, was rejected in 1895 by the Newcastle Liberal 'One Thousand', in opposition to their executive's advice, despite the fact that he held orthodox Liberal views on 90 per cent of the political issues which currently dominated national politics – although, in fairness, one must add that many, perhaps a majority, of the delegates responsible for this ill-judged action were themselves working men.[49] Middle-class prejudice was even more blatantly displayed when Bradford's Liberal Executive Council refused in 1885 to allow the President of the Trades Council, a life-long Liberal, to stand as one of their candidates in the local School Board elections, and when Fred Mappin, the leader of the local Liberal caucus, blocked attempts to run a working-class candidate in the Sheffield (Attercliffe) by-election in 1894.[50]

Why did Liberal management committees display so little vision? In some cases, it seems, they hesitated to put forward manual workers because they believed that lack of education and social standing were a disqualification from performing an MP's role. To put it another way, working-class Liberals were hampered in their political careers by considerable social prejudice. But there were also practical considerations. Not until 1912 did MPs receive a salary. They (or their backers) were also obliged before 1918 to pay the returning officer's expenses, as well, of course, as meeting the costs of the election campaign itself. Finally, to win all but the safest seats, a candidate was expected, before the campaign formally opened and restrictions on legal spending began to operate, to show generosity to a variety of local clubs and associations. The outlay could be daunting. In Lancashire, it cost a parliamentary candidate between £500 and £1000 to fight a borough and twice as much to fight a county division.[51] Little wonder that constituency associations tended to select wealthy men who could entirely or largely pay their own way.

The Liberals' parliamentary leadership was obviously aware of the importance of helping into the House able men of limited financial means. Some of the money accumulated by the party's Chief Whip was used to subsidise such men. However, it seems that most of the beneficiaries were impecunious young professionals, like C. F. G. Masterman, rather than manual workers.[52]

In any case, the party's Central Fund was raised by means of donations from wealthy supporters and sympathisers (some of them on the look-out for 'honours'). With the departure of so many of its landed members in 1886, this meant that the Party was falling dependent on a relatively small number of very wealthy businessmen. Some of these men, like the cocoa manufacturer, George Cadbury, were 'advanced Radicals' who genuinely wanted to see more working men in the House. But most were not. Moreover, in the long run it proved damaging to the Liberals that, despite their claim to be a 'democratic' party, they rested on so very plutocratic a financial base. So long as this situation persisted, it was unlikely that the Liberals were ever going to put up working men in significant numbers.[53]

A partial resolution of this difficulty eventually came about but in a very unlikely way. Angered by the Taff Vale Judgment which placed the very existence of independent trade unionism at risk, union leaders and socialists came together in 1900 to form the Labour Representation Committee (LRC), the forerunner of the modern Labour Party. When it became apparent that this new body, unlike earlier attempts to establish independent Labour associations, seemed likely to survive as an effective force, most Liberal politicians expressed some anxiety and disapproval. Even Lloyd George in 1904 professed bewilderment at this latest turn of events, calling the decision to 'go in for anything like independent class representation' 'a mistake': 'They will realise that sooner or later.'[54] The Liberals, as we will shortly see, disliked intensely the very idea of class-based parties.

Yet the Liberal organisers soon realised that, given their failure to put up working-class candidates of their own, there would be advantages in running them by proxy, as it were. An electoral pact with the LRC would not only avoid a splitting of the anti-Unionist vote, it would also align Liberalism with an authentic working-class organisation, thereby adding to its own popular electoral appeal. This formed the background to the signing of the Lib-Lab Pact in 1903, negotiated between Herbert Gladstone, the Liberal Chief Whip, and his assistant, Jesse Herbert, on the one hand, and Ramsay MacDonald, secretary of the LRC, on the other.[55] It was an informal understanding, which neither side could formally proclaim. The leaders of the two parties could thus exercise influence with constituency parties with the aim of avoiding electoral clashes, but the scheme rested very largely on the willingness of the activists in the constituencies to co-operate with one another.

Yet in England and Wales such co-operation was indeed

forthcoming. In the 1906 election, the LRC sponsored fifty candidates, of whom twenty-nine were returned. And of these, all but five were elected either in a straight fight against a Unionist or by the running of a single candidate in harness with one Liberal candidate in a two-member constituency (in Merthyr Tydvil Hardie was elected against the opposition of two Liberals but no Conservatives in a two-member seat). This set the pattern for subsequent Liberal-Labour co-operation (some call it the 'Progressive Alliance'), which survived, more or less intact, until the outbreak of the First World War.

But was it wise for the Liberals to have entered such an arrangement? Even at the time there were voices in the provinces raised against what they suspected was being done in their name, warning of 'nursing into life a serpent which will sting their Party to death'.[56] In Scotland, where Liberalism was strong and anti-Labour feeling among its activists ran high, the pact did not operate at all. Even in the north-east of England nineteen out of the twenty-three Presidents of Liberal constituency organisations opposed such an arrangement, while in the West Riding, firmly in the grip of wealthy industrialists, there was a similar reaction.[57]

The case against the 'Lib-Lab Pact' ran as follows. The Liberals, said the critics, should never have given a helping hand to this new party, which threatened in time to become a formidable rival. It was all the more dangerous in that, though the leaders of the LRC might find it expedient to present their party as a kind of working-class Liberal association, in reality it was very much more than that: for the LRC was a federation of affiliated trade unions and socialist societies, and, although most trade unionists may indeed have been 'sound' on the major political issues of the day, the same could not be said about the socialist elements – about ILP members like Keir Hardie, Bruce Glasier and Philip Snowden, for example, who, true socialists that they were, viewed both the 'capitalist' parties with contempt. In areas like Bradford, where the ILP had for many years been challenging the Liberals in local elections, this case was frequently made.

In retrospect, it can also be argued that the sacrifice of seats to the LRC was totally unnecessary. The LRC leaders were merely bluffing when they claimed to be able to control one million working-class votes; most of the ordinary trade union members had always voted Liberal in the past and would have continued to do so. Conversely, the result of the 1906 election seemed to confirm that the Liberals were strong enough to go it alone; LRC candidates had shown their utter incapacity to win seats through their own unaided efforts. Thus, the pact was a one-sided affair, from which the Liberals had secured little advantage.

But the arguments on the other side are equally strong. The danger of splitting the anti-Unionist vote was indeed a very real one, and this would have been a tragedy, given the fact that very little separated the LRC from the Radical wing of the party. From this viewpoint one cannot easily call the pact a 'betrayal' of the Liberal creed. Indeed, in 1900 Labour and the Radical 'Little Englander' wing of the party were so close to one another in their hostile stance towards the Boer War that in 1900 Keir Hardie actually suggested that Labour put itself under the leadership of John Morley – a declaration that was all the more startling, coming, as it did, from an avowed socialist.[58]

Over the next few years, on the most important issues of the day, education, licensing, and the tariff, nothing separated the Liberal Party from most Labour politicians. In London, where Liberals and Labour had been linked since 1889 through shared participation in the so-called 'Progressive Party', Radicals and Fabians were happy to appear on one another's platforms. A proof of what could be achieved by such co-operation was furnished by the Woolwich by-election of March 1903, when the Cockney Will Crooks was triumphantly returned as an LRC candidate – with a sympathetic Liberal Party forbearing to put forward a candidate of its own.[59] Even 'socialists', like Hardie, Snowden and (pre-eminently) MacDonald, took the Liberal side against the Unionists on almost every live political issue that counted. Campbell-Bannerman therefore had good reason to proclaim that Liberalism and Labour 'were both elements in the progressive forces of the country' who 'were going together nine-tenths of the way'.[60]

Moreover, granted that socialism posed a long-term challenge, the Pact could be defended as a cunning way of containing its advance. For the LRC, as we have seen, was a federal organisation, linking the trade unions to the important socialist societies. The Liberals, by reaching an informal alliance with it, would strengthen the 'moderate' trade unionists at the expense of those socialists who continued to believe, at a theoretical level, that nothing separated the two parties of 'capital'. An electoral understanding, from which the LRC had much to gain, would encourage it to emphasise those things which it had in common with the Liberal Party. 'Socialism' (in which most members of the LRC anyhow disbelieved and which was not so much as mentioned in the party's Constitution) would become nothing more than a misty aspiration.

Finally, there were more tangible advantages to be gained. If an informal pact with the new party could be negotiated, the Liberals, still hard-pressed for money, would, as Jesse Herbert of Liberal Central Office noted in March 1903, save £15,000 by leaving certain constituencies to be contested by their junior allies.[61] Nor was this all. In those parts of the country, particularly Lancashire, where the Liberal Party was weak and working-class Conservatism strong, the LRC with its class appeal might succeed in taking votes away from the Unionists which Liberal candidates would be unlikely to do. Indeed, almost all the seats where Liberal candidates stood down in 1906 were seats which the Liberals had been unable to win in 1900 and could not be sure of capturing the next time round: not much of a concession to the new party, some might think.[62] Finally, in return for ceding such seats to Labour, the LRC, for its part, would have to pay the price of recommending its working-class sympathisers, in constituencies where Labour was not standing, to vote Liberal. Quite probably the Liberals' vote was swollen in 1906 by the adhesion of working men who perceived the Liberals to be the allies of Labour. For a party concerned to maximise its working-class appeal, this was a powerful recommendation.

In the short-run the advantages of the pact to the Liberal Party undoubtedly outweighed its disadvantages. Its authors cannot, in any case, reasonably be criticised for misfortunes which befell Liberalism over ten years later in circumstances wildly different from anything that they could have envisaged in 1903. Indeed, the 'understanding' with Labour worked so well that, appropriately modified, it was also brought into operation in the two elections of 1910 and, but for the war, might have continued still longer. So great was the movement of the electorate towards the Liberals in 1906 that one can well say, with the wisdom of hindsight, that its existence contributed little to the Liberal victory of that year. However, that was emphatically not the case in the close-run contests of 1910, when Liberal-Labour clashes might have tipped the balance decisively in favour of the Unionists – to the detriment of both Liberals and Labour. Moreover, the very benefits which Labour gained from the Pact also indirectly helped the Liberals, since they made Labour leaders very reluctant to break free and try to take on all-comers. The fact that, following the landslide victory, the Labour MPs occupied benches on the Opposition side of the House was neither here nor there; where else could they comfortably have sat? Labour MPs, many of whom had obviously been returned on the strength of Liberal votes, would find it difficult to behave as members of the truly independent party which they still claimed to be.

Nevertheless the 'Progressive Alliance', even if the best that the Liberals could hope for under the circumstances, was far from ideal. As one historian argues, it conceded the formal independence of a separate working-class party and was thus 'a setback rather than a victory for the New Liberal point of view'.[63] The Pact had, after all, only come into existence because of the Liberals' failure to put up enough working-class candidates of their own. Moreover, when the Miners Federation of Great Britain (MFGB) finally decided to affiliate to the Labour Party in 1908, the last big industrial union to do so, most of the miners in the House transferred their allegiance from the Liberal Party and took the Labour Whip, so depriving the Liberals of almost all their working-class MPs.

It is true, as we shall see, that the Liberal governments of 1905–14 showed an acute concern for the problems of the poorer members of society.[64] But 'doing good' to the working classes was never an adequate substitute for helping (or allowing) working men and women to cater for their own needs. It is ironic that even the urban Radicals, who had never been happy with the notion of entrusting their welfare to 'enlightened' aristocrats, should not have seen that politically conscious working men would similarly resent a political system which did not allow people of *their* order a place of dignity and influence in the running of the country.

5
THE RADICALS IN OFFICE, 1905–14

So long as the Liberals were in opposition, or held office in precarious circumstances (as between 1892–5), what strategy Liberals should adopt was largely a matter for *debate*. It was quite otherwise with the formation of Campbell-Bannerman's ministry in 1905. For the next decade the Liberals held power. What use were they going to make of it?

To understand how the Liberals faced up to this dilemma one must take account of the rather odd circumstances in which the Liberals displaced their Unionist opponents. The reversal of party fortunes between 1900 and 1905 was both sharp and unexpected. So demoralised had the Liberals been in the 1900 ('Khaki') election that they had left 152 constituencies on mainland Britain uncontested (more even than in the disastrous year of 1895 when the figure had been 117); the outcome had become clear even before the polling booths opened. Over the next eighteen months Liberal fortunes reached the lowest point that they had yet touched, as faction fighting enveloped the party. It seemed as though the Unionists would remain in office for the foreseeable future.

In retrospect, one can see that this was an illusion. In fact, the vagaries of the electoral system produced a somewhat misleading result. Even in the highly disadvantageous circumstances of 1900 – a war in progress, weak leadership, deep divisions at all levels of the party – the Liberal vote had stood up reasonably well, amounting to 48.2 per cent in contested seats (44.6 per cent overall). Where the Liberals performed worst was in the densely populated constituencies which generally experienced low turn outs, which suggests apathy amongst potential working-class supporters – a situation that was remediable.[1]

Moreover, the relationship between the different wings of the Unionist Alliance was a fragile one. Once the 'danger' of Home Rule had been seen off, it was no longer clear quite what Unionism stood for. Tension between Radical Unionists, like Chamberlain, and more traditional Conservatives steadily increased. The climax was Chamberlain's launching of the Tariff Reform Campaign in 1903, in which he announced that Free Trade had outlived its usefulness and should be replaced by a system of 'Imperial Preference'. Such an attack on one of the most sacred Liberal tenets quickly re-united the Opposition party.

There followed a series of ministerial mishaps and blunders, all of which played into Liberal hands and made the likelihood of another Liberal ministry increasingly probable. In December 1905 Balfour resigned as Prime Minister. Campbell-Bannerman, having quickly quelled a half-hearted mutiny from the old Liberal Imperialist faction,[2] was able to form an extremely strong government – it contained three future Prime Ministers, Asquith (Chancellor of the Exchequer), Lloyd George (President of the Board of Trade) and Winston Churchill (Under-Secretary at the Colonial Office), as well as Edward Grey (Foreign Secretary), Haldane (War Secretary) and John Morley (Indian Secretary).

Early in 1906 Parliament was dissolved, and the Liberals were confirmed in office with the second biggest landslide achieved in any twentieth-century election. The Unionists were reduced to a rump of 157 MPs, while Liberals won many apparently 'safe' Conservative seats, like Bath, Salisbury and Exeter.[3] In the excitement of the moment it was difficult for Liberals to make sense of what had happened. But enthusiastic Radicals felt that a new age of rationalism and enlightenment had dawned. Disappointment was bound to follow.

It is often said that parties never win elections, though they sometimes lose them. That adage applies very well to 1906. Not only did Tariff Reform tear the Unionists into antagonistic factions. The Unionists had also managed to alienate almost every conceivable interest group in the land. The Nonconformists were furious over the 1902 Education Act, and their anger deepened with the passing of a licensing measure in 1904 which could plausibly be denounced as a sell-out to the drink trade. Organised Labour was aggrieved over the government's refusal to reverse the Taff Vale Judgment and at its employment of indentured 'Chinese Labour' in the South African gold mines. Even natural supporters of the government were disheartened when they looked back on the bungling, incompetence and inadequate preparations which had marked the military campaigns in the recent South African War. In these circumstances, the Liberals did not need to formulate an alternative programme or even an alternative strategy.

It is sometimes claimed that the Liberal victory of 1906 represented a popular mandate for sweeping measures of social reform. There is very little truth in this. The landslide victory swept into Parliament a motley crowd of enthusiastic reformers of one kind or another, among whom can be identified a group of 'Social Radicals', between twenty-five and forty in number, who had made a serious study of urban social problems.[4] But the front benchers were ominously non-committal about social reform, even about old age pensions, which had been on the political agenda for nearly twenty years. The emphasis fell upon retrenchment and economy, not on a programme of state-aided welfare that was bound to be expensive. As George Bernard Shaw correctly observed, the 1906 election was a triumph for conservatism with a small 'c'.[5] It was quite clear what the Liberals were *against*. They were against Tariff Reform: against high arms expenditure: against Chinese 'slavery': against the 1902 Education Act, and so on. The Liberals had even promised not to introduce a Home Rule Bill within the lifetime of the forthcoming Parliament: a promise which probably reassured the nervous and destroyed Balfour's frenzied attempts to frighten the electorate with his last-minute claims that the Union was in danger. But what were the Liberals *for*?

Certainly, there was a mood of expectancy in the air in 1906.

But no detailed commitments had been made. Nor is it easy to extract a class meaning from the 1906 election results. Clearly, the majority of working men cast their votes for the Liberals – while another 11.5 per cent or so supported the recently formed Labour Representation Committee, which, as we have seen, was linked to the Liberal Party through an informal electoral alliance. On the other hand, the Unionist government's affront to Non-conformist sensibilities and the attack on Free Trade had between them driven a large block of middle-class voters, including businessmen, into the Liberal camp.

In 1906, then, the Liberals enjoyed popularity with electors from a wide variety of social backgrounds. But it soon became apparent that the Liberal triumph had been brought about by an unusual combination of circumstances that were unlikely to recur. Moreover, the Liberals, having won power, had to make up their minds what they were going to do with it. As soon as they did that, the rather spurious sense of 'national unity' seemed likely to evaporate.

With Campbell-Bannerman failing to give a firm lead, the first couple of years of Liberal rule was a period of aimlessness and drift. Important decisions were taken in foreign affairs, but in domestic politics no clear pattern emerged. In 1906 Campbell-Bannerman threw over his own law officers and, with the Trades Disputes Act, gave trade unionists what they had been demanding ever since the passing of the Taff Vale Judgment: an unconditional restoration of their immunities in the event of a strike. This perhaps denoted an eagerness to propitiate the Labour Movement both inside and outside the House. The same might be said of the 1906 Workmen's Compensation Act, which extended Chamberlain's 1897 measure. The Liberals also took over a private Bill introduced by a Labour backbench MP which permitted local authorities to provide meals for necessitous schoolchildren, using a rate subsidy if necessary.

But the main legislative priority, if indeed there was one at all, seemed to involve the paying-off of political debts to the Liberals' Nonconformist followers. 'We have been put into power by the Nonconformists', Campbell-Bannerman is alleged to have said.[6] An Education Bill, aimed at ending the 'obnoxious' features of the Balfour Bill, was the principal government measure of the 1906 session.[7] A major Licensing Bill shortly followed. But when, to no-one's surprise, the House of Lords obstructed the passage of the Education Bill, the Liberals declined to dissolve, fearing to jeopardise their majority over an issue which, they suspected, aroused little popular enthusiasm in the country at large. Moreover, this Bill (through its Clause 4) had made provision for the public funding of church schools in urban areas should four-fifths of the parents petition for it – a clear attempt to curry favour with the Irish Nationalist Party, and something which damaged the Bill in Dissenters' eyes. Thereafter, the educational grievance was given low priority, and the Dissenters soon found that they could do little to pressurise the government into changing its mind. Nonconformity's later disillusionment with Liberalism can be traced back to this initial failure.[8]

Other government Bills, like the 1906 Plural Voting Bill, made no better progress, coming up, as they did, against the Opposition veto in the Upper House. The Liberals also suffered a humiliating setback over their Irish Council Bill of 1907, a botched attempt to extend Irish local government without going the length of Home Rule; the measure had to be withdrawn in the face of furious protests from the Nationalist leaders.[9] Such events badly undermined the morale of Liberal backbenchers, and by the spring of 1908 the fortunes of the party were at a low ebb.

But there was another reason for this. In 1907 the economy had started to go sour. A cyclical depression, originating in America, was producing bankruptcies, falling profit margins and mounting unemployment. Contemporaries called it 'the Rich Man's Panic'. By 1908 unemployment among trade unionists had gone up to nearly 8 per cent, its highest point since 1886. These economic circumstances had immediate political consequences. The government started to lose a string of by-elections. Three seats were won by the Opposition in early 1908 on swings of between 3.5 and 6.5 per cent. There were two by-elections in which an independent socialist did the damage,[10] but the real threat to the Liberal position in 1907 and 1908 came from the Unionists. Now recovered from their stunning defeat in 1906, the Tariff Reformers saw that the Depression gave them the opportunity they needed. They began to take control of the Opposition party, with Balfour's grudging acquiescence, shrilly blaming the unemployment on to the Free Trade system. Tariff Reform, they promised, meant work for all.[11]

At just this moment, in April 1908, the dying Campbell-Bannerman submitted his resignation. Asquith, as expected, succeeded to the Premiership. The Cabinet reshuffle which followed saw Lloyd George promoted from the Board of Trade to the Treasury and his close friend, Winston Churchill, enter the Cabinet for the first time in Lloyd George's old post. The period of drift and uncertainty was over. The Radical crusade was about to resume.

In the new Asquith government the drive was increasingly provided by Lloyd George himself, a complex figure who arouses among historians, as he did among his contemporaries, feelings of both admiration and disgust.[12] But, faced by a rejuvenated Opposition fighting for Tariff Reform, Lloyd George did at least have the imagination to see that a negative defence of Free Trade would not suffice. Instead, he decided to take up the gauntlet thrown down by the House of Lords and to make a new determined assault on aristocratic privilege and, at the same time, to seek to broaden the Liberals' electoral appeal by a constructive policy of social reform.

Lloyd George's own background and personality help explain why he was determined to combine these two campaigns. Although by no means a typical product of the Dissenting communities of rural North Wales, Lloyd George nevertheless did feel instinctively that the Liberal mission was to undermine the Anglican establishment, destroy the remnants of the pre-industrial aristocratic order – or 'feudalism', as he liked to call it

82

– and to create a society in which there would be equality of opportunity and men and women would be valued for their intrinsic qualities without reference to their ancestry or social status.

An insensitive observer, listening to Lloyd George's emotional and demagogic platform orations, might suppose that he was an egalitarian. The Welshman certainly hated, with fierce hatred, what he called 'privilege', and boasted that he was better qualified than most politicians to speak for 'the People', since he was one of the children of the People. Like a number of left-wing politicians, Lloyd George invented, as he grew older, an almost entirely spurious childhood, supposedly marked by poverty and suffering. Having got to the top, he boasted, with pardonable but childish pride, of the dizzy social ascent he had had to make. In fact, Lloyd George's background can best be described as 'petit bourgeois'. He started life as a small-town solicitor. By no conceivable stretch of the imagination can Lloyd George be called working-class. In fact, growing up in the area around Criccieth, the Welshman seldom came into contact with the proletariat proper, and some historians would say that he never really understood the psychology of the unionised industrial worker.

It is perhaps worth remembering at this point that Lloyd George, though his speeches were soaked in class feeling and often lifted his audience into a state of great emotional excitement and anger, never used the language of class in its *modern* sense. As with so many nineteenth-century Radicals before him, he saw himself as leading 'the People', with a big P, against the forces of privilege. His bogies were landlords, peers, brewers, publicans, priests. But he had no quarrel with capital. Providing that businessmen, bankers, and shareholders acknowledged their social responsibilities, he was happy to defend their role as a necessary and beneficial one, and he did not begrudge them very large incomes if they earned these incomes by a constructive contribution to the production of wealth. Essentially, Lloyd George was trying to create a unity of the so-called 'productive classes', by which he meant the industrial workforce, and capitalists, entrepreneurs, managers and shareholders. This pan-class alliance he then wanted to lead in a fight against parasitic monopolists and idlers, notably the landlords, who battened on the country's wealth, but did nothing to create it. In a way Lloyd George was therefore picking up the Unauthorised Programme which Chamberlain had dropped in 1886, when his attention had been distracted by Ireland.

Lloyd George had first achieved national prominence by the zeal with which he had led the Welsh Nonconformists in their impassioned protests against the Balfour Education Act. Although he had lost his Christian beliefs at some point in early manhood, all his life Lloyd George strongly identified with the world of the Baptist Chapel, in which he had spent his formative years. Listening to sermons and hymn-singing remained one of his favourite pastimes. The great Baptist preacher, Dr John Clifford, was so impressed by this aspect of Lloyd George's character that he assured a political rally in 1910 that 'Lloyd George was in politics as Mr Gladstone was in politics, that he might serve God in politics'.[13]

Even had he wanted to break free from his chapel connections, Lloyd George would have found it difficult to do so. But he had no such wish. Apart from anything else, Lloyd George knew that pushing forward Nonconformist demands helped to preserve the *balance* in the Liberal programme, which was necessary if its traditional middle-class supporters were to be kept loyal to the Party[14] – something which, on both practical and ideological grounds, was indispensable to Liberalism's survival.

But what Lloyd George also saw was that sectarian issues by themselves were not enough. The events of 1906–8 had proved that. Without ever quite renouncing the enthusiasms which had brought him into politics in the first place, Lloyd George outgrew them to some extent. If the Liberal Party were to have a future, it needed to move in a Radical direction, and its Radicalism would have to acquire a social, as well as a political, conscience.

What was true of Lloyd George was broadly true of the Edwardian Liberal Party as a whole. And so the years between 1908 and 1914 saw two parallel campaigns: the final assault on 'feudalism' and an earnest attempt to tackle the 'social problem', along the broad lines already laid down by the 'New Liberal' intelligentsia. The two campaigns sometimes became inter-woven. Lloyd George's famous 'People's Budget',[15] for example, exasperated the landed interest but caused corresponding delight to the party's traditional Radical supporters by including, not only a number of land taxes, but also provision for the valuation of all land. Increased duties on tobacco and spirits could be counted upon to please the Dissenting teetotallers, as could provisions for increasing the cost of licenses issued to licensed premises (a provision partly taken from the Government's 1908 Licensing Bill, which the House of Lords had rejected). Yet, if these proposals seem to look back to a nineteenth-century conception of Radicalism, the introduction of a 'super-tax' of 6d in the £ on incomes over £5,000 and a move towards a more sharply graduated income tax system seem to point to the future. So did the government's establishment of the Development Commission.[16] A similar ambiguity surrounded the later Land Campaign and Lloyd George's other highly innovative Budget of 1914.[17]

Edwardian Liberalism, in short, was Janus-faced: it looked back to the great Radical tradition of Cobden and Bright, but it also looked forward to the social democratic policies promulgated by later twentieth-century governments. At the risk of some simplification, it seems sensible to take these two aspects of Liberalism one by one, starting with the final 'assault on feudalism'.

The Assault on Feudalism

The assault began in earnest in 1909 with the first of the eight Budgets which Lloyd George prepared. This 1909 Budget, the so-called 'People's Budget', contained along with other controversial proposals, a group of land taxes and a scheme of land valuation. The Radical backbenchers were delighted, the Conservative Party predictably enraged. The land taxes themselves were moderate enough; in fact, in time they were to be repealed by the post-war coalition government, of which Lloyd George was the head, on the ground that the revenue which they brought in did not warrant the administrative costs involved in their collection. But it was the provision for land valuation which caused all the furore; for once valuation had been completed, a Radical government had a number of extreme options available to it, including land nationalisation itself, which was actually backed by nearly 130 MPs, most of them Liberals.[18] Characteristically, Lloyd George, though by temperament and conviction an ardent land reformer, had only the haziest idea exactly what sort of reform he wanted. Equally characteristically, he concealed his imprecision under a flood of emotional rhetoric. Here many landlords played into the government's hands by the extravagance and bad temper with which they attempted to justify their traditional privileges. Their outspokenness enabled Lloyd George to reply with a platform invective which, even over the years, still gives off a charge of violence and excitement.

The fight over the Budget had an important, but not entirely planned, outcome. The House of Lords, with the blessings of the Conservative leadership, broke a constitutional convention of nearly 200 years' standing by rejecting the Budget. An earlier view that Lloyd George cunningly framed the Budget in order to precipitate this response now finds little favour. But the Lords' decision greatly pleased most members of the Liberal Party and no-one was more pleased than Lloyd George himself.

The Constitutional Crisis which followed is one of the most familiar episodes in British political history.[19] Summarised baldly, the defeat of the Budget forced Asquith to dissolve Parliament. The Liberals were returned in the January 1910 general election in roughly equal numbers to the Unionists, with Labour and the Irish Nationalists, who held the balance of seats, keeping Asquith in power. The Budget, now that it had received a popular endorsement, soon became law. But Asquith's freedom to move against the House of Lords was hampered by the insistence of the King that *another* election must take place before he would use his prerogative to create enough Liberal peers to swamp the Opposition in the Upper House when – as would inevitably happen – their Lordships refused to consent to their own emasculation. Following the death of Edward VII in May, a constitutional conference was held in an attempt to break the deadlock. The conference failed, and Asquith promptly asked for a dissolution and also for an advance promise ('the contingent guarantees') that the royal prerogative would be used for a mass creation of Liberal peers if and when the need for this arose.

The result of the second 1910 election closely followed the first. The government introduced its Parliament Bill; the Unionist Opposition objected, but, informed at the last minute of the King's promise, prudently gave way – though only after an internal party dispute which cost Balfour the Conservative leadership. In August 1911 the Parliament Bill became law. Under its terms the right of the Lords to throw out Bills passed by the Commons was replaced by a suspensory veto; the immunity of Finance Bills from interference by the Lords was formally affirmed; and the life of Parliaments was reduced from seven to five years.

While the Constitutional Crisis was in progress, Lloyd George, at least in public, gave the impression of greatly enjoying himself. Some of his sallies against the landed aristocracy and against the Upper House have become legendary. He and other Radicals could also take satisfaction from the final outcome of the struggle. The curbing of the powers of the House of Lords had been something which all nineteenth-century Radicals had thirsted to achieve. To have brought it off was something of a triumph for 'the People'. Moreover, the Lords' loss of its absolute veto enabled the Liberal government to promote legislation which would otherwise have been doomed to failure. In 1912 a measure for the disestablishment and disendowment of the Church in Wales was introduced. It was rejected by the Lords, but under the terms of the Parliament Act a measure which passed through the Commons in three successive sessions would automatically become law. In fact, the Bill received the royal assent in September 1914, although its operation was suspended due to the recent outbreak of war.[20]

At the same time Lloyd George was pressing forward with his Land Campaign, an ambitious attempt to revolutionise the countryside, involving security of tenure for farmers and the creation of Wage Boards for the fixing of a minimum wage for agricultural labourers. This constituted a serious electoral threat to the Unionist Party since, although the Opposition had won about two-thirds of all English rural constituencies in December 1910, its leaders felt that their hold on many of these seats was 'precarious'.[21] A delighted Masterman was writing to Lloyd George in 1913, 'Create an organisation to spread the "Virus" in every village, even the neighbourhood of Hatfield [home of Lord Salisbury], and we will at least stir things a bit before we die!!'.[22] The prospect of harassing the aristocrats in the heart of their great estates was a highly pleasing one to Radicals. Indeed, there is evidence that the campaign went down very well in Scotland, though in England it enjoyed mixed fortunes.[23] In addition, together with slightly improved agricultural conditions, these anti-landlord agitations had the effect of encouraging land-owners to put part of their estates on to the market. By late 1914 some .800,000 acres of English land had changed hands – a sign of the loss of confidence felt by many great aristocrats in the future of landed property.[24]

Nevertheless, something had gone wrong with the Radical crusade. For the 'destruction of feudalism', if that is what it was, did not, at least in the short run, seem to be doing much to boost the Liberal Party's fortunes.

There are broadly two reasons for this. The first is that the Liberals were only able to reduce the powers of the Lords with the help of the Irish Nationalists, and the Irish, in return for their help, exacted an assurance that Home Rule would again be brought out of cold storage. When the first of the two general elections of 1910 left Redmond, the Irish leader, holding the balance of seats in the Commons, the Liberals found that they had fallen dependent upon the Irish, a situation which many of them resented. Indeed, the Constitutional Crisis, almost from the start, became overshadowed by the Irish issue. In early 1910, for example, there were a number of ministers, among them Grey, the Foreign Secretary, who did not want to reduce the *powers* of the Lords but preferred to alter the *composition* of the Upper House. This might mean anything or nothing, but the Irish reckoned that even a 'reformed' Lords would probably be hostile to Home Rule, and held out for removing the Lords' veto. Indeed, Redmond threatened Asquith that if the government did not commit itself to the removal of the veto his party would refuse to vote for the 'People's Budget' when it was reintroduced into the Commons. The threat was a plausible one, given the unpopularity of the Budget in Nationalist Ireland. There was even a brief moment in the spring of 1910 when it seemed possible that the Asquith ministry might fall, to be replaced by a minority Conservative administration enjoying temporary Irish support.

Although on this issue the Liberal Cabinet gave way and secured the passage of the Budget by a public commitment to the policy of veto, the constitutional conference of the summer saw them once more trying to back away from the strategy to which Redmond and the Irish were trying to pin them. No Irish MP was invited to the constitutional conference, which was ominous in itself; had any been present, he would have been enraged to learn that, unbeknown to the wider public, the delegations were discussing the so-called 'Ripon Plan', a scheme for resolving deadlocks between the two Houses by special 'joint sessions'. The Liberals were even prepared to debate an Opposition proposal that 'organic' (or 'constitutional') Bills, which might possibly include a Home Rule Bill, should be accorded special treatment by being first referred to the judgement of the people in the form of a referendum. In the event, the Liberals turned down this suggestion; had they done otherwise, their alliance with the Irish Nationalists would have come to an abrupt end.[25]

But before the conference had finally collapsed, Lloyd George had secretly approached Balfour with the proposal that a 'National Government' be set up to dispose of all the outstanding issues of the day. This episode, like so many of Lloyd George's escapades, is surrounded to this very day in ambiguity and confusion. But what is not in doubt is that Lloyd George had floated the possibility that the Irish Question be resolved within a larger measure of 'Home Rule All Round' or 'Devolution' – that is to say, that other parts of the United Kingdom as well as Ireland be given subordinate assemblies, prior perhaps to an attempt to federate the entire Empire. Such an arrangement, even if it had been practical, would have been entirely unacceptable to the Irish Nationalists, who, facing opposition within their own country from separatists and physical force nationalists, could not afford to be too accommodating. But, of course, if a coalition of the two main parties had been formed, the Irish could have been left to 'stew in their own juice', as Lloyd George remarked to one delighted Conservative MP who was 'in the know'.[26]

The Secret Coalition talks petered out after some desultory discussion. The parties returned to their battle stations. But, as many Liberals had predicted would be the case, Asquith's Third Home Rule Bill, first introduced in 1912, brought the ministry nothing but trouble. In the north-east of Ireland what amounted to a pan-class rebellion of the Protestant Loyalists took place. Indeed, between 1912 and 1914 the threat of civil war in Ulster overshadowed all other political issues. It was in vain that Lloyd George launched his Land Campaign in October 1913. His speeches received disappointing coverage in the press. People were not interested in the plight of tenant farmers whose crops of mangel-wurzels had been destroyed by pheasants when Carson's men were drilling in Belfast and angry Conservatives were openly advertising for strong and willing men prepared to cross the Irish Sea and join the Ulster Loyalists in armed rebellion to Home Rule.

On several occasions the Liberal ministry almost broke up under the strain of the Irish crisis, as its members hunted desperately for a compromise solution of the difficulty which they could recommend to their supporters without too much loss of face. Lloyd George showed himself to be particularly eager to devise an expedient which might meet the anxieties of the Ulster Protestants, albeit at the cost of watering down the original Home Rule measure.[27]

For the fact was that Irish Home Rule did not command that much support in mainland Britain. The stubborn refusal of Asquith even to contemplate a national referendum on the question may in part reflect his lawyer-like antipathy towards constitutional innovation, but it is also evidence that, like his colleagues, he was not prepared to risk the future of his government on what was seen as being a vote loser. In any case, there was some sympathy, even within sections of his own party, with the plight of Ulster Protestants fighting for the retention of what they considered to be their 'civil and religious liberties'. It is particularly significant that the Liberal backbencher who first publicly suggested that the predominantly Protestant counties of Ulster should be allowed to opt out of a Home Rule settlement was the MP for Mid-Cornwall, Agar-Robartes, who in turn was reflecting the anxieties of his Nonconformist constituents over the sectarian implications of the government's Irish policy. To use armed force against these 'Loyalists' was politically hazardous. Yet to defy the wishes of Redmond and the Irish, who naturally insisted that Ireland be treated as a unity, would probably mean their own ejection from office, since the government depended very largely on Irish Nationalist votes.

How the Cabinet twisted and squirmed as it attempted to grapple with this dilemma and how it attempted to manoeuvre its Irish allies into accepting at least some measure of *temporary* partition falls outside the scope of this book. In any case, the belief of an earlier generation of historians that the government's floundering over Ireland between 1911 and 1914 constitutes evidence of the 'failure of Liberalism' no longer seems very plausible. After all, no subsequent government has been any more successful in reconciling the divergent claims of Irish Nationalists and Ulster Unionists, and the Asquith ministry was simply unfortunate to be caught in the way it was between these two intransigent forces.

However, in the short run, these Irish difficulties damaged the Liberal Party, and certainly took the shine off their recent triumph over the House of Lords. Since at the same time they were faced with trouble from militant strikers and suffragette outrages, the impression was occasionally given in these years that the country had become ungovernable on traditional Liberal lines – the origins of George Dangerfield's far-fetched thesis concerning the 'Strange Death of Liberal England'.[28] Liberal policies also had the effect of arousing nationalist feelings in both Scotland and Wales which the government was not then able to satisfy.

But this leads on to the second reason for the relative failure of the Radical assault on feudalism. Both in the Constitutional Crisis, and in the struggle over Ireland which followed it, the

Radicals found that the forces which opposed them were surprisingly strong and self-confident. To some extent Lloyd George had made the mistake, common among politicians, of taking his own rhetoric too seriously. In his great platform speeches he had portrayed landowners and peers as an anachronistic and useless caste, whose attempts to obstruct reform could no longer be tolerated by 'the People'. But, as the general elections of 1910 showed, the electorate did not altogether share his view. True, the Liberals, with their Labour and Irish allies, managed to win a conditional victory in both elections, which was better than they could have hoped for in 1908, but their success was far from overwhelming. Why?

The question can be answered on a number of levels. But it does seem clear that the social forces represented by the House of Lords were, oddly enough, stronger in 1911 than they had been in the 1880s. For in the intervening period a silent but important social transformation had occurred. One historian has graphically called it 'the Gentleman's Revolution'. Despite the continuing depression in agriculture, the big landowners had *not* gone under. On the contrary, with remarkable resilience they had adapted to their straitened circumstances and, after a fashion, come to terms with the modern world. Many landowners, overcoming their instinctive aversion to self-made men and financiers, made a prudent accommodation with the new wealth. For example, some sold off parcels of land and invested the capital in stocks and shares. Others exploited the many lucrative offers that came their way and served as guinea-pig directors on company boards. In short, landed society became fused with financial wealth to form a new governing class – the plutocracy. The aristocracy underwent a profound change. But they were, to some extent, strengthened by that change and acquired important new allies.[29]

Finally, there is one respect in which the great landed families remained true to the traditions of their class. They were nearly all involved, in one way or another, in military or naval life. Some had distinguished service records; most had sons or relatives serving in the officer corps. A high proportion enlisted in Haldane's Territorial Army, the new home defence force. Indeed, about three-quarters of all landed Unionist MPs during the Edwardian period were connected, directly or indirectly, with the armed services. Landowners were also the life and soul of local rifle clubs, Boys Brigades and other organisations designed to promote the martial arts. For the British aristocracy was, first and foremost, a *military* caste. This showed through even in its social pastimes. Of course, Radicals realised quite well that landed society, in its devotion to blood sports, was displaying its characteristics as a military caste. Radicals hated this 'militarism' and all that it implied. How horrible, they lamented, that in an advanced civilisation like that of industrial Britain well-educated gentlemen should devote so much of their time, money and energy to slaughter.[30]

Lloyd George himself often derided the aristocracy in these terms. But surely in doing so he was getting dangerously out of touch with the spirit of the age and indeed with much of public opinion. For in 1912, 1913 and 1914 professional soldiers, Territorial officers and the like did not strike most Britons as comic, anachronistic or sinister, rather the contrary. For these years saw a resurgence of patriotism in the face of the German challenge. From 1908 or 1909 onwards, if not before, the newspapers were full of the threatening international situation and of the risk of war. Invasion scare stories poured off the presses, and readers thrilled as they read fictional accounts of German Armies jackbooting their way through Surrey or the eastern counties. There were outbreaks of mass neurosis; the excitable and suggestible reported sighting Zeppelins hovering mysteriously over the English countryside. Right-wing editors worried over the presence of so many German waiters and musicians in British holiday towns, suspecting them of being an embryonic fifth column.[31]

All of this was hysterical nonsense. Nevertheless, in 1911 Britain came close to being involved in war with Germany at the time of the Agadir Crisis, and, interestingly enough, one of the most hawkish ministers during this crisis was Lloyd George, a recent but ardent convert to the view that German expansion threatened the very existence of the British Empire. Was this quite the right moment to pillory and attack a social class – the landed aristocracy – which would inevitably provide the country with leadership in war, if and when the long-awaited clash with Germany finally occurred? The 'Diehard Peers' had no doubt about their own importance. In fighting against the Parliament Act of 1911 and in resisting Home Rule, these men did not see themselves as defending, in a spirit of selfish obstinacy, a social order whose usefulness had passed. They believed – and with some reason – that they occupied an important position of trust in national life, that upon their shoulders rested, in large part, the security, and hence the prosperity, of the entire Empire. They hated Liberals, not least because they thought the political ambitions of these men were leading them into actions prejudicial to vital national interests.[32]

What particularly angered the Diehards were the activities of the Radical backbenchers in attempting to force their leaders to adopt policies more likely to avoid the horrors of war (only a small·minority, mostly Quakers, were doctrinaire pacifists). This was also a constant source of embarrassment to the pre-war Liberal Cabinets, not least because some ministers sympathised with the backbenchers' complaints or, like Lloyd George, found it politically expedient to pretend that they did so. In 1909 and again in 1914 the party was honeycombed with disaffection at all levels, as 'economists' and peacemongers tried to stop the escalating naval arms race with Germany. In fact, most Radicals strongly believed in the desirability of Britain's continuing naval supremacy; they simply did not believe the claims of Admiralty and Opposition that that supremacy was in serious jeopardy. There was also disquiet over Grey's anti-German foreign policy, which involved the consolidation of the French Entente (through the military talks of 1906) and the 1907 rapprochement with Tsarist Russia (which was particularly obnoxious, on moral grounds, to nearly all Radicals).[33]

In practice, the 'anti-War' Radicals achieved few, if any, of their objectives. On the other hand, their activities contributed to a picture of Liberal disunity, and, especially once war had broken out, the Opposition critics were able to claim that the Asquith government had been paralysed in its dealings with the German threat by the 'Potsdam Party' within its own ranks. A sense that the patriotism of the Liberals was in doubt and that the party could not be trusted with the defence of the Empire, however unfair it may have been, undoubtedly seriously damaged it after 1914, but it also encouraged open displays of disaffection from many members of the Opposition even before hostilities commenced.[34]

Thus, many of the great landlords and their dependants, confident about their own indispensability and convinced of the righteousness of their cause, came out in revolt against the authority of the elected government in 1913 and 1914, ostensibly over Home Rule, but more fundamentally to mark their contempt for parliamentary institutions and radical demagoguery. The prospect of civil war breaking out in Ireland and spilling over on to the mainland frightened some right-wing peers and landlords, but others welcomed the drift to violence as a refreshing contrast to the cant and hypocrisy of party politics.[35]

But this 'Revolt of the Right' was not confined to aristocrats, army officers and other traditional members of the country's ruling elite. It cannot, therefore, truly be characterised, as has recently been done, as 'the politics of paranoia', the death throes of an obsolete social order.[36] For associated with landowners like Willoughby de Broke in this challenge to the Liberal government were angry patriots from other social backgrounds and different political traditions. Together these people formed what has recently been called the 'Radical Right': 'a collection of super-patriots unable for one reason or another to identify with their "natural" party': 'a movement of rootless nationalists who felt alienated to a lesser or greater extent from *all* the major political organisations of the day'.[37]

The Liberal government and Liberal values generally proved to be strong enough to survive the 'Revolt of the Right' in Edwardian Britain. But, momentarily, Liberalism was weakened by the force of the reaction which it had provoked. Meanwhile, how successful was the Asquith ministry in its attempt to consolidate the relationship between the Liberal Party and the working-class electorate?

6
LIBERALISM, LABOUR AND SOCIAL REFORM, 1905–14

The landed aristocracy did not topple over, politically, when attacked, as perhaps some Radicals had intended. But there was at least this satisfaction to be derived from the situation. Organised Labour – and the clear majority of working-class voters – sided with the Radicals. The assault on feudalism, though it led to complications aplenty, at least helped Lloyd George in his attempts to win over the working man. For the Constitutional Crisis raised issues of fundamental importance to ordinary working people. After all, it was very much in the interests of Labour that Radicalism should prevail. The Labour Movement, for example, had a vested interest in securing a reduction in the powers of the House of Lords. Many Labour MPs would have preferred the total abolition of the Upper House, but they saw a removal of its absolute veto as a step in the right direction. Irish Home Rule was viewed with greater ambivalence. Labour supported Home Rule, but one senses a certain weariness with the everlasting complaints of relatively prosperous Irish tenant farmers. Perhaps what most brought the British Labour Movement out in warm support for Asquith's Home Rule Bill between 1912 and 1914 was the unconstitutional nature of the opposition which it encountered.

For, although, as we will shortly see, Labour was throwing up from its own ranks rebels against the parliamentary system on the eve of the First World War, the leadership, including nearly all Labour MPs, were parliamentarians to the core. They hated violence and illegality of any sort. So, in a way we have in these years an odd reversal of roles. The Conservatives were in open defiance of the parliamentary system, proclaiming the need for revolutionary action, while the decent, dull trade union officials and socialist journalists (all manual workers by background) showed a thoroughly bourgeois sense of social and constitutional propriety. Violent parliamentary scenes like the shouting-down of Asquith by Conservative backbenchers in July 1911 (the House had to be adjourned in disorder) simply made Labour politicians aware of how deeply attached they were to constitutionalism and to Liberal values generally, and this in turn helped to cement the alliance between Liberals and Labour. In other words, the 'Revolt from the Right' provided them with a common enemy which, as progressives, they could combine to fight.

But this, by itself, would not ensure that the Liberal Party remained the 'people's party', to which the working-class electorate would instinctively turn for protection. Strong claims have been made for the electoral popularity of the Land Campaign.[1] But even Lloyd George seems to have sensed that, if Liberalism were to have a secure future, it would have to prove its legitimacy in the eyes of the working man by showing an entirely new kind of sensitivity to the problems thrown up by *industrial* society. This, though not the only one, was a principal source of the social legislation which characterised the 1908–12 period. In rapid succession the Liberal Ministry carried old age pensions (1908), the establishment of labour exchanges (1909) and of trade boards (1909), an ambitious National Insurance scheme covering sickness, invalidity and unemployment (1911), and a Miners' Minimum Wages Act (1912), to mention only the most important of these schemes.[2] The tax system also changed, with the introduction of differentiation between earned and unearned income (1907) and steeper graduation. The percentage of income derived from direct taxes also increased sharply: from 44 per cent to 60 per cent between 1888 and 1914, mainly, though not entirely, as a result of Liberal reforms.[3]

But did these reforms fulfil their main purpose? In other

words, were the Liberals able to demonstrate that a Radical Party, enjoying mass support but under the direction of a progressive middle-class leadership, could be a viable proposition by the early twentieth century? Did welfare legislation slow down the growth of socialism?

At first sight the answer would appear to be an unqualified 'Yes'. Historians who have studied the 1910 elections are generally agreed that, although the Liberals lost ground in the south of England in predominantly rural and suburban constituencies, the Party held its own very well in working-class areas, especially those in the industrial north. The fact that in December 1910 plural voting seems to have given the Unionists some thirty seats which they would not otherwise have picked up provides further evidence that Britain's political system was becoming more 'class-based' – or so, at least, many historians believe. (No wonder the Liberal government tried, albeit unsuccessfully, to abolish plural voting and to establish 'one man, one vote'.)[4]

Yet these developments, it has been claimed, proved highly beneficial to the Unionist Opposition, which was able to rally to its support middle-class groups frightened by the 'predatory socialism' of the government. Tariff Reform, so decisively rejected in 1906, actually enjoyed a new lease of life in 1908–9. Its attraction was that it provided a way of raising additional revenue which promised to shield the rich from any personal discomfort or inconvenience. Unionists contrasted the painless strategy of 'making the foreigner pay' with the horrors of the People's Budget, which had raised income tax to what many contemporaries thought the punitive level of 1/2d (6p) in the pound, as well as introducing surtax – the City had been particularly angered by this.[5] The almost equally radical Budget of 1914 (1/4d in the pound on earned incomes over £2500, as well as surtax)[6] seemed to supply confirmation of these fears. In fact, according to some historians, what was happening in the years after 1908 was a polarisation of society along class lines, with the Conservatives and Unionists increasing their appeal to the middle-class electorate and becoming more than ever before the party of property: all property, landed, commercial and industrial. The Liberals' abandonment of the ideology of retrenchment

98

and their reduced emphasis upon the paying-off of the National Debt also contributed to this realignment.[7]

Yet, interestingly enough, in a political system where class allegiance was becoming more important, the working-class party in 1910 seemed not to be the Labour Party, which only ran fifty-six candidates in December 1910, in all but eleven cases with Liberal support. Most manual workers who had the parliamentary vote were still supporting the Liberals. It seemed as if the combination of social reform plus the commitment to mildly redistributive fiscal policies was making Liberalism the popular cause. Indeed, so successful was Lloyd Georgian Radicalism that some Labour candidates in 1910 found it difficult to carve out a distinctive niche for themselves. Many were driven into claiming credit for popular measures, like old age pensions, which the Liberal government had recently passed; as one historian has noted, there were some constituencies in which an ignorant observer might have supposed from the election literature put out by the Labour candidate that *Labour* had been in office for the previous four years![8]

It would be churlish to deny that the Liberals had achieved a considerable success. But how durable and significant was it likely to prove? Here historians differ dramatically. Some (the 'revisionists') argue that the Liberals had converted themselves by 1914 into a kind of 'social democratic' party, with strong popular support. From this they draw the deduction that the eventual Liberal collapse did not have profound socio-economic causes since the Liberals, far from being destroyed by the advent of class, had successfully adapted themselves to its requirements. Such an interpretation leads logically on to the claim that only the 'accident' of the Great War brought about the Liberals' eventual downfall.[9]

On the other hand, there are historians who admit the importance of the Great War, but insist that it merely speeded up a Liberal disintegration of which there were already abundant signs *before* 1914. The debate is nicely poised, and seems unlikely ever to be resolved to everyone's satisfaction, since much depends upon one's assumption about what course British politics would have taken if the First World War had not broken out when it did. But there are two kinds of challenge with which Liberals were grappling before 1914. Firstly, could they hold on to a modicum of middle-class support, at the same time as wooing the working-class electorate with a policy of social reform? Secondly, would the working classes continue to be satisfied with the kind of reforms which Liberal Ministries were likely to produce? In the words of a leading Liberal, Herbert Samuel, it was 'the abiding problem of Liberal statesmanship to raise the enthusiasm of the working class without frightening the middle classes'.[10] Had the Liberals brought off this difficult trick?

Holding on to some middle-class support was clearly essential to the long-term survival of the Liberal Party. But it also posed serious problems. After 1906 a plethora of middle-class defence groups came into existence, like 'the Middle-Class Defence Organisation', the 'Income-Tax Reduction Society', and the 'Anti-Socialist League', all of them avowedly anti-Liberal in their politics. Some traditional middle-class Liberal supporters, especially in London, were bound to be unsettled by the activities of these bodies and by reading articles such as 'The Bitter Cry of the Middle Classes', which a Liberal paper, *The Tribune*, was publishing in July 1906.[11]

It was partly to counter these complaints and to rally the faithful that ministers took up the Nonconformists' various grievances. Indeed, the assault on the House of Lords during the Constitutional Crisis vividly recalled to many Liberal activists, the Dissenters especially, the struggles of their ancestors against the tyranny of Strafford and Laud.

But even as early as 1910 this strategy was running into difficulty. Some leading Dissenters were beginning to express alarm over Radical demagoguery and the contents of Radical social legislation. A straw in the wind was the formation in 1909 of the Nonconformist Anti-Socialist Union, organised and financed by wealthy Methodist businessmen, among them Robert Perks (leading to Lloyd George's public taunt that he wished that Sir

Robert 'would not always talk as if the Nonconformist conscience were locked up in his City safe'.[12]) Even some Congregationalists and Baptists, the sects closest to Liberalism, were losing the enthusiasm which had brought them on to the hustings in support of Liberal candidates four years earlier. In fact, by 1910 Nonconformist clergymen who abused the pulpit by indulging in party political propaganda sometimes had the disconcerting experience of seeing wealthy laymen rising to their feet and marching out of the chapel in protest. On the other hand, Primitive Methodism, which had a strong working-class following among groups like north-eastern coalminers and Norfolk farm labourers, was moving to align itself with the Labour Party. It would be broadly accurate to say that, on the eve of the Great War, issues of class were beginning to supplant the old church/chapel rivalry, and that this spelled trouble in the long run for the Liberal Party.[13]

Yet very few of the Radical MPs concerned with social legislation were themselves trade unionists or manual workers by origins. At parliamentary level, the Liberal Party was overwhelmingly middle-class. In particular, only one Cabinet minister came from a working-class background: the reactionary and inefficient President of the Local Government Board, John Burns, about whom it was unkindly remarked that he did at least drop his 'aitches' and so was regarded by Asquith as the authentic voice of Labour.[14] Despite some democratisation at local level, particularly in areas where traditionally Liberalism had been weak, for example, the East End of London, the Liberal Party gives the impression of being an overwhelmingly middle-class organisation.

With what section of society, then, was Liberal social reform especially associated? Historians are generally agreed that the impetus behind the 'New Liberalism' came from the *professional* middle class: from journalists, writers, and lecturers, plus certain lawyers and doctors with a social conscience. Men like L. T. Hobhouse provided the intellectual rationale for the new welfare politics, as we have already seen. From a recent study one gets a vivid picture of these men: high-minded intellectuals, living in spacious but draughty houses in Hampstead or the Manchester suburbs (fresh air was valued as a stimulus to progressive thought), eating raw fruit, and thinking ruthlessly about the political problems of their age.[15] There were men of this ilk in the parliamentary party as well, mainly on the left-wing social reform side of the party – for example, C. F. G. Masterman, who became the close friend and ally of Lloyd George and who did much of the preparatory work on the National Health Insurance Scheme, for which he eventually became the government's parliamentary spokesman.[16] Some historians go so far as to claim that the New Liberalism was the ideology of the professional middle class and that social reform brought both emotional satisfaction and enhanced career prospects to that particular segment of British society. Though an exaggeration, this claim has some validity.[17]

The involvement in Liberal politics of 'caring' professional men and women and of the progressive intelligentsia undoubtedly gave the party its intellectual vitality; all suggestions that Edwardian Liberalism was an obsolete or bankrupt creed must be summarily rejected. But could, in the long run, the viewpoint of the intelligentsia be harmonised with the class needs of the business community upon which the historic Liberal Party had been heavily dependent?

The Liberal Party and Business

This is an issue on which historians wildly disagree. Roy Hay, in an important essay, has argued that 'social reform' in some respects met the requirements of capitalism, serving as an instrument of 'social control': it helped stabilise the social system at a time of considerable class tension, as well as integrating certain groups of manual workers into the existing economic system. Indeed, says Hay, many Edwardian businessmen had, for that reason, become converted to the necessity of social welfare (of the kind pioneered by Bismarckian Germany) and actually contributed to its implementation before 1914.[18]

However, the empirical evidence to support this thesis is not strong. Most of the businessmen Hay cites in his article turn out

102

to be Unionists, not Liberals. And although certain individual businessmen, with Radical convictions, can be found supporting social reform,[19] it is much easier to find contrary examples. The Employers' Parliamentary Association, for example, was set up in 1911 to resist further social legislation, the costs of which, it claimed, were burdening British industry. This pressure group was centred upon the Lancashire textile industry, where the links with the Liberal Party had traditionally been strong.[20]

Moreover, within the House of Commons itself businessmen soon began to display their restlessness over social reform. On the eve of the war a 'cave' of about forty MPs had formed, under the leadership of a wealthy Liverpool shipowner and backbench MP, Richard Holt, mostly composed of businessmen who feared that the Asquith government was destroying business confidence and frightening capital out of the country.[21] There is reason, then, for supposing that social radicalism was drifting apart from what passed for commonsense among the Party's business backers.

But historians who take this view are divided over its significance. According to H. V. Emy, social reform both reflected and contributed to a drift of businessmen out of the Liberal Party. Safe Liberal seats in northern England, he says, tended, once the businessmen representing them had retired, to pass into the hands of professional men. But although this development strengthened 'Social Radicalism', it still further alienated businessmen from Liberalism and boded no good to the party; traditional wealthy supporters were lost, whilst the working-class votes thereby gained could not be relied upon, since Social Radicalism could only make an electoral appeal to manual workers for as long as a distinct Labour machine failed to emerge.[22]

Some of this analysis is shared by the arch-revisionist, Peter Clarke, but Clarke goes even further. The years after 1908, he claims, saw a fundamental class realignment in British politics. 'Economic Liberalism' collapsed as businessmen abandoned the Party for the security offered by the Conservatives and Unionists. Indeed, so disaffected were these deserters from Liberalism that they were ready to embrace Tariff Reform, since they were now thinking, not in terms of the well-being of the industries that employed them, but in terms of their personal class needs. And, faced by an apparent choice between free trade plus social re-form (which many of them equated with socialism) versus pro-tection and economic individualism (which in practical terms meant low taxation), many opted for the latter combination.[23]

But Clarke radically differs from Emy in going on to argue that this development was a sign of *health*, not a symptom of decline, since the loss of these businessmen was a necessary outcome of the Liberal Party's transformation into a modern 'social democratic party'. Only the mishaps which befell it dur-ing the First World War prevented the Liberals from playing the sort of role in twentieth-century politics that the Labour Party has played since 1945.

The Emy–Clarke disagreement largely centres around the question of how attractive Liberal social reform actually proved to·be to the working-class electors it was designed to attract. To that question we will shortly turn. But before doing so, it is worth questioning whether the larger claims which both historians are making stand up to close examination. Two specific questions must be asked. Did businessmen, as voters, really switch over from Liberalism to Unionism? And did the proportion of business-men within the parliamentary party really fall?

In the absence of opinion polls, the first question is difficult to answer. Certainly the 1910 election results reveal a well above-average swing against the Liberal Party in middle-class sub-urban areas in southern England, particularly in London, the cathedral cities and the seaside resorts. But in the northern manufacturing districts Liberalism fared relatively well in *all* types of constituency. Peter Clarke attaches particular signifi-cance to the Liberals' loss, in by-elections in April 1908 and August 1912, of the Manchester North-West constituency, the business heart of the city which, more than any other, had become closely identified with the Free Trade cause.[24] Yet both defeats occurred in mid-term, when the Liberal government was going through a temporary period of acute unpopularity. In the two general elections of 1910 the seat reverted to the Liberals; indeed, in the second of these elections, the Liberal candidate,

Sir George Kemp, a local cotton spinner, succeeded in beating off a strong challenge from one of the Unionist Party's most prominent figures, Andrew Bonar Law, soon to become its leader.

Moreover, although Kemp was a somewhat reluctant candidate and retired from politics in 1912, this by no means formed part of a decisive trend. True, some Liberal business MPs opted not to stand again in January 1910 because they disliked the tone and contents of recent government legislation: the percentage of retirements was proportionately nearly double that in the Unionist Party.[25] Yet well-to-do businessmen had been deserting the Liberal Party ever since the Party had been founded, without dramatic consequences (just as ambitious working-class politicians have often deserted the Labour Movement as they have risen in the world). In any case, the Liberal Party had no difficulty in finding new candidates from business backgrounds. An analysis of the parliamentary party indicates that the social balance of power within the Party was almost static. MPs drawn from a business career continued to make up nearly 40 per cent of the parliamentary party (compared with little over 23 per cent of Unionist MPs).[26] At local level, too, councillors and activists were often businessmen of one sort or another, especially in the West Riding (though there is some evidence of their being displaced in the immediate pre-war years).[27]

What animated these business Liberals remains slightly unclear. Radical social policy is unlikely to have proved the *attraction*. Probably many businessmen who had traditionally supported the Liberal Party continued to do so, either because they set high store by Free Trade (which the Unionists were threatening in 1910) or because they perceived the Unionist Party as 'alien': which to most Dissenters, and many Scotsmen, Welshmen and Jews, for example, it long continued to be.[28] But it is the existence of these Liberal businessmen, not their motivation, which matters to the present argument.

It has further been suggested that the Liberal Party was being damaged on the eve of the war, not because of its increasing detachment from the business community, but because, in some respects, the links with businessmen were unhealthily close.

Even Lloyd George, despite his Radicalism, was spending much of his leisure time in the company of self-made millionaires. This was important inasmuch as such social activities laid Lloyd George wide open to the charge of hypocrisy. It was all very well for him to extol the simple lives of the poor and to preach the need for a reduction in the inequalities which disfigured society. But these words sounded strange in the mouth of a man who spent so much time in the company of his newly acquired pluto-cratic friends. The Conservative Press mercilessly pilloried Lloyd George (or £loyd George) and his £iberal friends for their use of double standards.[29]

The Opposition similarly seized with delight on the Marconi Scandal which broke in 1912–13. For it not only revealed three leading Liberal ministers (Lloyd George, Rufus Isaacs, the Attorney-General, and the Master of Elibank, the former Chief Whip) as deeply implicated in the buccaneering world of Edwardian capitalism, but it also showed them as benefiting from the tips of their business friends – in fact, using 'inside' information to have a flutter on the Stock Exchange. This be-haviour, if not corrupt, was surely highly improper.[30]

But it was not just *individual* ministers who relied on business support of one kind or another to keep them in the comfort to which they had grown accustomed. Some constituency parties were making a determined effort during the Edwardian decade to broaden their social base. But at central level, the Liberal Party was still being largely funded by wealthy businessmen. The impressive election campaigns of 1910 were only made possible because of heavy donations from this quarter – from the 'Radical plutocrats' and 'cosmopolitan millionaires', as the Opposition dubbed them. Moreover, a high proportion of these subscribers subsequently featured in the Honours Lists – as knights, baronets, and, indeed, as privy councillors and peers of the realm. By 1913 even loyal backbenchers and sympathetic pressmen could hardly deny that the government was cynically exchanging titles and honours for cash – and doing so more brazenly and on a much larger scale than any other government had done before. On the eve of the war, the Liberal government, rocked by the Marconi Scandal and plagued by complaints about honours trafficking, was becoming associated in the public mind with scandal and corruption.[31]

The Liberals could ill-afford to receive this sort of publicity, given their claim to be the party of public purity and morality. The Nonconformists were especially upset. But, more importantly, perhaps, any suggestion that the Liberal Party was implicated in the seamy side of capitalism was bound to weaken the 'Progressive Alliance' and shake the confidence of working-class electors in the Liberal ministry. Left-wing socialists, who had always disapproved of the Lib-Lab Pact, were quick to exploit an episode like the Marconi Scandal because it beautifully illustrated their contention that the Liberal Party was a capitalist party, and a corrupt one at that, with which no self-respecting class-conscious worker should have any dealings.

This leads on logically to the second part of the enquiry. What about the workers? Would Labour consent, for ever and a day, to have its interests represented by its Liberal 'friends', or would working men, sooner or later, insist on taking full control of their own destinies?

The New Liberalism, Social Policy and the Labour Movement

The answer to these questions depends, in part, upon whether one believes that the nature of the Liberal Party really had been transformed in the years immediately preceding the outbreak of the First World War. Without in any way denigrating the importance of the welfare legislation passed by the Asquith government, several aspects of the Liberal politics of this period give one cause to doubt the validity of the wider claims that have been made by the 'revisionists'.

Firstly, the government, as a whole, does not seem to have been that committed to the welfare reforms. Nearly all the great welfare measures originated with Lloyd George and Winston Churchill, helped by Masterman and a few other junior ministers. These Bills were obviously endorsed by the Prime Minister and the Cabinet. But, significantly, the People's Budget had

encountered fierce initial criticism (in private) from more 'traditional' Liberals, like Runciman, Bryce, Loreburn, and Morley.[32]
Moreover, as one historian has noted, it is a little startling how
small many of the welfare initiatives bulk in the correspondence
of most Cabinet ministers: 'The men who ran the Edwardian
party show in their private archives virtually no sign of progressive motivation.'[33] This may explain in part why no coherent welfare strategy developed in these years. In any case,
there was no reform programme as such – rather a patchwork
quilt of *ad hoc* measures, based on no single principle or philosophy, and sometimes colliding with one another. The desperate
plight in which the Party had found itself in 1908 allowed ministers who wanted to address these social problems to do so; other
ministers, with different personal inclinations, like Burns at the
Local Government Board, were similarly allowed to go their
separate ways. Hence the failure of Poor Law Reform, which
would have required co-ordinated action across a range of
Whitehall departments.

Moreover, in the first of the two 1910 elections the government
focussed on the constitutional outrage which the peers had committed in rejecting the Budget; in the second election the main
plank in its campaign was a call for a mandate to curb the
powers of the Upper House.[34] Indeed, once the 1911 National
Insurance Act had been carried, the impetus behind social reform seems to have slackened to some extent. For although in
June 1914 Asquith did give his support to the idea of a minimum
wage, as recommended by Lloyd George's committee into the
problems of urban land, it is unclear whether this would have
become a central plank in the Liberal programme had war not
broken out when it did.

True, there is some evidence that social radicals were entering
Parliament on the Liberal side in greater numbers after 1908,
especially in Scotland, encouraged in some cases by the Whips'
Office.[35] But even revisionists concede that the position of the
'New Liberals' was precarious in the sense that they lacked an
institutional power base and depended far too heavily upon
personal contacts and the attractiveness of their ideas.[36] All of
this perhaps goes some way to explaining the sudden disappear-

ance of welfare politics from the Party's agenda during and immediately after the Great War – a development which otherwise seems rather mysterious.

At the local level, the impression is still more strongly conveyed that the New Liberalism and the policies based upon this reformulation of the Liberal creed had done little to break the traditional political mould. Many local Liberal newspapers and the local Liberal activists were far more solidly committed to the old sectarian objectives than to old age pensions, to say nothing of labour exchanges and the promise of social insurance. In February 1909 the *Leicester Daily Mercury* could still list the issues which required immediate attention as follows: 'monopolies in land, in liquor, in ecclesiasticism, in electoral machinery, and in the House of Lords, which is the very holy of holies of monopoly'.[37] In Wales, too, the New Liberalism made comparatively little impact. Lloyd George, it has been claimed, was 'a new liberal in England, an old liberal in Wales'.[38] Even the Young Scots, a radical pressure group, attached as much importance to temperance as to all other social issues combined, judging by their speakers' lists of 1911–12.[39] Clearly, nationwide generalisations are hazardous. The Liberal Party was a shifting coalition, and its character varied from one region to another. In areas where Liberalism had been traditionally weak, the East End of London, for example, New Liberalism seems to have been making progress in the immediate pre-war years. But in most of the Liberal heartlands there was no great pressure from below in support of new welfare initiatives. On the contrary, judging from the stance taken by a famous Liberal organ of opinion like the *Leeds Mercury*, the new welfare initiatives were deeply unpopular with many of the party faithful.[40]

This leads on logically to a further point. Whereas the Lib-Lab Pact was reactivated in the two 1910 general elections (and never more successfully than in December 1910), in *municipal* politics it was common for the Liberal and Labour parties to fight one another. This happened even in a town like Norwich, a two-member constituency where the 'Progressive Alliance' was working well in the parliamentary arena, but where the ILP's attack on the Liberals' failure to municipalise essential services, as advocated in its own 1903 programme, triggered off a fierce electoral battle.[41] In Leicester, too, the local Liberal dignitaries were divided, and 'socialism' proved to be a highly divisive issue. Let them 'have no more talk about "two wings of a Progressive party"', declared Councillor Kemp, a hosiery manufacturer, in April 1907; he went on to warn his fellow Liberals that if they did not fight off the socialists 'they would be wiped out'. Even sympathetic Liberals envisaged a subordinate position for Labour, whom they tended to address like children who needed to have their own best interests pointed out to them.[42] This led to predictable conflict. Moreover, in the matter of municipal contests, Labour had fewer inhibitions about 'going it alone' than it had in parliamentary elections, perhaps because many council wards were socially homogeneous and contained concentrations of groups like railwaymen and dockers, who were its natural supporters, unlike parliamentary constituencies where a broader appeal was needed for success.[43]

Admittedly, one can find other towns (Wigan and Gloucester, for example) where a municipal electoral alliance between Liberals and Labour was being successfully operated.[44] On the other hand, an anxiety to hold down the rates and keep Labour at bay led in many parts of the country (notably Bradford, Leeds, large areas of London, and Glasgow) to informal electoral understandings between the Liberals and the *Conservatives*.[45] The Labour press alleged that such anti-Labour alliances had existed at one time or another in no fewer than thirty-two different municipalities in England and Wales – to say nothing of Scotland.[46] Some of these arrangements, as in Glasgow, were of long standing, but others came about as a response to the heightened social and industrial tension of the immediate pre-war years and seem to foreshadow the Anti-Labour Alliances that sprang up all over the country in the wake of Labour's advance in the 1919 municipal elections.

All of this raises two fundamental questions. How long would it be before the 'class' issues which were creating animosities in local government elections spilled over into the parliamentary arena? Secondly, does not the story of municipal politics suggest that the Labour Party's co-operation with the Liberal government at national level owed less to their shared commitment to the creed of 'Progressivism' based upon welfare reform than to a common interest in triumphing over the House of Lords and safeguarding Free Trade?

But this, in turn, leads on to the issue of how popular social reform was amongst the working-class electors whom the Liberals were trying to attract. The first thing to note is that the Liberals did not do quite as well in working-class constituencies in January 1910 as the revisionist thesis might lead one to suppose. In many ways all that happened in that general election was a reversion to a more 'normal' pattern of behaviour; middle-class seats which the Liberals had won for the first time in the 'freak' contest of 1906 nearly all returned to their former Unionist allegiance, while the Liberals held on to constituencies where they had earlier been strong. In fact, the outcome of the two 1910 elections quite closely followed that of 1892. It can be argued, in other words, that, in so far as pre-war politics had become class-based at all, this had occurred in the immediate aftermath of the Home Rule schism, long before the New Liberalism had made any serious impact on the Party's policy agenda. Nor was the New Liberalism of any help to the Liberals in the working-class constituencies of Liverpool and Birmingham; on the eve of the war the former were still totally dominated by the Conservatives, the latter by the Liberal Unionists.[47]

Is there even any evidence that sizeable numbers of working-class voters *were* attracted by social reform? This is a tricky question to answer. There seems little doubt that old age pensions (although Labour politicians criticised them for being niggardly) were immensely popular with working men and women. Significantly, the normally unflappable Balfour showed great agitation when a junior Liberal minister alleged in the run-up to the first 1910 election that a future Unionist government would repeal the Old Age Pension Act: a 'frigid lie', he called it. But the National Insurance Act was not initially popular and Unionist candidates claimed it had brought them by-election success.[48]

Writing to a close political friend in November 1911, Asquith said that there could 'be no doubt that the Insurance Bill [was] (to say the least) not an electioneering asset'.[49] Lecturers had to be paid to tour the country in an attempt to 'explain' the measure and persuade the people of its merits. The main reason for this popular antipathy was that, whereas old age pensions had been financed out of general taxation, National Insurance involved contributions from the insured workers, as well as from the employers and the state, and the resulting deductions from the weekly pay packet came as an unpleasant surprise. Many trade unionists, too, harboured deep suspicions about labour exchanges being possible weapons in the hands of strike breakers, suspicions which ministers tried hard but not entirely successfully to allay.[50]

The ministers involved in the welfare reforms had certainly started off with the *belief* that they would be attractive to the working-class electorate, although they also had other aims in view (promoting national efficiency, pure humanitarianism etc.). Lloyd George wrote privately to his brother in May 1908, *a propos* of old age pensions, that it was time that something was done that 'appealed straight to the people' and would 'help to stop the electoral rot'. Churchill wrote to Asquith at about the same time in similar vein.[51] But had Liberal ministers, in their benevolent aloofness from the lives of the urban poor, miscalculated? All that can confidently be said is that working people seem not to have had any particular view about social reform as such, but simply discriminated on the basis of whether they thought that specific measures would, on balance, help or hinder them. Trade unions took the same pragmatic approach.[52]

But what is equally clear is that the greater security in everyday life which the Asquith ministry's welfare legislation undoubtedly did provide mattered less than the preservation of living standards, and these in turn mainly depended upon the level of real wages. So much became apparent when, only a year after its 1910 electoral successes, the Liberals found themselves enveloped in what has gone down in the history books as the 'Great Labour Unrest'. Over the next two and a half years strikes and lockouts affected a large section of industry. Historians have offered different explanations for this outbreak of working-class militancy, but undoubtedly the most important cause was inflation, which depressed real wages and caused discontent; moreover, since unemployment in these years was low, union leaders knew that in bringing their men out on strike they were running fewer risks than usual.

Some of these industrial disputes were conducted in a mood of intense class bitterness. The Merseyside dock strike of August 1911, for example, spread panic and confusion. At the request of the Mayors of Liverpool and Birkenhead the government despatched a warship to the Mersey. Lord Derby wrote personally to Churchill, the Home Secretary, complaining that people in London did not realise that this was no ordinary strike riot, but that 'a revolution' was in progress. In August 1911 200 people were injured in the disturbances, two of them fatally.[53]

Dock strikes were traditionally violent affairs. But the railwaymen were also involved in serious rioting, especially in South Wales, where the miners were also simmering with anger. Indeed, in 1912 there was a nation-wide coal strike which was largely free from violent incidents but which had a devastating impact on the economy, throwing thousands of men from other industries out of work. Even more alarmingly, in 1913 moves were made for co-ordinated strike action between railwaymen, miners and transport workers, who linked up in the so-called Triple Alliance. Meanwhile the syndicalists, a revolutionary sect, were calling for the overthrow of capitalism by means of a general strike and for the establishment of a workers' state.

For the government this was a disturbing development. When Lloyd George, Churchill and Masterman had made their bid to secure the working-class vote, they had not expected to be faced with this kind of assault from below. Concessionary social reform, it seemed, was not working.

How did this affect the relations between the Liberal and Labour Parties? It may have done so in many different ways. Most obviously, the class tension of the 1910–14 period weakened the Liberal Party by creating antagonisms in many areas of the country between Liberals and Labour. At parliamentary level the moderate and dispirited group of Labour MPs, led after 1911 by the cautious Ramsay MacDonald, might still cling to the Progressive Alliance, but in many coalfields, for example, industrial tension was undermining the position of union moderates, as militant socialists rose to prominence.[54]

Moreover, not even left-wing Radicals were likely to welcome working-class militancy, especially when this was expressed in the language of syndicalism, with calls for 'Direct Action' and 'Workers Control' and with vague threats to overturn the capitalist system by means of a general strike. Faced with such declarations of class war, the most 'advanced' Liberal politicians and intellectuals were prone to recoil in horror. For example, L. T. Hobhouse, philosopher of the New Liberalism, who found himself on the receiving end of a piece of working-class militancy from the London coal porters, an experience he did not enjoy, angrily dismissed the views of those who argued that nothing was to be gained except by fighting: 'The moment you convince me of this', he wrote in a private letter, 'I shall shut up shop as a radical or socialist or anything reforming, for I shall be convinced that human nature is hopeless, and that the effort to improve society had better be left alone.'[55] Hobhouse was a reformer, but he wanted orderly change after rational debate and by constitutional methods. He emphatically did not approve of assertions of working-class power.

But Hobhouse's discomfiture over the latest turn of events was nothing compared with the embarrassment of the Liberal government, which found itself being drawn willy-nilly into industrial conflicts where it would have to take sides – which, in practice, often meant offering resistance to the striking men. Most governments, faced by such situations, tend to flounder, and the Asquith administration was no exception. It was especially unfortunate, from the Liberal point of view, that the Home Secretary in the crucial years of 1910 and 1911 was Winston Churchill, who took an obvious and rather childish delight at moving troops about the country to enforce law and order in troubled areas. Such Napoleonic moods and gestures made the worst possible impression on the Labour Movement. Even MacDonald turned angrily upon Churchill in the House of Commons and reminded him that he was not the Tsar of Russia.[56]

The effect of the labour unrest was to make the Labour Party more militant. For example, in areas like South Wales militant miners began to ask themselves whether it made sense to go on co-operating politically with a Liberal Party whose local leaders were often coalowners (among them, the hated Lord Rhondda, head of the Cambrian Combine, who, as D. A. Thomas, had recently been the Liberal MP for Merthyr).[57] Moreover, industrial unrest tended to increase the influence of left-wing socialists within Labour's affiliated organisations and gave rank-and-file members in the constituencies the confidence to take on all-comers.

How far had this challenge to the party leadership gone by 1914? Here historians are in disagreement. Some, notably Ross McKibbin, believe that there is evidence that the Lib-Lab Pact was disintegrating in the by-elections which occurred in 1912, 1913 and 1914. In five of the seats lost to the Unionists in these years, a Labour candidate, intervening for the first time, secured more votes than the margin of victory – a sign of how damaging this development was to the Liberal Party. True, in all these by-elections Labour came bottom of the poll. But, in McKibbin's view, since many of these contests took place in the Midlands coalmining belt, which was untypical in many ways, this does not conclusively prove that Labour's level of support in the country as a whole was low. Arguably, these Labour candidates did quite well considering that they were contesting their particular constituencies for the first time. In any case, the important feature of these contests, to historians like McKibbin, is the fact that Labour were even *willing* to make a dash for 'independence'.[58]

Meanwhile at grass roots level the Labour Party's membership was being swollen by trade union expansion, and, following the passing of the 1913 Trade Union Act, all these new affiliated members would be paying a 'political levy' to the Labour Party unless they specifically 'contracted out'. The extra money encouraged Labour to extend its organisation in the country (many unified local Labour Parties date their origins to this period, including the London Labour Party, set up in May 1914), and this, in turn, increased the probability of Labour's mounting many more candidates than the paltry fifty-six which had stood in December 1910. Had a general election been held in 1915, alleges McKibbin, Labour would probably have fielded between 120 and 150 candidates, many of whom would have had to face sitting Liberal MPs, so forcing the Liberals to retaliate.[59] In short, it is arguable that the pattern of Progressive politics was at last breaking up.

But McKibbin's views have recently come under powerful challenge from Duncan Tanner. The level of Liberal–Labour conflict in by-elections was no worse in 1911–14 than it had been during the corresponding period of the previous Parliament, argues Tanner.[60] Moreover, most of these Labour 'interventions' had been sanctioned by MacDonald and the NEC of the Labour Party in a calculated bid to put pressure on the Liberal organisers, with the aim of securing a more favourable allocation of seats at the next general election. But Tanner's meticulous examination of electoral arrangements at constituency level leads him to the conclusion that, after a process of negotiation and 'pruning', Labour would probably not have fielded many more than the sixty-five candidates already sanctioned once Parliament was dissolved – certainly nothing like McKibbin's figure.[61] This would have permitted the perpetuation of the Lib-Lab Pact – albeit on terms slightly more advantageous to Labour. Militant socialists might well have grumbled at this outcome, but, Tanner believes, the anti-MacDonaldites were far from being in the ascendant throughout the Labour Movement, and most activists realised that the party was still nowhere near ready for a total breach with Liberalism at the level of national politics. Indeed, despite its organisational reforms, Labour still had no significant presence over much of the country, and where it *was* active it too often gave the impression of incoherence and factionalism.[62] (Nor was Labour's performance in local authority elections anything other than disappointing, even in industrial areas where it must have hoped to do very well.)[63]

Which of these two historical interpretations is correct? The PLP, as so often, was split over what strategy to pursue – and the rank-and-file even more so. But whereas most ILPers wanted Labour to behave with true 'independence', MacDonald and the bulk of the trade union MPs knew how risky this would be. Given the fact that in December 1910 none of its forty-two MPs had been returned in a genuine triangular contest (though two had had straight fights against a Liberal), all-out war against the Liberals in a general election threatened the PLP with obliteration. Ever since 1910, when Labour had found itself, along with the Irish, holding the balance of seats, it had given general support to the Asquith ministry. Symbolically, Labour MPs now sat on the government side of the House. Thus MacDonald's ploy was, on the one hand, to maintain his party's organisational independence, coming down hard on trade union mavericks who failed to toe the line, while at the same time 'buying' favours off the government: for example, payment of MPs and the 1913 Trade Union Act (both made necessary by the 'Osborne Judgement') as a reward for supporting the National Insurance Act.[64]

It was an adroit balancing act. But for how much longer could it have been carried on? Some historians believe that by 1914 Labour had reached the point where it either had to move closer to the Liberal government or disentangle itself completely from the 'Progressive Alliance'. Significantly, some Liberal leaders seem to have been thinking in the same way. Twice in 1912 and again in 1914 ministers put out 'feelers' as to the willingness of certain senior Labour politicians to join the Asquith ministry. MacDonald was tempted by the third of these overtures, made in March 1914, but Keir Hardie had it killed off.[65] Yet simultaneously MacDonald was coming under pressure from some of the rank-and-file to try and go it alone. The resolution of this dilemma would have fateful consequences, not only for the future of his own organisation, but for that of the Liberal Party as well.

Tantalisingly, from the viewpoint of the historian, the Great War then broke out, transforming the entire political landscape, before the decision could be made. Inevitably, confusion and uncertainty still surround the question of how strong the Liberal Party still was in 1914 and whether it would have 'survived' but for the war. Even the result of the general election, due to be held by late 1915 at the latest, cannot be predicted with any certainty. The Liberals (and their Labour allies) had done badly in by-elections between 1912 and 1914, even where triangular contests had not occurred. But something similar had happened in the middle of the 1906 Parliament, and the Liberals had then gone on to secure their qualified 'win' in January 1910.[66] The same might have happened again. Nor would the loss of the election in itself necessarily have proved fatal. On the contrary, the disturbing actuality of a Unionist administration might well have shocked the two 'parties of progress' into recreating their alliance – supposing that it had been in abeyance during the election. Alas, all this cannot be other than speculation.

But a few concluding remarks may be hazarded. It now seems likely, in the light of Tanner's researches, that, even though the outcome of the 1915 election must remain wreathed in mystery, the Lib-Lab Pact, in some form or another, would still have operated. In that sense, 'Progressivism' may have been alive and well in 1914. But the perpetuation of the pact does not, as most historians assume, have any very great bearing on the question of the success or otherwise of the New Liberalism. After all, MacDonald and Herbert Gladstone had reached their 'understanding' in 1903 at a time when the Liberal agenda was still heavily dominated by the old issues: the need to rectify Nonconformist grievances and to defend Free Trade. The Liberal government's subsequent espousal of social reform may have facilitated co-operation with Labour, though this is unclear. But far more important to the pact's survival was the mutual recognition that each party needed the other (Labour's need, of course, was much the greater) if the Tories were to be defeated.

In fact, the co-operation between the two parties operated smoothly at national (though not at local) level precisely because each complemented the other so well. Labour was able to make progress in the former Tory strongholds and in many working-class areas where the Liberals stood little chance of success. Conversely, the Liberal Party continued to appeal to groups like middle-class Nonconformists whom Labour was unlikely to reach.[67] Even on the eve of the war the Liberals were still deriving almost one-quarter of their English seats from heavily rural constituencies, mostly in East Anglia, Lincolnshire and Cornwall, which later proved to be unrewarding territory for

Labour, while national sentiment gave Liberalism a popularity in Scotland and Wales which often overrode the class factor; indeed, in January 1910 the Liberals managed to win all but ten of the seventy Scottish seats, a better result than they had achieved in 1906.

In short, the Edwardian Liberal Party cannot easily be portrayed as a precursor of the late twentieth-century Labour Party. It operated from a different social base (especially in municipal elections[68]) and was making a rather different electoral appeal. In the short run, this did not matter. Indeed, as with the Liberal-Irish Nationalist alliance, the two 'parties of progress' worked together reasonably well because they were *not* direct rivals. Paradoxically, the Lib-Lab Pact might have been less effective if New Liberal ideas had achieved a greater centrality in the Liberal Party's thinking.

But the long-term prospects of Liberalism were more problematic. Social reforms like old age pensions and the National Insurance Act were important measures in their own right, but it is questionable whether they did the Liberals much good in a narrow party sense. Their introduction frightened off some former middle-class adherents, including Dissenters whose support was essential to the Liberals' self-image as a 'national party'. Yet Edwardian Liberalism still had deep roots in the business world and, at least at central level, was financially dependent on a handful of rich business backers. Meanwhile, by 1914 social reform – distrusted by many middle-class Liberals – was not proving to be the antidote to the growth of the Labour Party which it had seemed to be between 1908 and 1910.

Finally, although there are few signs that the Liberals were on the point of supersession in 1914, two developments within the Labour Party were taking place which threatened Liberalism's long-term future. Firstly, there was the danger that the formal adoption of socialism by the party as a whole (something which did not, in fact, take place until 1918) would turn Labour from being uneasy allies into overt enemies. But more immediately worrying was evidence that the Labour militants were attacking the Asquith government, not so much for what it was *doing*, but rather for what it *was*. As Ross McKibbin puts it, what fuelled the Labour Movement in these years was the working man's intuitive belief that he wanted to have a government of his own.[69] This was ominous for the Liberals because, whereas they could have settled policy differences with Labour through discussion and negotiation, they could do little about such class antagonisms. Thus did the earlier failure of the Liberal Party to match its enthusiasm for working-class votes with a willingness to put up working-class candidates return to haunt it.

7
LIBERALISM AND THE GREAT WAR

Historians may differ about the prospects of the Liberal Party on the eve of the Great War, but the Liberals were in office, as they had been for nearly nine years. In municipal politics Liberalism was in retreat.[1] On the other hand, many constituency parties, both in Scotland and in England, were expanding their member ship in the immediate pre-war years.[2] Compare this situation with what happened during the election which was held soon after the signing of the Armistice in December 1918. Although this election took place in somewhat unusual circumstances, it did, broadly speaking, establish the main lines of development for the entire inter-war period.

The Conservatives, in alliance with the Lloyd George wing of the Liberal Party, won a crushing victory, and for the next twenty years they remained the dominant group at Westminster. But challenging their primacy for the first time was the Labour Party. True, as a result of having to face a combination of their opponents, Labour won a modest number of seats, sixty-three in all. But they had polled an extraordinary 2,385,472 votes. With 388 candidates in the field (compared with only fifty-six in December 1910, the previous election), Labour were projecting a quite different image of themselves from pre-war days. Already the newspapers were speculating about who might be the first Labour Prime Minister.

And Labour's advance had seemingly been achieved at the Liberal Party's expense. The Coupon Election saw the Liberals divided, demoralised and ineffectual. The Party's official leader, Asquith, suffered the ignominy of being rejected by the electors of East Fife, who had regularly returned him to Parliament for the last thirty-two years (he was also injured by boundary changes).[3] Two former Liberal ministers, Runciman and Samuel, came bottom of the poll. Only twenty-eight Independent Liberals survived the holocaust. This, too, was a portent of things to come.

In the copious literature dealing with the Liberal Party during the First World War three broad explanations have been advanced for this decline. Some historians are impressed by the play of 'accidental' factors, the mixture of bad luck and poor judgment on the part of certain prominent Liberal politicians which contributed materially to the Party's problems. Others talk about an incompatibility between the Liberal creed itself and the requirements of modern war; this interpretation dates from the seminal study by Professor Trevor Wilson, *The Downfall of the Liberal Party 1914–1935* (first published in 1966). Thirdly, there is a school of thought which gives primacy to the social changes initiated by the war, which led, it is said, to a class-based political system to which the Liberals never quite succeeded in adapting. Let us take these interpretations one by one.

The Liberals certainly suffered more than their fair share of ill-luck between 1914 and 1918. Their central misfortune was to be in the wrong place at the wrong time. Frustrated patriots, who started off with the assumption that the war would quickly be over, understandably directed their rage against the Liberals, who, after all, had been nearly nine years in power and could reasonably be held responsible for the country not being better prepared. Something very similar happened to the Conservative Party in 1939.

But the strictures passed on the Asquith ministry by its opponents were largely unjust. Haldane's creation of the Expeditionary Force, the naval reforms passed in the pre-war years (including the launching of the Dreadnought battleships), the work of the Committee of Imperial Defence in preparing the 'war book', which detailed exactly what each department should do in the event of war, all give the lie to the charge that the Liberals had neglected the country's armed services. Indeed, Churchill's determination, when at the Admiralty between 1911 and 1914, to maintain Britain's naval superiority over Germany meant that, on the eve of the war (1913), £72,500,000 was being spent on the armed services – unprecedented for peacetime.

In retrospect, it is tempting to compare the hesitant and ineffectual handling of the economy in the opening months of war with the bold planning which characterised the 'war socialism' presided over by Lloyd George in 1917 and 1918. But this, too, is unreasonable. Had Asquith attempted anything of this sort in 1914 or early 1915 he would almost certainly have strained 'national unity' to breaking-point.[4] Nor is it at all likely that if the Unionists had taken the country into war, the country would have been any better prepared, either economically or militarily.

Indeed, had the war been the short affair which so many were expecting, the Liberals might well have gained considerable credit from the experience. Asquith, for example, had shown all his conciliatory powers to good advantage in holding the Cabinet together in August 1914, with the loss of only two Cabinet ministers (Lord Morley and John Burns).

But the failure to secure a quick and decisive victory – something beyond the reach of any British government – created problems for the Liberals, which Asquith perhaps exacerbated by placing too much trust in Lord Kitchener, his War Secretary. Military disappointment intensified the mood of dissatisfaction with the ministry. As early as 15 September 1914 a walk-out from the Commons of the entire Conservative Party led by Bonar Law over the decision to put the Home Rule Bill on to the statute book (although its operation was to be suspended for the duration of hostilities) showed how fragile was the Opposition's offer to provide the government with patriotic support from outside.

In May 1915 the government was rocked by the simultaneous eruption of two crises, one affecting the adequacy of the munitions being supplied to the British Army in France; the other caused by the dramatic resignation of the First Sea Lord, Lord Fisher, over the decision to send further naval reinforcements to take part in the controversial Gallipoli campaign, so weakening the home fleet. The Prime Minister was left with little choice but to invite the Opposition leaders into his government. Equally inevitably, many prominent Liberal ministers had to step down to make way for Conservatives. Unfortunately, at Conservative insistence, Haldane, the Lord Chancellor, was (most unfairly) forced out of office because of his alleged pro-German sympathies, and Churchill was demoted from the Admiralty (he soon afterwards retired to the backbenches). The Liberal parliamentary party was only narrowly dissuaded from passing a resolution condemning these events.[5] In retrospect, the unhappiness of the Liberal MPs seems well justified. The last purely Liberal ministry had come to an end; there has never been another.

The establishment in May 1915 of the first coalition government over which Asquith presided until December of the following year also had two other damaging consequences for the Liberal Party about which, again, it could have done little. Firstly, the alliance with the Irish Nationalists came to an end. Redmond, the Nationalist Leader, was offered a post in the government which the rules of his party prevented him from accepting. But his old enemy, Edward Carson, the Ulster Unionist Leader, entered the coalition as Attorney-General – a galling sight to the Irishmen. The Nationalist Party, all hope of Home Rule having disappeared for the immediate future, was left stranded, and moderate leaders lost control over nationalist feeling in their own country. There is no need to describe the sequel: the 1916 Easter Rising and the rapid supersession of the Irish Nationalist Party by Sinn Fein, whose aspirations went well beyond Gladstonian Home Rule.

In some respects release from the Irish commitment came as a relief to the Liberals, to whom the issue had brought little but trouble over the past thirty years. On the other hand, the eclipse of Home Rule did deprive the Party of a distinctive policy. Moreover, although the drifting apart of the Liberals and the Irish did not matter for the time being (since the coalition had been set up, the Irish had, of course, ceased to hold the balance of seats in the House), in the long run it would be important. For no longer would Irish voters living on mainland Britain be urged to vote for the Liberal Party as the only English party that could realistically be expected to satisfy Ireland's national aspirations. Indeed, after 1918 most of the working-class Irish vote in areas like Merseyside and Clydeside soon transferred itself to Labour; and in Glasgow, as one historian has noted, 'Irishmen who had formerly been United Irish League ward bosses resurfaced as Labour councillors'.[6]

Coalition also ended the 'Progressive Alliance'. The war-time electoral truce meant that Liberals and Labour now stood in no need of one another; besides which, the coming together of the two main parties meant that the PLP lost its former leverage over the Asquith government. Yet, unlike the Irish Nationalists, Labour were not left out in the cold. On the contrary, Arthur Henderson, the chairman of the Parliamentary party, was made President of the Board of Education, the first Labour politician to hold office. This was not because Asquith set much store by the PLP. Rather, the war effort required the active involvement of the Labour Movement, and senior Labour figures from trade union backgrounds were valued as agents who could help preserve the industrial truce and 'sell' necessary but unpopular industrial policies to workers on the factory floor.

This gave Labour an importance and an independent position it had previously lacked. A revealing incident came in the course of the political crisis of December 1916. In its early stages Henderson took counsel with the Asquithian ministers and was treated as though he were one of their number. But when the Liberal ministers made a decision that they would none of them serve in a Lloyd George ministry, Henderson announced that he would be guided solely by the wishes of the Labour Movement and by his own particular concept of the national interest. In the event, Labour chose to support Lloyd George's new coalition. And Henderson was promoted by being brought into the new streamlined War Cabinet of five members, which took overall political control of the running of the war.

Experience of office gave Labour a credibility in the post-war years which otherwise it would almost certainly have lacked. Trade unionists and working men had penetrated into the inner recesses of Whitehall, where they had performed with efficiency. This raised their status in the eyes of the electorate. It also gave senior Labour politicians a taste of office and power, which made them more ambitious; never again would they be content with the modest, subordinate role allotted to them in the Edwardian political system. In 1918 Labour felt that it had made a major contribution to allied victory. It now insisted on having a powerful voice in the re-shaping of the post-war world. Moreover, Lloyd George's foolish expulsion of Henderson in the so-called 'door-mat incident' in August 1917[7] simply made the Labour leaders all the more determined to build up their organisation to the point where they were not dependent on any other organisation. The 'Progressive Alliance' had collapsed and was never to be re-created.

There was yet another way in which a long-drawn out war was bound to damage the Liberal Party. One element in the political truce was an understanding that the 1911 Parliament Act, stipulating quinquennial elections, would have to be suspended for the duration of the emergency, in order to postpone the dissolution which would otherwise have taken place by December 1915 at the latest. But this, in turn, necessitated an annual suspending Bill, which needed the approval of both Houses of Parliament; and since the Lords, in which the Unionists retained a comfortable majority, had not lost their absolute veto but could still hold up legislation, the Liberal ministers were left at the mercy of their Unionist colleagues, who could, should they so choose, oppose the prolongation of the life of Parliament and force a dissolution at a time of their own choosing.

Yet in all the mishaps which befell the Liberal Party during the war which have so far been discussed, none (except Lloyd George's foolish treatment of Henderson) was the result of clear-cut Liberal mistakes. Rather, once the country had become embroiled in a long war, events acquired a momentum of their own which the party leadership was powerless to deflect.

But the Liberals did also compound their difficulties by making avoidable errors. Asquith, for example, was undoubtedly unwise in not showing more generosity to his erstwhile political opponents (who by May 1915 outnumbered Liberals in the House of Commons). The main posts in his coalition were almost without exception reserved for Liberals (Kitchener at the War Office was, of course, a non-party figure). Only Balfour, the former Conservative Leader, who became First Lord of the Admiralty, was put in a position where he could decisively affect the war effort; his successor, Bonar Law, was fobbed off with the Colonial Office. Asquith was also damaged by his unwillingness or his inability to adapt the machinery of government to the requirements of war. The large Cabinet of twenty-two members could not provide overall direction to the war effort, and smaller bodies like the War Council, the Dardanelles Committee and the War Committee, which might theoretically have performed this function, lacked real authority, since any decision that they reached could always be challenged in full Cabinet.

As a result, many prominent Conservatives felt little loyalty to Asquith's premiership; some actively intrigued to bring it down. But discontent also spread to the ranks of the parliamentary Liberal Party. In January 1916 a patriotic backbench ginger group was set up, the Liberal War Committee. To these Liberals the hero of the day was not Asquith, but Lloyd George, who, put in charge of the new Ministry of Munitions in May 1915, had achieved a remarkable success in organising the economy for war production on novel lines. By the end of 1915 Lloyd George was even beginning to endear himself to many *Conservatives*, not least because of his alignment with them in a campaign to replace the country's traditional system of voluntary enlistment by conscription. Mainstream Liberals might mutter about 'treachery'. But to many dispassionate observers the former Radical tribune was emerging as a genuinely 'national' leader, able to transcend the petty interests of party in his eagerness for victory.

Lloyd George's growing importance was confirmed in June 1916 when, following Kitchener's death at sea, he became War Secretary. He did so on the eve of the disastrous Somme offensive. This experience confirmed the War Secretary in his belief that strategic command would have to be wrested from the military and tansferred to a streamlined civilian administration. Yet such a reform Asquith was neither able, nor perhaps willing, to promote. The rift between the two principal Liberal statesmen began to assume serious proportions. In early May 1916 Lloyd George's henchman, Christopher Addison, helped by David Davies and Frederick Kellaway, began his somewhat mysterious informal sounding-out of Liberal backbench MPs to see how much support there would be for Lloyd George in the event of a breach with the Prime Minister.[8]

The events of the 'Buckingham Palace Plot' of December 1916, which led to Asquith's replacement by Lloyd George, have been subjected to minute examination.[9] This is understandable enough, for there were several occasions when it seemed that the disagreement between Lloyd George (working with his new allies, Bonar Law and Carson) and Asquith was close to being resolved. Indeed, provisional agreement had been reached, not on personnel, but on the powers of the new War Committee which Lloyd George had been pressing the Prime Minister to establish, before Asquith went back on the agreement, angered by a mischievous leader published in *The Times* (a leader actually inspired by Carson). Edwin Montagu, the Minister of Munitions, a prominent Liberal who liked and admired both men, spent the crisis running from Asquith to Lloyd George and back again, trying to avert a split which spelled personal tragedy for politicians like himself as well as danger to the Party. But the bond of trust between the two senior statesmen which had served the Liberal government well between 1908 and 1914 had broken down.

Historians disagree over which man was the more to blame for the perpetuation of what soon became a damaging vendetta. Although sorely provoked, Asquith it was who probably did more, in a formal sense, to create the division. For example, by deciding to retire to the backbenches if he could no longer serve as Prime Minister (rather than sit as Lord Chancellor in a Bonar Law ministry), Asquith effectively put Lloyd George into 10 Downing Street. Moreover, Asquith's resentment over the way in which he had been treated encouraged the other senior Liberal ministers (among them, Grey, Runciman, McKenna and Montagu) to join their Leader on the backbenches. And this, in turn, meant that, whether he liked it or not, Lloyd George, the new Premier, was heavily dependent on the Conservatives – a situation that changed only slightly when in mid July 1917 the Liberal element in the government was strengthened by the bringing in of Churchill to the Ministry of Munitions and of the conscience-stricken Montagu to the India Office.[10]

What made the future prospects of the Liberal Party so hazardous was that Asquith remained the official Leader of the Liberal Party, and, as such, the controller of party funds. Even as early as January 1917 Lloyd George's friends were talking of the need to get together 'the nucleus of an organisation' to support the Prime Minister, to counterbalance the Asquithian machine.[11] Yet until well into 1918 a schism within the ranks of the Liberal Party was far from inevitable. Many backbenchers sincerely professed their admiration both for the Liberal statesman who led the government and for the Liberal statesman who continued to lead their Party. The division between the two groups was anyhow hazy, since it owed little or nothing to social or economic distinctions and had no connection with pre-war disagreements.[12] The moment for decision, though, finally arrived in May 1918, in the so-called Maurice Debate, when Asquith's perhaps ill-judged challenge to the government's handling of the issue of troop reinforcements in France prior to the German Spring Offensive enabled the Prime Minister to stage a show-down with his party critics. In the event, the government won this crucial parliamentary division, with seventy-one Liberal MPs coming to its support but ninety-eight Liberal MPs, including tellers, voted with Asquith and another eighty-five abstained or were absent from the House.

Lloyd George was emboldened by his success to make preparations to fight an election in partnership with the Conservative Party, although it is important to recall that at this stage it was a war-time election that everyone had in mind. Even now, all hope of a party reunion had not been abandoned. In late September an emissary sounded Asquith out about his willingness to rejoin the government as Lord Chancellor, with the power to nominate a certain number of his colleagues.[13] An embittered Asquith rejected the olive branch. Events now developed with bewildering rapidity. The German army suddenly disintegrated; in October its military high command sued for peace; and within a few weeks of the signing of the Armistice the country was plunged into a general election campaign.

The 'Coupon Election' of 1918 (so called because Lloyd George and Bonar Law issued a joint 'coupon' to their favoured candidates) still further split the Liberal Party and intensified the bitterness between its two wings. In general those Liberals who had supported the government in the Maurice Debate received coupons and as a result were sheltered from the opposition of Conservative candidates, while those who had voted the other way were abandoned to their fate.[14] Not surprisingly, the new House of Commons had an overwhelming Conservative majority, but 133 'National Liberals' (i.e. supporters of Lloyd George) were returned, while the official Liberals were reduced to a pathetic rump of twenty-eight. Most prominent Asquithians (McKenna, Runciman, Simon etc.) lost their seats, as did Asquith himself. But the atmosphere of the election campaign mattered almost as much as the result. In the heat of the contest Lloyd George impugned Asquith's patriotism by alleging that he had tried to bring down the government for unworthy reasons at a critical point in the war. But to the official Liberals, the 'traitor', of course, was Lloyd George himself. The Party was now formally divided, and although, as we shall later see, reunion was achieved in November 1923, the scars of the wounds which the Liberals had inflicted on themselves in the last two years of the war never properly healed over.

With the Liberal Party visibly disintegrating, Labour was given a chance of establishing a claim to being the principal party of reform – the one serious alternative to the Conservatives. The imminent enlargement of the electorate may also have been a factor in Labour's decision to run several hundred candidates – in December 1917 Henderson mentioned to a startled Liberal sympathiser that these might number 'as many as 500', though perhaps this presupposed the introduction of the Alternative Vote (see pp. 161–2).[15] Some historians even believe that it was in order to take advantage of the Liberals' decline that Labour reorganised itself in 1918 and finally, through Clause 4 of its new constitution, made the commitment to socialism.[16] Thus there are grounds for arguing that Labour's rise to power came about because it consciously moved to fill the political vacuum left by the Liberal Party's various acts of self-immolation.

Yet there seems something unsatisfactory about an interpretation which lays such heavy emphasis upon accident and the vagaries of personality. Take, for example, the issue of the Asquith–Lloyd George quarrel. Why should the two men, whose differences of social background and temperament had made them complement one another so effectively between 1908–14, to the great benefit of the Liberal Party, have allowed their relationship to deteriorate seriously once war had broken out? It makes little sense to dwell on Lloyd George's slipperiness and ambition, since these character traits were of long standing. Why should Lloyd George's ambition have driven him to advance his career *through* the Liberal Party before 1914, while it drove him into actions damaging to Liberalism thereafter? Further explanation inevitably leads one to an examination of some of the more fundamental dilemmas which all Liberals were facing in these years.

Quite the most persuasive of such interpretations is the one furnished by Trevor Wilson in *The Downfall of the Liberal Party*. In a metaphor which has achieved fame, Wilson contends that the Liberals on the eve of War resembled a man experiencing symptoms of illness (Ireland, Labour unrest, the suffragettes, etc.), who then had the misfortune to be hit by a rampant omnibus (the Great War) which mounted the pavement and inflicted on him injuries from the effects of which he eventually died.[17]

Wilson's thesis is that the Liberals were ideologically ill-equipped for 'total war'. The successful waging of such a war, he says, seemed unfortunately to require the abandonment or at least the temporary suspension of nearly all the principles and values which Liberals held dear. The dilemma was raised most acutely by the issue of conscription, which the military high command insisted was essential to break the deadlock on the Western Front. It was hard for Liberals to deny the generals the extra men they said they needed, yet at the same time the adoption of conscription seemed a gross betrayal of the cause for which Britain had entered the war in the first place: the destruction of Junkerdom. What would be gained by an Allied victory if this involved the 'Germanisation' of the British people? Conscription was eventually passed in two stages in 1916, but one prominent Liberal, the Home Secretary, Sir John Simon, resigned, and only Asquith's parliamentary skill prevented others from following suit. The Liberal Party underwent a traumatic experience during the struggle over conscription: patriotic duty and the will to win the war pulled it one way, inherited traditions and beliefs pulled it another. It follows from this analysis that the leadership difficulties, and the Asquith–Lloyd George antagonism itself, should properly be interpreted as *symptoms* of a more fundamental malaise, not as its principal *cause*.

It can also be demonstrated that the Liberal Party found itself under similar strain over other issues. The Chancellor of the Exchequer, Reginald McKenna, instituted a departure from strict Free Trade (the 'McKenna Duties' of 1915) and there was talk in government circles of organising a trade war against Germany even after hostilities had ended. Encroachments on customary civil liberties, such as press censorship and the proliferation of Orders-in-Council issued under the Defence of the Realm Act, also violated the Liberal conscience.

As a consequence, the Party began to split into three separate groups. The more high-principled Radicals simply despaired of Liberalism altogether and began to desert their Party for

Labour. This was made easier for them because of the existence of a pressure group called the Union of Democratic Control (UDC), which MacDonald and a number of left-wing Liberals had created in the autumn of 1914 to express their hostility to Grey's conduct of foreign affairs. Dissident Radical intellectuals, like E. D. Morel, C. P. Trevelyan and Arthur Ponsonby, got into the habit of co-operating in the UDC with kindred spirits from the socialist movement, like MacDonald. In time many of them gravitated into the Labour Movement, as did Bertrand Russell, whose principal attachment was to the more uncompromising No Conscription Fellowship.[18]

Secondly, there were the middle-of-the-road loyalists. These men did their best to conceal their unhappiness, and continued to look to the Leader, Asquith, for guidance and inspiration. Asquith, his personal life in disarray, was not at this time an inspirational figure, but many Liberals (especially rank-and-file activists) went on backing him because they feared for what might happen were he to be overthrown.[19]

This position was in total contrast to that of a third group: a ginger group of 'patriotic' Liberals, some of them, incidentally, advanced Radicals before 1914, whose open exasperation with Asquith's 'wait and see' approach mounted the longer the war progressed.

The crisis of war certainly drove some highly unlikely people into criticising Asquith and calling for ruthless and decisive action. Even James Bryce, Gladstone's old friend, was once heard to observe: 'War is one of those things that if done at all ought to be done with all one's might'.[20] Patriotic zeal persuaded such men that the conscientious scruples of Liberals and maybe the short-term interests of the Liberal Party itself must be subordinated to the greater national good. They wanted the war to be won, and they failed to see how the Germans would ever be defeated by a government half paralysed by an over-developed moral conscience. Moreover, neither did these Liberals see why the Conservatives should be allowed to claim a monopoly of patriotism and belligerent ardour. Those who took this view of things soon became very powerful indeed, and no wonder, for these 'patriots' soon found a spokesman in Lloyd George.

Impatient with half-measures that threatened to prolong the war, Lloyd George identified himself in the public mind with a policy of 'Thorough', a dedication to efficiency which overrode all other considerations. In alliance with the Conservatives, it was Lloyd George who pushed a reluctant Asquith into adopting conscription in 1916. It was also Lloyd George, the high-minded opponent of British military operations during the Boer War, who proclaimed fifteen years later that he intended to make life very hard for the conscientious objectors. And it was Lloyd George who in November 1916 called for a 'Knock Out Blow' against the enemy – so quashing any possibility of a compromise settlement which might have ended the blood-bath.

From an orthodox Liberal viewpoint, this was shocking behaviour indeed. But even Radicals who distrusted Lloyd George personally could see that, while the very existence of the Empire hung in the balance, his approach offered certain advantages. In December 1916 the 'progressive' Barbara Hammond mused: 'the Asquith regime means certain & moderate disaster; the Ll.G. either absolute disaster or success'.[21] By the end of 1916 the country was in such desperate straits that it seemed worth taking a gamble on Lloyd George, and a significant number of Liberal MPs were ready to give him their support, even though they realised that this might mean a temporary breach with Asquith, the Party leader. Looked at in this way, however, Lloyd George was not so much 'deserting' Liberalism; rather, he was providing an alternative version of it suited to the prevailing circumstances.

Let us, however, focus more sharply on *The Downfall of the Liberal Party*. It is so persuasive a book that one is tempted to swallow its argument uncritically. Yet its interpretation suffers from certain limitations. For a start, it is a study of the morale of the Liberal Party which concentrates almost entirely on members of the Parliamentary Party. Opinion amongst Liberal constituency workers was probably different. For example, in a study of Yorkshire Liberalism, George Bernstein has suggested that, 'by focussing on the parliamentary party, historians have exaggerated the strains that war-time policies imperilling tenets of liberalism placed upon Liberal loyalties. This tension between policy and principle was a norm of Liberal politics'.[22] In any case, argues Bernstein, Liberal activists and pressmen were prepared to accept compromises from Asquith because they basically trusted him (although conscription and the formation of the coalition ministry created disquiet), and most went on following him even after the split in December 1916. In Bernstein's view, then, the real blow to Liberal unity did not come until the allocation of the coupon in December 1918: Wilson's war-time 'crisis of Liberalism' was not the decisive factor.

Moreover, it is also arguable that, in the nature of things, all three British parties suffered from the impact of war and the 'distortions' of political life occasioned by coalition government. The Conservatives, for example, were, like their Liberal counterparts, sharply divided between 'Westerners' and 'Easterners' (those who wanted to concentrate the fighting on the Western Front and those who favoured operations in other theatres of war) and could by no means agree over the desirability of conscription and the 'sacrifices' to property rights that needed to be made in the cause of military efficiency.[23] A few prominent Conservatives, like the former Leader in the Upper House, Lord Lansdowne, author of the famous 'Letter' of 1917, even questioned publicly whether the pursuit of total victory justified the enormous loss of men and money which was being sustained. In addition, the cessation of 'normal' political life weakened the authority of all party leaders; Bonar Law played a major part in the construction of both Asquith's and Lloyd George's coalition ministries, but in each case he did so partly to shore up his own declining authority.[24] Even the enlargement of the franchise, agreed to in the last period of the war, worried the Conservatives, who feared (needlessly, it later transpired) that the imminent arrival of 'democracy' would seriously damage their party's electoral fortunes.[25]

The Labour Party found itself in an even more precarious position. Indeed, after the establishment of the first coalition, Labour MPs were actually sitting on both sides of the House. The ILPers, among them MacDonald and Snowden, were so seriously estranged from Henderson and the bulk of the trade union members that the very survival of a united Labour Party sometimes seemed to be in question. The struggle for power between the shop stewards, articulating a primitive syndicalist philosophy, and the party leadership involved in membership of a coalition government whose policies they could only marginally influence, also illustrates the dilemmas facing the party in these years. These dissensions had the effect of hamstringing many of Labour's constituency organisations.[26]

Yet, helped in part by its federal Constitution, Labour managed to surmount its difficulties, and, following its reorganisation, was able to enter the electoral fray in 1918 in good heart. Of course, the extension of collectivist controls during the war removed much of the earlier feeling that socialism was merely 'utopian', a change of attitude that was very much to Labour's benefit. But the contrast between the two 'parties of progress' was not simply that the Labour Movement found it easier than the Liberals to live with the demands of total war. More important, the social changes, which the war accelerated, had created an environment in which Labour felt confident that it could operate with success, and this confidence gave its various factions an interest in minimising their differences and presenting a more or less united face to the wider world. True, Trevor Wilson acknowledges the significance of such developments, in one place in his book ascribing the Liberal decline to 'the impact of the war on the nation's economy' which 'so increased the importance of the trade unions, and so stimulated their political consciousness, that it correspondingly enhanced the position of the Labour party. . .'.[27] But this is an *obiter dictum* which his book in no way demonstrates.

The gist of the Trevor Wilson thesis is his claim that 'the Liberal Party fell . . . because of a revolution in ideas occurring in the minds of men'.[28] But this approach leaves questions of organisation and of class relationships entirely out of account. And it is to these that we must now turn.

Why, in the long run, did the Labour Party emerge from the war with increased strength? We have already seen that participation in the wartime ministries gave the Labour leadership a new self-confidence and ambition, and also that the very fact of coalition government forced the Party to free itself from an electoral alliance which, perhaps, had long been something of a trap. But, in addition, Labour's base was enlarged by the circumstances of war. The total number of trade unionists approximately doubled between 1914 and 1919, from about 4 million to nearly 8 million. And this enabled the TUC to claim, for the first time, that it represented the majority of working people, skilled and unskilled, women as well as men, over a wide range of industries.

Given the close links between the political and industrial wings of the Labour Movement, such a development, it has been argued, was bound to help the Party – not least because trade union expansion automatically enriched it, since all the big trade unions were affiliated to Labour and only a minority of workers chose to contract out of the political levy. By 1918 the Labour Party was flush with funds. The fact that early in the year Henderson was speaking confidently of Labour's ability to run up to 500 candidates at the next election is eloquent testimony of his party's new-found wealth.

But it is possible that the perspectives of the Labour leadership also changed because the working-class community itself was undergoing a profound transformation in these years. Most historians believe that the gap in living standards between the skilled man and the labourer considerably narrowed during the course of the war. This particularly happened in the so-called 'controlled establishments', factories doing contract work for the Ministry of Munitions under official supervision, where piece work and the bonus system squeezed income differentials hard. The semi-skilled machine operators who were recruited in large numbers into munitions production were often earning more money than the skilled craftsmen who were put in charge of them.[29] But that was not all. For the dividing line between the skilled and the unskilled was itself becoming blurred as a result of 'dilution', that is to say the breaking-down of skilled craft procedures into a series of simpler operations which could be performed by unskilled and semi-skilled machinists, many of them women. This had immediate social consequences. As one

137

well-placed observer later put it, the social barriers of caste between the skilled worker and the lower industrial grades were permanently lowered during the war; from then on 'the artisan felt less superiority, the labourer and semi-skilled man more self-assurance'.[30]

Average real wages increased during the Great War, but the main benefits accrued to the unskilled. Apart from anything else, it was the unskilled, the much-despised 'residuum' of Edwardian Britain, whose circumstances were transformed by the virtual disappearance of unemployment. The unemployment rate fell below 1 per cent in May 1915 and then stayed at a very low point for the rest of the war. There was now a chronic labour *shortage*. Work was available for all who were not suffering from some physical or mental handicap. The so-called 'unemployables' we're soon as busily occupied as anyone else. So, in many cases, were their wives, and the double income made possible a standard of living for the poor which before 1914 would have been inconceivable.

Admittedly, in the short run, such changes gave rise to a certain amount of friction within the working-class community. The newspapers during the war years were full of amazing revelations about unskilled workers, drawing good pay in the munitions factories, who were able to purchase luxury items like pianos and gramophones. Many 'labour aristocrats' agreed with middle-class moralists that it was a topsy-turvy world in which ordinary labourers could acquire these prestige consumer goods.

But, despite this sort of jealousy, the changes initiated by the war probably succeeded, in the long run, in uniting working people more than they divided them. It was a more cohesive Labour Movement, as well as a more broadly-based one, that was flexing its industrial muscles in the 1920s. For working-class groups that previously had had little in common with one another had been subjected during the war to similar experiences, and this welded them together and made them conscious, perhaps for the first time, of their identity as a class with interests that conflicted with those of other classes. To a large extent this new working-class culture also cut across the local peculiarities which had been so pronounced in the Edwardian period.[31] Such developments could not but help Labour. Buoyed up by a new mood of confidence, the Labour Party re-wrote its Constitution in 1918, which now contained the famous Clause 4 committing its members to socialism. It is unlikely that any of this would have happened so quickly if the First World War had not occurred.

Labour also improved its position during the war at the Liberals' expense by quickly seizing the initiative on social reform, agitating vigorously over practical working-class grievances, such as rent levels, food prices and profiteering. These activities, centrally co-ordinated by the War Emergency Workers' National Committee, on which all sectors of the Labour Movement were represented, also served the useful purpose of distracting attention from its own political divisions over the war.[32] The Liberals, by contrast, largely let these social and economic issues go by default. Many of the Radical activists most in sympathy with the problems of the poor had in any case already discredited themselves by opposition to the war, and some of them, on the point of being de-selected, now lived in a kind of political no-man's land. As for the bulk of the Liberals in the country, for them the main issue of the day seems to have been, not social reform, but the restoration of liberty.[33] Thus, whereas many Labour Party members hailed 'war socialism' as a proof of the practicality of socialism itself,[34] Liberals tended to see it as a 'Prussian innovation' which was both dangerous and inefficient. The recent wartime controls, opined Sir Thomas Whittaker, MP for Spen Valley, 'meant that all the foolish talk we had heard for years about Socialism had been blown to the winds'.[35] This was a dangerously negative stance to take, but one which the Liberals' parliamentary leaders did little to counter.

Finally, there is some evidence that, although businessmen did very well out of war contracts, many *professional* middle-class groups living on fixed incomes suffered a severe decline in their standard of living. If we are to accept Masterman's considered judgment that this stratum had provided the pre-war Liberal Party with its bedrock support, its later demoralisation may have had a damaging impact on Liberalism itself.[36]

Yet it is necessary to end on a note of caution. One should not be carried away by wisdom of hindsight into portraying an optimistic Labour Party surging irresistibly forward at the end of the war, sweeping aside all the obstacles in its path. A closer examination of developments in the constituencies does not confirm this picture. Many trade unions were still apathetic about electoral politics; party organisation was weak or non-existent in many areas; and the old ideological and sectional divisions had by no means disappeared. Although artificially boosted by the impact of total war, the Labour Party still had an enormous mountain to climb before it could establish itself as a party of government.[37] By the same token, there remained a possibility that the Liberals could recover much of their former influence. It is always a mistake to 'read off' political events as mere indicators of social change. In any case, many of the developments apparently favouring Labour between 1914 and 1918 had been reversed by the mid-1920s, when wage differentials were widening once more, unemployment was rising sharply, and so on.[38] Such changes did not lead to Labour's decline. Neither did economic circumstances by themselves decree the Liberal Party's downfall. All one *can* say is that the social environment created by the war was one which gave some help to the Labour Party, while Liberals would have had difficulty in coping with it, even had they avoided the ideological wrangling to which Trevor Wilson has rightly drawn attention.

8

THE 1920s

In many respects the Great War proved to be a disaster for the Liberal Party. Yet, paradoxically, it also accomplished many of the objectives which Liberals had always set themselves. The 'modernisation' of society, in fact, was speeded up by the war in a way that the Liberal Party had itself never succeeded in doing. The big landowners had been bringing their land on to the market from 1909 onwards, before heavy war-time taxation, high military casualties among the aristocracy and a temporary rise in demand for land provided a fine chance to rid themselves of what, in many cases, had come to be seen as a burdensome liability. Between 1917 and the end of 1921 one quarter of England probably changed hands. The whole aristocratic 'system', centred on the ownership of big estates, was irrevocably destroyed. By 1927 36 per cent of land was owned by farmer-proprietors, compared with 12.3 per cent in 1908.[1]

But this belated collapse of 'feudalism' was a mixed blessing for the Liberal Party, since it meant the loss of one of its great defining 'causes'. Thus, although Lloyd George launched a new Land Campaign in 1925, it soon petered out, being largely superseded by the Industrial Inquiry. The trouble with the Land Campaign was that its proffered solution, 'cultivating tenure', was not easy to understand and threatened to divide the interests of farmers from those of their labourers. In any case, an alliance between farmers and labourers would be more difficult than ever to construct, now that the economic power of landlordism, which had provided the common enemy before 1914, had been broken. In the 1920s the great landowners were objects of pity, rather than of hatred.[2]

Something similar happened in the sphere of sectarian politics. With the settlement of the Welsh Church issue on a compromise basis in 1919 and with temperance less of a public issue now that heavy drinking had been reduced by higher living conditions and more recreational outlets, as well as by tight restrictions of licensing hours, there was nothing very significant upon which the 'Nonconformist Conscience' could focus. True, Nonconformity still rallied to the party's support. But after 1924 there were more Dissenters, in absolute terms, on the Labour than on the Liberal benches – though proportionately they increased, as the Liberals were driven back into the 'Celtic Fringe'.[3] Even in Scotland many United Free Church ministers, who could once have been relied upon to support the party through thick and thin, had deserted it by 1924, a development likened by one historian to the Barbary apes leaving Gibraltar![4]

Yet it was these 'dying' issues with which the Liberals still felt most at home. Hence, the importance to the Party of the atrocities committed in nationalist Ireland in 1920–1 by the notorious 'Black and Tans', the hastily assembled auxiliary police force, which revived a historic Liberal cause and gave Asquith an opportunity to attack the coalition government with real verve and effectiveness – rather as, when a young man, he had attacked the Unionists' 'coercion' in Ireland. Baldwin's challenge to Free Trade in 1923 had similar consequences. Indeed, the final abandonment of Free Trade in 1931–2 was to deal the Party a frightful blow, since it entailed the disappearance of the issue which, more than any other, had given the Liberals their identity.

Unfortunately, the zest with which the Liberals threw themselves into these familiar controversies tended to give them a somewhat dated appearance. It is hardly to be wondered at that one Liberal candidate should have had his election meeting disrupted by his working-class audience bursting out into the hymn, 'Tell me the old, old story'! It may be significant, given this context, that the Liberals seem to have had some difficulty in enlisting young recruits for municipal contests; in Wolver-hampton, for example, the average age of new Liberal council-lors during the 1920s was forty-nine, ten years older than that of their Labour counterparts.[5]

This did not mean that there was necessarily no place for the Liberal Party in the post-war world. As their defence of Free Trade in 1923 showed, Liberals still performed well when they could launch a principled attack on the Conservative Party from a broadly 'conservative' position. But such opportunities would only arise infrequently. Given the rise of the Labour Party, the Liberals' best bet was thus to try to carve out a role for them-selves as a centre party – mediating between the two extremes of Conservatism and Socialism. But was such a strategy feasible? And, even if feasible, did it offer the Liberals a chance to re-establish themselves as a party of government?

It might be thought that the facts spoke for themselves. Up until October 1922 the Liberals remained divided, with Lloyd George continuing to head a coalition government, while the 'Wee Frees', as the Independent Liberals were called, lan-guished in impotent opposition. Even with the fall of the coali-tion, the two parties led almost entirely separate existences. True, the Conservatives, by clumsily challenging Free Trade, brought about the Liberal Reunion of late 1923, shortly to be followed by a general election in which the Liberals were only narrowly beaten into third place. But that was the best electoral performance that they were to achieve in the entire decade. After 1929 (and perhaps by late 1924) a new two-party system had come into existence, centring around Conservatives and Labour. In municipal politics, too, the Liberal decline proceeded apace. By 1930 Huddersfield was the only English borough where the Liberals held control, though they were the largest single party in another five.[6]

But, once again, the subject is one over which historians have sharply differed. To illustrate these differences I shall first present the 'pessimistic' case, then suggest that a more 'optimis-tic' view of the Liberals' survival chances is possible, before concluding with an interpretation which combines elements of both.

The Pessimistic Case

Some historians believe that the Liberal Party never recovered from its war-time divisions. The perpetuation of the coalition in 1918 was a great disaster; it would have been better if a reunited Liberal Party had suffered a severe electoral defeat rather than undergoing a schism which left some of its prominent leaders reliant on the Conservative Party to keep them in office. Not surprisingly, the split within the Party later deepened as the 'official Liberals' took stock of their situation. At the Leamington meeting of the NLF in May 1920 the party faithful booed and hustled out of the hall those Liberal MPs who were supporting Lloyd George. The National Liberals (i.e. the Lloyd George Liberals) were denounced as 'traitors' to their party and their creed. These bitter divisions spilled over into the country. In Scotland, for example, seventeen constituency parties were disaffiliated in the post-war years for supporting the Prime Minister, and in the 1922 general election there were sixteen constituencies where Liberals fought one another.[7]

The Asquithian contempt for the coalition Liberals was not entirely justified. Some of the Liberal ministers, notably Montagu at the India Office and Addison, the first Health Minister, worked with courage and determination in pursuit of genuinely progressive policies. But all of this was eclipsed in the minds of the Independent Liberals by the atrocities committed by the 'Black and Tans' against Sinn Fein sympathisers, as the government sought to crush nationalist resistance to British rule in Ireland; it was all the more humiliating that the Irish Secretary responsible for these activities happened to be a National Liberal, Hamar Greenwood. The 'Liberal' credentials of the Prime Minister were then further undermined when he abandoned, first, Addison in July 1921, and then Montagu in March 1922, in a vain attempt to appease his restless Conservative 'allies'.[8]

All of this, the Irish issue in particular, gave Asquith a splendid opportunity for launching an attack on the immorality and unscrupulous attachment to power of the Prime Minister. Returned to the Commons once more in February 1920 at the Paisley by-election, Asquith took back the chairmanship of the parliamentary party from its stopgap leader, Donald McLean (who had, in fact, done surprisingly well), and for a brief time an Independent Liberal revival seemed possible. But disillusion with Asquith's tired performances soon set in: in 1921 and early 1922 serious moves were afoot to replace him by Grey as leader of a new 'centre' grouping which would also take in 'liberal' Conservatives, notably Lord Robert Cecil.[9] These intrigues came to nothing, and it was the revamped Labour Party which was the better placed to take advantage of the government's unpopularity. Consequently, when the coalition finally fell in October 1922, Asquith and his friends could do little but watch from the sidelines.

From the Liberal point of view, it was particularly unfortunate that the coalition's demise came about, not by Lloyd George breaking free from his Conservative allies (as he had sometimes threatened to do), but because of a Conservative revolt against his own leadership. For the impression was given that Lloyd George and his friends, who maintained their own 'National Liberal' organisation, had only returned to Liberalism because more promising options had temporarily been closed down. How long would it be, many people wondered, before Lloyd George once again tried to link up with his many Conservative Party friends (Austen Chamberlain, Balfour, Lord Birkenhead among them)?

Since Asquith's inner circle continued to view Lloyd George with suspicion and contempt, the Liberal schism continued for the next twelve months. Reunification, when it came in November 1923, owed more to Baldwin's incompetence than to any desire for reconciliation, and, although in many constituencies the old camaraderie was quickly restored, at national level the new-found unity of the Party (which Asquith formally led) was never anything other than superficial. The Asquithians, particularly close associates of the leader like Herbert Gladstone and Vivian Phillipps (the 'Holy Family'), continued to view Lloyd George with loathing, and Lloyd George, for his part, showed his own distrust by refusing to hand over to the official Liberal coffers the very sizeable fund which he had amassed over the previous few years (not least by the sale of honours during the period of the post-war coalition!) until the party machine had been organised to his satisfaction – a transparent device for increasing his own authority within the Party.

Lloyd George's behaviour only makes sense if one supposes that he was 'riding for a fall', confident in the knowledge that he would be able to seize control of the Party in the wake of another election defeat. If so, the scheme was well planned. When a snap election was called in October 1924, financial uncertainty meant that the Liberals were only able to field 340 candidates, 113 fewer than had stood in the successful campaign eleven months earlier.[10] Even before the polling booths had opened (shades of 1900) the Liberals had publicly renounced any ambition to form their own government.

The 1924 election reduced the Liberals from 158 MPs to forty. Asquith lost his seat, though he took a peerage (becoming Lord Oxford and Asquith) and remained the titular party leader. Day-to-day running of the parliamentary party devolved on to Lloyd George, the chairman of the Liberal MPs. It was almost an exact re-run of the unhappy period of 1894–5 when Rosebery tried to lead the Liberals from the Lords, in the face of obstruction from Harcourt, the Leader in the Commons. Haggling over the disposition of the by now notorious 'Fund' continued to poison the atmosphere of Liberal politics: Asquith's friends insisted that it needed to be 'pooled' (in effect be handed over to them), but Lloyd George clearly had no intention of losing control over a fund which, he believed, guaranteed him a continued political career in a hostile environment.

The existence of the 'Fund' was damaging to the Liberal Party for three reasons. First, it meant that a party which prided itself on being the embodiment of morality in public life (the association with Nonconformity strengthened rather than weakened in these years, Dissenters comprising over a half of all Liberal MPs after 1924) had become associated in the public mind with chicanery and corruption. Secondly, the Fund made it difficult for the Liberals to put their finances on to a sound footing. Asquith's officials tried, belatedly in 1925, to raise a central fund from a number of small subscriptions (the 'Million Fund'), but sympathisers with Liberalism, affluent or otherwise, felt understandable reluctance to dig deep into their pockets to help the party when a sum of money, rumoured to amount to some £3 million, was in existence to which access was being blocked (according to sources close to Lloyd George) by the petty-mindedness of the Asquithians. The Liberals, it seemed, were damned whether they accepted Lloyd George's 'tainted' money or whether they refused it. But the 'Fund' was also damaging to Lloyd George himself for a rather different reason. Public discussion of the matter kept alive in the electorate's mind memories of the circumstances in which it had been accumulated and drew attention to Lloyd George's coalition past even when the Welshman sincerely wanted to be seen as a 'man of the Left'.[11]

A resolution of sorts was achieved in the summer of 1926 when differences between Asquith and Lloyd George over how to respond to the General Strike led to the final showdown, resulting in Asquith's retreat into private life. Now that Lloyd George had become the undisputed party leader, his commitment to a Liberal revival dramatically increased, and, although he continued to the end of his life to cling tenaciously to his separate Fund, he began making generous disbursements from it to improve the party organisation and to help the intellectuals of the Liberal Summer School movement formulate a modern programme. But, to the Asquithian faithful, their once great party had been 'bought' by an unprincipled adventurer. In 1927 these men formed the Liberal Council, under the presidency of the aged Grey, to keep 'independent Liberalism' alive. As a result, when the Liberals fought a spirited campaign in the 1929 election, with their bold 'We Can Conquer Unemployment' slogan, the effect was marred by the more-or-less open scepticism expressed by old Asquithians like Runciman and Simon.[12] In any case, by this time Liberal fortunes may have sunk too low for them to be revived by any party campaign, however inspired.

Over Liberal politics in the 1920s there hangs, in Michael Bentley's telling phrase, an atmosphere of 'regret and re-crimination'.[13] The Asquithians' sense of outrage at what they considered the 'betrayal' of their party and their creed never really abated, and, for some of them, like Lord Cowdray, the 'feud' against the Welshman became the main purpose of their existence.[14] The depths of this bitterness can be seen from the fact that when in 1927 the right-wing newspaper, the *Morning Post*, ran a series of articles about the 'Fund', some of its material was being secretly provided by Vivian Phillipps, while other Liberals cheered him on in his attempt to drive their 'Leader' from public life.[15] Moreover, many Liberals succumbed to a mood of self-pity, in which nostalgia for a supposedly glorious past was combined with a stubborn pride in resisting the wiles of the sordid post-war world. 'You have helped the remnant of us to think rightly and to hold out', one Liberal intellectual, Gilbert Murray, wrote to Asquith in 1925.[16] Faced by such a frame of mind as this, do we need to look further for an explanation of the Liberals' failure to return to power?[17]

Once again, however, Liberal factionalism may have been in part the symptom of a deeper demoralisation. Liberals had good grounds for querying whether after 1918 Lloyd George was truly committed to their party; in 1920 he was saying privately to his 'National Liberal' colleagues: 'Liberal labels . . . [lead] nowhere; we must be prepared to burn them'.[18] But *why* did Lloyd George feel this way? Can it not also be argued that the introspective quarrelsomeness displayed by the Liberals for most of the 1920s was as much the consequence, as it was the cause, of the Liberals' failure to win power?

In two respects the Liberals were faced by an entirely new challenge after the First World War, with which, in the opinion of some historians, they were ill-equipped to deal: a mass electorate and the Labour challenge. Let us take these one by one.

In the summer of 1918 Parliament passed the Representation of the People Act, which, for the first time, gave the vote to all adult men and many women, so trebling the electorate at a stroke. In a famous article Matthew, McKibbin and Kay have claimed that the Conservative and Labour Parties were able to appeal to this new mass electorate more effectively than their Liberal rivals, and this for two reasons. First, the newly enfranchised voters naturally inclined towards Labour, which was thus able for the first time to exploit its class appeal to the maximum. Secondly, Liberals, or so it is claimed, were too rational to make emotive appeals to less educated voters, unlike Labour, which could employ class slogans, and unlike the Conservatives, with their patriotic appeal.[19]

Both claims are shaky. For a start, the assumption that the 1918 Act enfranchised a hitherto excluded 'class', the casual poor, has been shown to be false. In fact, (excluding the plural voters) the Act raised the working-class proportion of the electorate from 76 per cent to 80 per cent, hardly a dramatic increase. In any case, the Labour Party did not do significantly worse in municipal elections, where a franchise similar to the 'household franchise' of pre-war days was still in place.[20] Indeed, if one statistical analysis is to be believed, 'the more new voters, the *less* the constituency tended towards the Labour Party'.[21] If Labour benefited from the new electoral system at all, this, it seems, was mainly because of the changes made to constituency boundaries.[22]

As for the relationship between the Liberal Party and the new electorate (and women, of course, were now voting for the first time), Asquith certainly seems to have privately viewed them with a mixture of detached amusement and mistrust: the women were 'hopelessly ignorant of politics, credulous to the last degree, and flickering with gusts of sentiment like a candle in the wind'; the Irish working class were at the mercy of their 'bosses', and so on.[23] But Lloyd George, author of the slogan of '9d for 4d' (when promoting Health Insurance after 1911) had never been averse to a spot of vulgar demagoguery in the past, nor did he become austerely scrupulous after 1918. Indeed, the opposite criticism of him was often made. Asquith's daughter wrinkled up her nose during the 1923 Election at Lloyd George 'cartwheeling round the country with his apparatus of loudspeakers, journalists, jokes, etc.', and Herbert Gladstone worried lest Lloyd George's 'American' campaigning methods would alienate the 'high-brows'.[24] The relevance of all this to the survival chances of the Liberal Party is unclear.

The rise of Labour, on the other hand, really did present the Liberals with a major problem. For the Liberals could not easily decide whether Labour should be treated as allies, rivals or enemies. Their uncertainty on this issue was, of course, bound up with the difficulty which they had in defining their own political position.[25]

Given the problems faced by their party in the 1920s, it was natural that many Radicals should look back nostalgically to the old 'progressive alliance' with Labour and try to recreate it. This was a favourite idea of C. P. Scott, the influential editor of the *Manchester Guardian*, who pressed it on moderate Labour politicians like Henderson. L. T. Hobhouse, who could never quite bring himself to join Labour as other New Liberals had done, would also have welcomed such a development. He even speculated privately about what he regarded as a logical party realignment, in which the 'bad Liberals' would join up with 'ordinary Tories', while 'good [i.e. progressive] Liberals' would fuse with 'ordinary Labour', leaving both Diehards and theoretical socialists on the political fringes.[26] It seemed to him absurd that the forces of progress should, through their divisions, play into the hands of the Conservative enemy. A number of historians, including Trevor Wilson, have agreed.

But these were mere paper schemes. The last thing that Labour wanted was a reversion to the pattern of pre-war politics, and, as they steadily built up their popular vote, they had no need of support from the Liberals. So much became apparent when MacDonald formed his minority ministry in 1924 after Asquith had made his fateful decision to 'put Labour in'. Far from being grateful for Asquith's assistance, the new Cabinet took its own line of conduct and refused even to consult with the Liberal MPs on whose votes it depended. Backbench Labour MPs were equally unaccommodating. Thus, when a Liberal brought forward a Bill to establish proportional representation, twenty-eight Labour MPs voted in its favour, but ninety-one went through the 'No' lobby (there was a free vote). Most galling of all, Liberal MPs found that, while they had been staying up late into the night sustaining MacDonald in office, the Labour Party was preparing to run candidates against them at the forthcoming election – even when this meant intervening in a constituency for the first time and thereby almost certainly handing it over to a Conservative (as happened in the Oxford by-election in June).[27]

Too late Asquith and Lloyd George recognised that they had walked into a trap. If the Labour ministry displayed moderation and acted in ways of which Liberals approved, as happened with Philip Snowden's Budget or with MacDonald's attempts to act as a conciliator between the French and German governments, the Liberals found that a rival party had stolen their clothes. But when the Labour ministry seemed to be pandering to its 'extreme' socialist backbenchers, for example, through its attempts to reach a commercial and financial settlement with the Bolshevik regime in Russia, the Liberals could do little about it, yet were open to the taunt that it was *they* who bore responsibility by having put these dangerous revolutionaries into power in the first place. Indeed, Labour showed by its behaviour during the 'Campbell Case'[28] that it was even prepared to countenance its own ejection from office if this would damage the Liberals. Relations between the two parties were little better between 1929 and 1931, when the Liberals, holding the balance of seats, once again installed Labour in government.

But there was more to Labour hostility than mere scepticism over whether a bargain with the Liberals was worth pursuing. For in the mind of Henderson, in many ways the key Labour figure in the 1920s, the memory of the 'doormat incident' still rankled. Moreover, Lloyd George's cynical attacks on 'Bolshevism' during the coalition years had alienated nearly all those active in the Labour Movement.[29] Finally, with the adoption of Clause 4, an ideological chasm now separated the two parties in a way it had not earlier done.

Yet this was not really the main obstacle. Socialism, important at a rhetorical level, did not mean much in practice, and at Westminster there was still a great deal that the Liberals and the Socialists had in common in policy terms. As we have seen, it was this very closeness of view which made for so much rivalry between the two parties. Conversely, Labour dreaded a Liberal revival more than it did the Conservative challenge, precisely because it realised that Liberals and Labour were, to some extent, 'fishing in the same pond' – in policy terms, at least.

The Liberals also caused offence, mainly unwittingly, by their patronising attitude towards the Labour Party, which they

151

pitied for being so raw and inexperienced. Asquith's private reference to Labour's Commons performance in 1920 – the Labour people 'know as much about Parliamentary politics ... as a hen does of Astrology'[30] – expressed a deep contempt which he scarcely bothered to conceal in public. Masterman's ostentatious 'coaching' of Labour ministers in 1924 also lacked tact (as did Keynes , who wanted some kind of 'alliance' with Labour yet showered its spokesmen with ridicule for their stupidity and philistinism).[31] Most Labour politicians were very touchy on these matters, and MacDonald was speaking for many of his colleagues when, during the 1923 election, he compared the dishonourable behaviour of the Liberals with that of the Conservatives, who had at least fought like gentlemen.

Thus, rational calculation and emotion alike suggested that Labour's policy should be one of treating individual Liberals considerately in the hope of persuading them to join its ranks, while treating the Liberal *Party* with bitter hostility. In any case, the Labour leaders believed the Liberals to be historically doomed, and so were tempted to behave in such a way as to make these predictions come true.

But even if Labour had proved more co-operative, it is not clear that this would have been acceptable to the bulk of the Liberal Party. The loss of several thousand disillusioned leftwing Radicals to Labour between 1917 and 1919 (one historian thinks that 2,000 joined the ILP alone) had undoubtedly shifted the political centre of gravity within the Liberal Party.[32]

This quickly manifested itself at the level of political thought. Michael Freeden, author of a study of the Edwardian New Liberals, has noted how much less adventurous were what he calls the 'Centre Liberals' of the 1920s. The latter tended to treat economics as something lying outside the control of governments and of society. This more conservative intellectual approach was in part a reaction against war-time controls, but it was reinforced by the slump, which destroyed the earlier Liberal belief that the problem of production had been largely solved and all that now mattered was how to redistribute wealth. 'The grievances of today are mainly economic', said the Yellow Book. In practice, this meant that Liberals now sought to restore capitalism's lost dynamic (re-discovering 'economic man' in the process) and correspondingly neglected social reform: for there was a reluctance to divert money into welfare work away from productive investment. The improvement of industrial relations, on the other hand, greatly interested Liberals – perhaps because it cost nothing! No-one expressed this new emphasis better than the Liberal Party's most distinguished intellectual, John Maynard Keynes. It is particularly significant, thinks Freeden, that Keynes and his Summer School friends seem to have been totally unaware of many of the important pre-war writings of Hobson and Hobhouse. A challenging, even subversive, element in Liberal thought had, at least for the time being, disappeared.[33]

Indeed, far from wanting any kind of co-operation with Labour, a not inconsiderable number of Liberals after 1918 hoped to make resistance to socialism the cornerstone of their politics. Shocked by the astonishing success of the Labour Party in the 1919 municipal elections, the Liberals joined the Conservatives in many parts of the country, either forming 'anti-Socialist' parties, like the 'Hull Municipal Alliance', or operating an informal pact, as in the Bristol region, Merseyside, western Scotland, and parts of West Yorkshire.[34]

Nor was this merely something which was happening in municipal elections. In the twelve two-member 'territorial' constituencies which had survived the 1918 Redistribution, it is possible to analyse the way in which electors divided their votes between the three parties. In most of them, there was a strong tendency for the Liberal vote to be shared with the Conservatives rather than with Labour. This even happened in a city like Norwich, which, as we have seen, had been one of the boroughs in which the 'progressive alliance' had worked very effectively before 1914.[35] But the result of this was that, for example, only nine of the Liberals who survived the *débâcle* of 1924 had had to fight a genuine triangular contest; of the rest, all but two had been spared the ordeal of fighting a Conservative opponent.[36] In the long run, this boded ill for the future of the party.

Can we be more specific about where the Liberal Party's electoral support was located? This is not an easy question to answer, since Liberalism meant different things in different parts of the country: for example, the old Lib-Lab parliamentary pact largely survived in Preston throughout the 1920s.[37] (Indeed, in one historian's opinion, the sporadic electoral successes which the Liberals enjoyed during the 1920s 'appear to have been partly fortuitous or the result of local initiative', not something which had much connection with the actions of the national leaders.)[38] But an analysis of the general elections between 1918 and 1929 shows clearly that the regions in which the Liberals enjoyed the highest success-rate were rural Wales and the Scottish Highlands, followed by the Western Peninsula (Cornwall and parts of Devon). It seems, in fact, as if constituencies with a very high percentage of the population working in agriculture were especially prone to elect Liberals. In 1923, for example, over one half of the country's rural constituencies were won by the Liberals.[39] By contrast, the party was generally weak in urban Britain, though it retained a powerful presence in some industrial towns, for example, Huddersfield, Middlesbrough, Preston, and Bethnal Green. Indeed, areas where the Liberal Party had hitherto been dominant, like Clydeside and South Wales, quickly became Liberal 'deserts', following Labour's breakthrough in the 1922 general election.

The omens, then, were not very promising for the electoral chances of the Liberals, for the kind of constituencies where they performed best were few in number – thus, their three strongest areas only returned thirty-two MPs in total. Labour and the Conservatives had a much stronger platform from which to launch their assault on power. This is what clearly lies behind the interesting statistic, that whereas the Liberals in the 1920s were quite successful in *winning* seats (they won 281, compared with Labour's 304 and the Conservatives' 445), their problem was rather one of *holding on to their gains*: in only forty-one seats did they win in four or more general elections, compared with 112 for Labour and 259 for the Conservatives.[40] Even in 1929, when the Liberals achieved a net gain of nineteen seats, they still managed to lose nineteen of the forty seats which they had won in the disastrous election of 1924. In other words, the Liberals had nothing equivalent to Labour's mining seats or the Conservatives' strength in the wealthy suburban districts of Outer

London. This put the Liberals at a permanent disadvantage in the sort of class-based politics which characterised Britain in the 1920s.

The Liberals liked to believe that they were able to transcend these class divisions with an appeal that reached out to all classes in the community. This was true, up to a point; in 1923 the defence of Free Trade enabled them to pick up seats in both counties and towns in all regions of mainland Britain. At the same time, the Liberals could not, after 1922, boast many secure working-class seats. Where they were successful in working-class constituencies, this usually owed a lot to the personal popularity of a particular MP, for example, Percy Harris, who had built up a strong rapport with the poverty-stricken people of South-West Bethnal Green. As for municipal contests, Chris Cook has shown that in Manchester the Liberals actually enjoyed less success in poor working-class wards than the *Conservatives*, let alone Labour, and that they fared only slightly better in Leicester.[41] Indeed, there were times in the 1920s when the Liberals looked like becoming 'a bourgeois special interest party' – which was why they posed such a serious potential threat to the Conservatives.[42]

At the parliamentary level, too, Liberalism in the 1920s gives the appearance of being a party of the right rather than a party of the left. Only a handful of Liberal MPs throughout the decade came from the working class; Barnet Kenyon, a Primitive Methodist who was President of the Derbyshire Miners and MP for Chesterfield, was a highly untypical Liberal member. In sharp contrast to the PLP, the Liberal parliamentary party was an overwhelmingly middle-class body.

The right-wing tendencies within Liberalism were exposed by the events of 1924. True, the leadership decided to allow Mac-Donald to create a minority ministry, but the decision was not popular in all quarters of the parliamentary party; ominously, ten Liberal MPs voted against the Liberal motion which destroyed Baldwin's government (another seven were absent unpaired).[43] Amongst the activists in the country, too, there was much dismay. Asquith had received a letter from five leading local businessmen in his Paisley constituency (both Liberals and

Conservatives) appealing to him to keep Labour out of office, and when he ignored this advice the leading Liberal newspaper in the Glasgow area, the *Daily Record*, threw in its lot with the Unionists.[44]

Opinion among the Liberal MPs soon polarised. Time and again Liberal MPs found themselves going through different division lobbies. A few of them (including initially Lloyd George himself) protested that Labour was behaving with shocking moderation, but a larger number were clearly unhappy about Labour being in office at all. These disaffected right-wing Liberals were already embarking on a political journey that was to end with them joining up with the Conservatives. When Parliament dissolved in October, many of these men were allowed by their Conservative friends to stage a straight fight against Labour. Of course, such behaviour disgusted most of the party's remaining working-class supporters in the country, who seem to have regarded it as a betrayal.

There were three further stages on this journey to the right. Firstly, there was Lloyd George's Land Campaign of 1925–6, which alienated some party members and provided the occasion for the defection to Conservatism of Hilton Young and Alfred Mond, the great chemicals magnate. Secondly, there was the 1926 General Strike when, despite the backing given to Baldwin's government by most senior Liberals, especially Asquith and Simon, some Liberals reached the conclusion that the enemies of Labour could not safely stay divided. For example, in the immediate aftermath of the Strike the Conservatives managed to persuade several prominent members of the Leeds City Council (including the leader of the Liberal group) to defect.[45] And finally there was the creation of the National Government in August 1931, when the 'Liberal Nationals', led by Simon, effectively abandoned the historic Liberal Party and joined forces with the Conservatives.

The General Strike was particularly disruptive to Liberalism because it forced the party to do what it had always tried to avoid: take sides in a stark confrontation between capital and labour. As we have seen, when this happened, Asquith took the former side, Lloyd George the latter. But the split was not confined to the leadership. For while many Liberals felt that the crisis obliged them to throw in their lot with the Conservatives, some genuine Radicals, including the Liberal MP for Central Hull, Commander Kenworthy, formally joined the Labour Party. It was (to use one of their own favourite metaphors) a classic example of the Liberals being crushed between the 'upper and nether millstones'.[46]

The Optimistic Case

But this is going too far in the direction of pessimism. In 1923 the Liberal vote was only fractionally less than Labour's: 4,311,147 as compared with 4,438,508. If one makes allowance for un-contested seats (eleven Liberal, as against three Labour), the two parties were virtually running neck and neck. In Scotland, the Liberals regained their old ascendancy over the Tories, win-ning twenty-two seats to their rivals' fourteen. It has been argued that the Free Trade issue artificially revived Liberal electoral fortunes in 1923, but, then, the same thing had been said about the 1906 victory. There is something unsatisfactory about simply *assuming* the Liberals were losers, as a consequence of which all successes have to be dismissed as 'aberrations'. True, the 1924 election was a disaster, but some good by-election performances, following the publication of the 'Yellow Book' in early 1928 (see below),[47] suggested that the electoral corner might once again have been turned. Indeed, in 1929 the Liberals polled more votes than ever before in their history, over five and a quarter million (admittedly on a wider franchise). The bias of the electoral system (of which more in a moment) cruelly dis-guised the underlying Liberal strength. Whatever socialist theory might have predicted, the Liberals took a long time to die – no wonder that they were viewed by their opponents (until late 1924 anyway) with deep fear.

It is still less convincing to present Liberalism as a 'Victorian' creed, of no relevance to post-war needs. For example, the popu-larity of the League of Nations, acknowledged by both Labour and Conservative front benches, testified to the continuing vitality of an essentially liberal approach to the problems of international life. Admittedly, in matters of economic management the Liberals were less favourably situated. Under Asquith's leadership the party seemed to be living on past memories. But, as Masterman ruefully conceded, 'When Lloyd George came back to the party, ideas came back to the party'.[48] The first of the annual Summer Schools took place in 1921, when the movement was associated with Liberal intellectuals generally sympathetic to Asquith, but by the middle of the decade it was Lloyd George who was treating the Summer Schools as a kind of 'think tank'.

Two groups can be identified in the Summer School movement. On the one hand, there was a group of radical Manchester businessmen, led by E. D. Simon, whose main interest lay in the re-structuring of industry with a view to creating a more co-operative relationship between capital and labour. On the other, there were the Cambridge economists, led by Hubert Henderson (who had replaced Massingham as editor of the revamped *Nation*) and John Maynard Keynes. To the latter group the primary task was the formulation of a reflationary financial and fiscal strategy, the implementation of which could lift the country out of Depression.[49] Both groups made their contribution to the so-called 'Yellow Book', *Britain's Industrial Future*, which, published in 1928, provided the Liberals with the economic proposals on which they fought the 1929 election. According to one historian, it was the most intellectually distinguished manifesto ever put before the British voters.[50]

More recently, economists who have fed the Liberal programme into a computer model of the economy have expressed scepticism over the Liberals' pledge to 'conquer' unemployment (Lloyd George spoke on the eve of the election of reducing it within the space of two years to 'normal dimensions'). Apart from anything else, in the absence of tariffs (and the Liberals remained a Free Trade party), a reflationary programme would probably have run quite quickly into severe balance of payments problems.[51] A question mark also hang over the commitment of the party as a whole towards the implementation of the radical economic ideas that Lloyd George and his Summer School friends had imposed upon it.[52]

All the same, the Liberals had the energy and the boldness to confront what was an unprecedented economic situation, and they did at least try to do something about the slump, unlike their opponents, most of whom were sunk in apathetic fatalism. Lloyd George and his friends certainly went out of their way to make the electorate draw such a contrast. It was Socialists and Conservatives, mocked the Liberals, who were living in the past: 'We refuse ... to spend time or energy over the controversy between Individualism and Socialism. ... If it ever were a real issue, it is certainly now obsolete'.[53] The fight between *laissez-faire* capitalism and capitalism, they claimed, was anyhow a bogus fight: businesses had been 'socialising themselves', as more and more were converted into joint stock companies, with the result that the capitalism which socialists were attacking had already been largely superseded – something which only a devotion to dogma prevented them from seeing.[54]

Underlying such gibes, of course, was the traditional Liberal belief that class divisions were either mischievous or unimportant. The 'Yellow Book' pitched its appeal to the intelligent and public-spirited from all social backgrounds – to people who were tired of class animosities and party political cries. Nor was this studied 'classlessness' (an index of the Party's own lack of a clear class base) to be seen necessarily as an unmitigated weakness. As the Liberals themselves realised, there was a growing class of white-collar workers and professional people unable to identify with either the Labour Movement or with big business. The 'Yellow Book' tried to tap precisely this social grouping with its references to 'the "third party" in industry' (the managerial and technical staffs) who were being left out of the process of collective bargaining between organised bodies of employers and workpeople.[55] Finally, the very depth of bitterness aroused by such episodes as the General Strike created a widespread yearning for social and political reconciliation which the Liberals were better placed than the other parties to exploit.

In the view of the 'optimists', then, there is nothing 'inevitable' about Liberal decline, which came about, rather, as a result of a series of mistakes. Even as late as 1923–4, they claim, the Liberals still had a good chance to re-establish their credentials as a party of government. Certainly, at the start of 1924 Asquith seemed to have the ball at his feet. Indeed, it was widely predicted that since the Liberals held the balance of seats in the Commons and no new dissolution could take place for many months, it was quite possible that, perhaps following a short-lived Labour administration, the King would turn to Asquith to form a caretaker ministry, for, of the three party leaders (Baldwin and MacDonald being the other two), Asquith was, of course, quite the most experienced and able. That the Liberals would have been pushed back by the end of the year to the margins of the political system, with a mere forty MPs, was not an outcome which seemed 'inevitable' or even probable at the time, and only the wisdom of hindsight makes it seem so today.[56]

In the view of several historians, the real rot only set in after Asquith had made the fatal mistake of putting Labour into office. True, the Liberals, having just fought an election on the issue of Free Trade versus Protection, had little option but to throw their weight, for the time being, on the side of Labour, another Free Trade party, rather than prop up the Conservative administration. But it is arguable that neither Asquith (nor, indeed, Lloyd George) took sufficient account of the dangers they were running. At the least, they should have pressed Labour for an 'understanding' that could have formed a basis for their support of the new government. If, as seems probable, Labour had then refused to strike any deal, the public would at least have been left in no doubt as to who was responsible for the resulting deadlock.[57]

But if a failure of strategy did indeed take place, then this owed something to the bad relationship between the two Liberal factions, which found expression in internal wrangling and introspection, and militated against a cool appraisal of the wider political situation. Nor can this internal squabbling easily be accepted as a manifestation of deep-seated ideological fissures within Liberalism. True, the final split between Asquith and Lloyd George took place on an issue, the General Strike, involving two quite different conceptions of what Liberalism meant.

But this was atypical. In any case, although on this occasion Lloyd George seemed to be articulating a 'radical', 'left wing' point of view, *most* of the Liberals closely associated with the Welshman, like Freddie Guest and Sir William Edge, were on the right wing of the party and eventually landed up in the Conservative (or Liberal National) Party. Inasmuch as the Asquith–Lloyd George dispute was largely a personal vendetta, the Liberal Party can be said to have been the author of many of its own misfortunes.

But there is yet another way of looking at the subject. The question of whether or not the Liberal Party could have 'survived' depends very much on what one means by 'survival'. Given the 'first past the post' system, there was little room for a Liberal Party which had sunk to the level of 'perpetual thirds'. But electoral reform would have transformed the Liberals' prospects. This is no mere debating point. For the Speakers Conference, whose Report laid the basis for the 1918 Representation of the People Act, *unanimously* recommended the adoption of Proportional Representation (PR) on the Single Transferable Vote (STV) system in all boroughs currently returning three or more MPs, while a majority also recommended the Alternative Vote (AV) in the remaining constituencies.

Unfortunately for the Liberals, Lloyd George, then Prime Minister, neither made these recommendations part of government policy nor even, when the matter came before the House, declared his own personal commitment to a fundamental change in the voting system in the way that he lent his authority to the enfranchisement of women. This probably accounted for the loss of the various PR amendments – one of which was defeated by only eight votes. An extremely confused parliamentary situation then developed, with much cross-party voting. To simplify slightly, the House of Lords resolved in favour of PR, the Commons insisted on replacing this with the AV, and eventually a compromise was reached, whereby PR was adopted for the seven university constituencies, while the *status quo* was otherwise maintained until further investigations had been made. By the time the matter was next reviewed, the majority of MPs had lost interest in change.[58]

In retrospect, it seems ironical that the Liberal leaders did not more quickly grasp the importance of electoral reform. Perhaps in 1918 Asquith could not have been expected to foresee the imminent Liberal decline which soon made this innovation so necessary to the party. As for Lloyd George, he was preoccupied in 1918 with the running of the war, and had little leisure to study electoral reform; perhaps also he instinctively distrusted any change which would have meant the handing over of seats in rural North Wales, 'his' fiefdom, to the old Conservative enemy.[59] Whatever the explanation, the fact is that the Liberals, as a party, only became keen about electoral reform (they preferred PR but would have welcomed AV as a second best) during the course of 1924 when they started to worry in earnest about their long-term survival. But this very situation meant that Labour's former support for electoral reform quickly evaporated. Why should Labour have made its own quest for power more difficult by throwing out a lifeline in the direction of the Liberals? True, the second Labour ministry did agree in 1930, under strong Liberal pressure, to agree to a scheme of AV, but the Bill embodying this was held up by the House of Lords and was lost when the government collapsed the following year. Thus, against all expectations, the traditional electoral system managed to survive. No-one could seriously claim that this outcome was in any way 'inevitable'.

Yet the consequences for the Liberals were serious. AV would have helped them considerably, since most Labour and Conservative voters would probably have chosen the Liberal candidate as their 'second choice'. It has been calculated that its likely effect would have been to raise the number of Liberal MPs from 159 to 217 in 1923, from forty to seventy-four in 1924, and from fifty-nine to 137 in 1929. PR would have been even more advantageous. The best informed guess is that it would have left the Liberals holding the balance of seats, not just in 1923 and 1929, but in 1922 and 1924 as well. Moreover, all such calculations probably underestimate likely Liberal gains, since a change in the electoral system would have altered political behaviour: the Liberals would have been encouraged to put up more candidates and, with the disappearance of the 'wasted vote' argument, electors would have been more likely to vote for them.[60] In these circumstances, Britain might well have had something resembling the political system of post-Second World War Germany, in which the 'Free Democrats' have allied themselves sometimes with the Left and sometimes with the Right but have been almost continuously in office. Would such a development have constituted a Liberal 'survival'?

However, there is yet another way in which the Liberal Party might have survived, albeit in a different guise. In the immediate post-war years, the Conservative Party did not look well equipped to cope with the Labour challenge. This was one reason why the life of the Lloyd George coalition was extended in the first place. In Scotland, for example, the Unionists had little confidence in their ability to go it alone in this traditionally Liberal terrain and so tended to support the coalition to the very end.[61] Moreover, the old issues which had formerly divided Conservatism from Liberalism seemed to many observers to have fallen into permanent abeyance. If this were so, how absurd for the two 'capitalist' parties to maintain their vendetta, thereby playing into the hands of a radicalised (some called it 'Bolshevik') Labour Movement. The obvious answer, then, seemed to be a 'fusion' of 'Coalition Liberalism' and 'moderate' Conservatism into a new broad-based Centre Party.

Lloyd George personally had a strong interest in encouraging such a political development. Having been partly responsible for splitting his own party, his personal survival depended upon splitting the Conservatives. Moreover, had the much-vaunted Centre Party come into existence, Lloyd George, its natural leader, would presumably have been Prime Minister for as long as his health held good.

But strangely enough, the Prime Minister was able in early 1920 to talk prominent Conservatives, even a somewhat reluctant Bonar Law, into endorsing such an initiative. More strangely still, when 'fusion' finally collapsed in March, it did so because of the hostility of most Coalition *Liberal* MPs and ministers, the two groups which, one would have thought, had most to gain from the arrangement. The opportunity to restructure the party system never arose again – at least not until the 1980s. The Conservatives thereafter drifted more or less steadily away from the coalition towards the idea of resuming their own independent existence, leaving Lloyd George in a very exposed position. The events at the Carlton Club in October 1922, when the Conservative MPs defied their leader, Austen Chamberlain, and voted to break with Lloyd George, finally put paid to the Coalition experiment itself.

What, in retrospect, is so fascinating about the 'fusion' talks, however, is the element of accident which shaped the outcome. In his two meetings with supporters, Lloyd George, normally so adroit and sensitive to the 'atmosphere' of his audience, seems to have presented his case ineptly, gratuitously alarming Liberals nervous of severing their links with the Liberal past. Some also disliked what they saw as an attempt 'to divide the nation into two camps, the "haves" and the "have nots"', a division which they thought 'would inevitably lead to a bitter class war'.[62]

In consequence, a chain of events was set off which eventually led to the establishment of a reunited but impotent Liberal Party. Liberalism itself, of course, did not disappear. Its Radical elements became incorporated into the moderate democratic socialism espoused by MacDonald's Labour Party, while its 'anti-socialist' strands formed an essential part of Baldwinian Conservatism. This might be seen as testimony to the continuing resilience and vitality of the Liberal creed. But it was Liberalism without the Liberal Party. A long chapter of British history had come to an end.

9
CONCLUSION

In politics all success is ephemeral. Parties may achieve electoral triumphs and fulfil some of their goals, but they satisfy transient needs and in time, having lost their *raison d'être*, they are replaced. Sometimes this is disguised by the accident of institutional survival. There is a party which calls itself a Conservative Party today, just as there was in the 1840s; but little connects the two organisations except the name and a few hazy historical memories. Nor would Keir Hardie and other Labour pioneers easily recognise any affinities with the political party which now bears the 'Labour' title. The once-mighty Liberal Party of Gladstone, Campbell-Bannerman, Asquith and Lloyd George served its turn before fading into insignificance. Does that make it any different from other political parties? What should be avoided is allowing our knowledge of eventual decline to distract attention from the very substantial achievements which the Party had earlier secured.

For a start, the Victorian and Edwardian Liberal Party, in its heyday, was highly successful at winning elections. It was in power with only a few brief interruptions from 1846 to 1886, and, despite a twenty-year period in the doldrums following the Home Rule split, re-emerged to win another three general elections in a row. Compare this record with that of the twentieth-century Labour Party which, at the time of writing, has only won two decisive victories in parliamentary elections in nearly 100 years of existence. As an institution capable of winning power and keeping the Conservatives at bay, the Liberal Party has never had an adequate successor. Lloyd George thus had a valid point when he warned in 1906: 'You are not going to make socialists in a hurry out of farmers and traders and professional men in this country, but you may scare them into reaction'.[1]

Moreover, the Liberal Party put its electoral success to effective use. It presided over the development of industrialisation, creating the conditions for spectacular economic growth. It helped 'modernise' society by removing or reforming older social practices and institutions that threatened to weaken Britain's competitiveness. It helped establish a concept of citizenship and of individual rights and gave them a central position in political life. In the early twentieth century it also laid the foundations of what later became known as the 'Welfare State' (to use an anachronistic expression) by making public provision for certain categories of disadvantaged people: for example, the sick, the aged and the unemployed.

Paradoxically, the Liberals may have eventually weakened themselves by dint of their own successes – a common fate of reforming parties. For the more completely they removed 'abuses', the less clear did it become what their aim in life now was. This particularly affected the always intimate relationship between Liberalism and Nonconformity. 'It is perhaps harder to be a Nonconformist today than it has ever been in the history of England', one of their ministers said in 1897. 'The very decay of the disabilities from which our fathers suffered has made it harder for us than it was for them to dissent.'[2] The same was perhaps also true of the Liberals themselves. As we have seen, the end of the war brought about the long-awaited 'fall of feudalism' (though this owed more to agricultural depression and the impact of the war itself than to the Liberals' own policies). Thereafter, the Liberal Party was no longer a party of radical change; the sense of intellectual adventure was still there, as the work of the Summer Schools bore witness, but Liberals no longer wanted to make fundamental institutional changes (except to the voting system) and their posture accordingly became a defensive rather than an aggressive one. But did this change of circumstances condemn the party to near extinction?

Certainly, prophets of doom were to be found from the 1880s onwards, some of them Marxists predicting the inevitable triumph of the proletariat, others Conservatives who, looking at the plight of many Liberal Parties on the European Continent, concluded that Liberalism was irreconcilable with the twin demands of democracy and popular nationalism. In a way, the latter groups proved to be the more assertive. Long before the Radical mission had been accomplished (Lloyd George's Budget and Land Campaign had still to be launched), Radical Tories were voicing the view that Liberalism was a 'Victorian' creed, incapable of coping with the demands of the new century. Thus, in the aftermath of his party's defeat in 1906, George Wyndham, could write to his mother, lambasting 'the blatant, lower-middle-class, fraud, called Liberalism, or "Free Trade"':

Two things – that are real – emerge: –
Labour and Imperialism. . . . I believe in my method. They believe in their method. . . . But whether we are Socialists or Imperialists, we are living men.
The others are old women and senile professors. . .[3]

Such prognostications had two practical consequences. Firstly, in times of adversity like the early 1920s some Liberals themselves seriously wondered whether Liberalism had not outlived its usefulness; perhaps, they mused, it was too noble a creed to prosper in the modern decadent world. But, secondly, such a view of politics often encouraged members of the other two parties to act in such a way as to make their predictions of Liberal decline come true. Thus, Maurice Cowling has argued that in the late summer of 1924 the minority Labour government 'colluded' with the Conservative Opposition in engineering its own defeat, knowing that in the resulting general election the Liberals would be the real losers.[4] Irritated at the 'survival' of a party they believed to be historically doomed, Labour showed in 1924 that it was prepared to put up with a (hopefully temporary) loss of office and reduction of representation if this helped extinguish the recent Liberal revival. The Conservatives showed similar animosity; thus, L. S. Amery warned Baldwin in December 1923 not in any circumstances to offer any support to the Liberals: 'the real healthy and *natural* [my emphasis] division of parties in this country is between constructive Conservatism on the one side and on the other Labour-Socialism'.[5] Contrary to the popular view that the Liberals committed suicide, there is an equally strong case for saying that they were murdered.

On the other hand, the warning of what had happened abroad did not simply encourage the enemies of Liberalism: it also stimulated the Liberals into working hard to save their own skins. Some Liberals drew a 'conservative' moral from their contemplation of overseas' events. 'The fate of the Liberal Party, unless experience teaches it wisdom, will doubtless be that of the German National Liberal Party which coquetted with Socialism till Socialism, grown strong, destroyed it as a political force.'[6] But the possibility that, to quote Rosebery's words, Liberalism would disappear 'leaving the two forces of socialism and Reaction face to face',[7] spurred many Liberals, Lloyd George included, into seeking to modernise their party's programme and to adapt themselves to the changing world.

Before that enterprise is dismissed as an impossibility, it is worth remembering that the Conservatives were not necessarily better placed than the Liberals to cope with social and economic change. Indeed, over-dependent as they still were in the Edwardian period on the landed classes, Conservatives had good reasons for fearing the advent of 'democracy'. Yet they worked hard – and, subsequent history would suggest, successfully – to refurbish their image and to broaden their appeal. Why, despite all their efforts, did the Liberals fail to ensure their survival as a party of government?

To the generation of historians growing up in the aftermath of the Liberals' humiliations in the early 1930s, the answer presented few difficulties. Liberal failure seemed to have been preordained – not just for the reasons given by Marxists – but because by then Liberalism itself had taken on a dated appearance. The great Liberal statesmen of the Victorian and Edwardian eras now looked, to those whose memories of the period were non-existent or vague, to be both quaint and absurd – custodians of an old-fashioned creed with an aura surrounding it redolent of top hats and mutton-chop whiskers. Mocking the values and idols of one's parents' generation is, of course, a favourite pastime of the young. It is precisely such attitudes which inform George Dangerfield's famous book, *The Strange Death of Liberal England*, first published in 1935, which combines a modishly psychological interpretation of the subject (England on the eve of the Great War was experiencing a 'nervous breakdown') with a sub-Lytton Strachey vein of 'debunking'.[8] Of course, the wheel has now turned full circle, and in many ways Dangerfield's book seems much more of a period piece than the objects of his mockery.

However, in the 1960s and 1970s a belief in the obsolescence of Liberal values gained new adherents. More was involved here than the renewed interest in Marxist theory. For, in addition, historians of various political persuasions were concerned to show that, in the Edwardian years in particular, Britain had shared in the same 'crisis' which had afflicted many Continental states, particularly Germany, and, like them, had seen a determined assault on earlier liberal practices and values. Accordingly, historians made their readers' flesh creep with their lurid accounts of 'anti-Liberal' ideologies, chronicling not only the rise of revolutionary socialism (though that was a familiar theme) but also bringing out the contemporary importance of 'Radical Right' causes like National Efficiency, Imperialism, militarism and eugenics.

This was a healthy reaction against an earlier view of the British past which had rather smugly emphasised Britain's virtuous attachment to parliamentary institutions and to liberal values and its good fortune in being insulated from the murderous 'illiberal' ideologies which were wreaking havoc on the Continent. But this historiographic reaction was undoubtedly carried too far. After all, the Edwardian 'crisis of Liberalism' was a relatively minor affair: the impotent rage of opponents unable to dislodge the popular Liberal Party from power. Liberalism, to use a Gramscian phrase, was still the hegemonic creed. And, in a way, it never subsequently lost that position. True, the later abandonment of Free Trade in 1931–2 represented a repudiation of a cardinal liberal belief. But most other elements of the creed survived. In fact, to this very day, few British politicians of any substance have chosen to assault Liberal values head-on, and those who have done so (Oswald Mosley comes particularly to mind) have not fared well.

Indeed, far from Liberalism having become discredited, it is easier to maintain the opposite case: namely, that most liberal beliefs and values came to be so widely accepted that there seemed no need for a separate party to campaign on their behalf. By the 1920s it could almost be claimed that 'We are all Liberals now'. After all, both Labour and Conservatives drew heavily in their policy-making and in their thinking upon the Liberal tradition. Writing about the late 1920s, Michael Bentley has drawn attention to this very paradox: 'Everyone believed in liberalism but no one would actually vote for it'.[9] Ten years later even a Communist and Marxist, like Stephen Spender, who wanted to go 'forward from Liberalism', did not propose to abandon it – appropriately enough, since his father and uncle were both prominent Liberal journalists, on close terms with the party leadership. Writing in 1937, Spender could dismiss Liberal politicians with contempt as 'capitalist hirelings',[10] but the classless society he advocated was to be an extension of the Liberal state, not a complete repudiation of it. Peter Clarke goes further. The post-Second World War Labour Party, in his view, was an uneasy coalition of socialists, trade unionists and 'social democrats' in which the latter, who really owed more to the Liberal tradition than to socialism, had simply attached themselves to Labour because the decline of the Liberal Party had, for the time being, left them with no alternative.[11]

The fact is that there are two ways of viewing Liberalism. It can be seen as an economic theory which expressed the interests of a particular social class, the urban middle class. Alternatively, its main mission may have been the creation of social conditions in which individuals had the greatest possible chance of self-realisation, in which case, as Michael Balfour has argued, Liberalism 'is a permanent rather than a transient creed, which changes its detailed aims from period to period in accordance with changes in the general environment'.[12] And if this be true, then there seems to be no *necessary* reason why the party with which it was identified could not have survived.

Yet it is self-evident that by 1935 the Liberal Party *had* virtually disappeared as a significant force in British politics. Why did this happen and at what point did the process of Liberal decline become irreversible?

Basically, the explanations furnished by historians fall under three heads. Some see the Party's collapse as the consequence of a deep moral or ideological crisis, a loss of belief in Liberalism as a creed; they accordingly emphasise the emergence of a 're-visionist' school in the 1890s (i.e. Liberal Imperialism), the later cult of efficiency, the 1910 Secret Coalition talks, and, of course, the damage wrought by the 'rampant omnibus'. Other historians draw attention to class divisions, though they disagree over when the Labour Party made its crucial breakthrough – the formation of the LRC in 1900, the return of twenty-nine Labour MPs in 1906, the Great Labour Unrest of 1911–14, or the industrial conflicts which culminated in the 1926 General Strike. By contrast, a third historical school (the 'accidentalists') emphasises matters of contingency, individual decision and chance. Would the Liberal Party, they ask, have floundered so badly in the 1890s but for Gladstone's Home Rule bombshell? Or would Liberalism not very possibly have bounced back in the 1920s but for the fateful 'mistake' of putting Labour into office in early 1924? The Liberals seem also to have inflicted deep injury on their own party by the quarrels which rent the leadership in the 1890s involving those three prima donnas, Harcourt, Rosebery and Morley, followed a quarter of a century later by the implacable vendetta waged between the followers of Asquith and Lloyd George. It is also possible, of course, to combine two or more of these interpretations in a variety of ways.

So complex are these issues and so difficult is it to hazard an intelligent guess of what, say, might have happened but for the outbreak of the Great War, that historians are unlikely ever to reach unanimity. What follows are only a few personal observations.

171

Clearly, Winston Churchill was right when he percipiently observed in 1906: 'War is fatal to Liberalism'.[13] The Great War wreaked great damage on the Party. Nevertheless, there was still plentiful scope for a Liberal recovery. In the 1918 general election the two halves of the divided Liberal Party had polled over 350,000 more votes than had Labour, which was perhaps significant given the edgy relationship between many 'Lloyd George Liberals' and the Conservative Party and the widespread belief (especially in Scotland) that the coalition was only a temporary arrangement.[14]

It is therefore tempting to assume that the Liberal Party's collapse was due to some more profound cause, perhaps to its inability to adapt to changes in the structure of capitalism. An examination of the exact backgrounds of Liberal businessmen lends some support to this contention. Right through its history, the party made an appeal to 'petit bourgeois' groups, like small retailers and shop-keepers, who belonged to a dwindling sector of the economy. The Liberals also continued to do well in the manufacturing districts of northern England. Yet, from a very early stage, Liberalism started to lose the confidence of people engaged in the financial services sector; for example, no Liberal was returned for the City of London constituency at any time after 1880.

Yet this does not mean that by the start of the new century the Liberals lacked support in the world of corporate capitalism. For example, the great industrialist Alfred Mond, the creator of ICI, did not desert the Liberal Party for Conservatism until as late as 1925. Indeed, Mond's case is also a reminder of Liberalism's formidable powers of adaptation. Traditionally, Liberals had been proponents of a market ideology, which extolled competition and sought to maximise its scope. This continued to be the case. But at the same time some Liberals, like Mond himself, had come out by the 1920s in favour of a 'managed capitalism' and were advocates of 'Rationalisation' – which they saw, in quintessentially liberal terms, as a way of tempering the excesses of competition by the application of reason and science.[15] A similar emphasis marked the Liberals' Industrial Inquiry in the late 1920s. Thus did early twentieth-century Liberalism bequeath to posterity a legacy of *laissez-faire* (to be revived by 'neo-Liberals' like Hayek in later decades), while also providing a rationale for economic planning and pioneering the welfare capitalism which dominated the political agenda of Britain (and many other industrialised countries) in the period following the Second World War.

Unfortunately for the Liberals, they seem to have been slower to have grasped the *political* implications of the emergence of the rise of the corporate economy. Thus, whereas J. C. C. Davidson, the Chairman of the Conservative Party, made great efforts to tap the big industrial and financial companies in the run-up to the 1929 general election, the Liberals continued, despite the 'Million Fund', to look to sympathetic entrepreneurs to replenish their central war chest.[16] This was an unsatisfactory arrangement, not least because many of these individual subscribers were looking for 'recognition'. The Liberals were unwise to have risked incurring another 'Honours Scandal' like the one which had so damaged Lloyd George's reputation in 1922. In consequence, unwilling or unable to modernise their fund-raising methods, the Liberals became stuck in what one historian has called the 'Plutocratic Era', without properly making the transition to the class-based system adopted by Labour (reliant on trade union subventions) and by the Conservatives (closely connected to big business).

But this, in turn, takes us on to what was perhaps the Achilles' Heel of Liberalism: its particular attitude towards class. 'The Liberal Party is not to-day, it never has been, and so long as I have any connection with it, it never will be, the party of any class, rich or poor, great or small, numerous or sparse in its composition. We are a party of no class', Asquith was still defiantly telling the faithful in 1921.[17] Lloyd George did not dissent. To quote from a historian who has made a specialised study of Preston: 'The Liberals remained essentially populist, being unable to make any specific appeals to members of the working class as such, and this allowed leading Liberals to present themselves as leaders of a popular coalition which did not in fact exist'.[18]

Now, admittedly, it was a convention of British political life, observed by all Conservatives and many Socialists, that parties should deny any intention of furthering the interests of any one social class. Even Ramsay MacDonald, the socialist, took this line.[19] Yet no-one was in any doubt where the sympathy of the Labour and Socialist movement lay. The Conservative Party provided a mirror image of this. Leaders like Baldwin denounced 'class politics' as essentially 'un-English', a foreign commodity imported from Russia. But while managing to attract a considerable working-class following, the Conservatives owed most of their electoral success to the skill which they played upon middle-class anxieties. Thus they were able to have their cake and eat it.

But the Liberals had little chance of pulling off a similar trick. Theoretically, they could have consolidated their position as the party which traditionally most manual workers supported by establishing formal links with the trade union movement, while at the same time protesting their devotion to the interests of the 'nation' as a whole. But though they were willing to reformulate their programme in order to accommodate the new welfare issues, the Liberals could not bring themselves to make any very great effort to place significant numbers of working-class candidates in winnable seats.

Moreover, whereas the Conservative Party enjoyed close ties with big business (though it was usually deemed prudent not to draw public attention to this fact), the Liberals continued, right until the end, to have very ambivalent feelings about trade unionism. In most of the big industrial disputes of the period, the Liberals were at best neutral and more often hostile to the cause of the strikers. These were the circumstances in which the Labour Party was able to establish itself in the affections of many working-class communities. And as Labour extended its organisation in the 1920s, the old working-class Liberal vote atrophied. True, the rise of Labour also created hostility to Socialism which the Liberal Party might have successfully exploited; indeed, many of their municipal and parliamentary candidates did precisely this. Yet, when all is said and done, by the 1920s the Conservatives were better placed than the Liberals to function as a 'party of resistance'; for, in Ross McKibbin's words, 'it was *known* that the Conservative Party was the party of bourgeois propriety and dignity'.[20]

Even so, electoral reform could still have saved the Liberals. But luck was not on their side. The traditional 'first-past-the-post' system militates against a third party acquiring a representation commensurate with its electoral support in the country as a whole. Hence, the narrow failure to carry either the Alternative Vote or Proportional Representation in the years following the Great War left the Liberals in a very weak position, while the bungling of the attempts at 'fusion' in the spring of 1920 shut off the possibility of a rather different kind of come-back.

Finally, the Asquith–Lloyd George feud further weakened the party at a crucial historical turning-point, for the collapse of the coalition ushered in a confused phase of three-party politics between 1922 and 1924, the outcome of which could not easily be foreseen. Yet the Liberals, given a great opportunity in early 1924, had blown their chances before the end of the year. By the time the party had reorganised itself around a new leader and a new programme, it was too late to break up the Conservative–Labour duopoly presided over by MacDonald and Baldwin. Despite the creation of the 'Alliance' in the 1980s and the subsequent formation of the Liberal Democrats, this is the political system within which we are still living.

NOTES

1 INTRODUCTION

1. Wilson, T., *The Downfall of the Liberal Party, 1914–1935* (London, 1966), pp. 15–16.
2. See Clarke, P. F., 'The electoral position of the Liberal and Labour parties, 1910–1914', *English Historical Review*, 90 (1975), pp. 828–36.
3. Though Roy Douglas has written a mischievous article, entitled 'Labour in Decline, 1910–14', in Brown, K. D. (ed.), *Essays in Anti-Labour History* (London, 1974), pp. 105–25.
4. Cooke, A. B. and Vincent, J., *The Governing Passion: Cabinet Government and Party Politics 1885–86* (Brighton, 1974), p. 164.
5. See the first three essays in Langan, M. and Schwarz, B. (eds), *Crises in the British State 1880–1930* (London, 1985), which provide a more sophisticated 'modern' Marxist reading of the turn-of-the-century British Liberal Party.
6. The most important book in this 'school' is that of Clarke, P. F., *Lancashire and the New Liberalism* (Cambridge, 1971). This interpretation is examined later in the book, especially in Chapter 6.
7. For example, Roy Douglas was a prominent Liberal activist in the 1960s, standing on five occasions as a Liberal parliamentary candidate, an experience which in places colours his *The History of the Liberal Party, 1895–1970* (London, 1971).
8. See Chapter 7.
9. See Chapter 8.
10. A useful recent survey of the literature, which focusses on the Edwardian period, is Thompson, J. A., 'The Historians and the Decline of the Liberal Party', *Albion*, 22 (1990), pp. 65–83.

2 THE RISE OF THE LIBERAL PARTY

1. For a vivid, if exaggerated, view of the power and prestige of the landed aristocracy before 1880, see Cannadine, D., *The Decline and Fall of the British Aristocracy* (New Haven, 1990).

2. Inglis, K. S., 'Patterns of Religious Worship in 1851', *Journal of Ecclesiastical History*, 11 (1960), esp. pp. 82–6; see also Pickering, W. S. F., 'The 1851 religious census – A useless experiment', *British Journal of Sociology*, 18 (1967), pp. 403–5.

3. In any case, the removal of Nonconformist disabilities did not immediately obliterate them as political issues. Alfred Illingworth, the Bradford millowner, a Congregationalist who later became a Liberal MP, singled out the requisitioning of his father's goods in 1866 (for non-payment of church rates) as the most important factor in determining his own political career (Jowitt, T., 'Patterns of Religion in Victorian Bradford', in Wright, D. G. and Jowitt, J. A., *Victorian Bradford* [London, 1981], p. 42).

4. Barker, M., *Gladstone and Radicalism: The Reconstruction of Liberal Policy in Britain 1885–1894* (Hassocks, 1975), p. 39.

5. Taylor, A. J. P., *The Trouble Makers: Dissent over Foreign Policy 1792–1939* (London, 1957).

6. Cobden to F. Cobden, 11 Sep. 1838, in Morley, J., *The Life of Richard Cobden* (London, 1881; 1896 cd.), Vol. I, p. 130.

7. There were important respects, however, in which Chamberlain differed markedly from Cobden. See below and Chapter 4.

8. For example, Edward Baines of Leeds, the leader of the 'voluntaryists': that is to say, those Dissenters who wanted education to be entirely separate from the state.

9. Hurst, M., 'Liberal Versus Liberal: The General Election of 1874 in Bradford and Sheffield', *Historical Journal*, 15 (1972), p. 669. Among the early defectors from within the northern business community were H. W. Ripley of Bradford and Edward Akroyd of Halifax. The latter had always been an Anglican; the former left the Congregational Chapel in which he had been brought up for the Church of England.

10. Howe, A., *The Cotton Masters 1830–1860* (Oxford, 1984), esp. Chapter 7.

11. On Whiggery's capacity to survive and adapt, see Jenkins, T. A., *Gladstone, Whiggery and the Liberal Party 1874–1886* (Oxford, 1988). An older, but still very valuable, study of the subject is Southgate, D., *The Passing of the Whigs 1832–1886* (London, 1962).

12. A Cornish squire, Sir John Trelawny, was the parliamentary

leader of the agitation against church rates, but he baulked at Disestablishment. See Jenkins, T. A. (ed.), *The Parliamentary Diaries of Sir John Trelawny 1858–1865* (London, 1990).

13. John Vincent, *Pollbooks: How Victorians Voted* (Cambridge, 1967), *passim*.

14. Lubenow, W. C., *Parliamentary Politics and the Home Rule Crisis: The British House of Commons in 1886* (Oxford, 1988), pp. 178–82.

15. Jenkins, *Gladstone*, p. 3, fn. 10.

16. Bagehot, W., *The English Constitution* (London, 1867; Fontana ed., 1963), p. 175.

17. Perkin, H., *The Origins of Modern English Society 1780–1880* (London, 1969; 1972 edn), p. 380. Unfortunately, neither of the two outstanding recent studies of Gladstone cover the entire span of his career. See Shannon, Richard, *Gladstone, Volume 1 1809–1865* (London, 1982); Matthew, H. C. G., *Gladstone, 1809–1874* (Oxford, 1986).

18. Barker, *Gladstone and Radicalism*, pp. 250–1. Steele, E. D., 'Gladstone and Ireland', *Irish Historical Studies*, 17 (1970–1), pp. 58–88.

19. Southgate, *Whigs*, p. 372.

20. Ibid., p. 374. But note Jenkins's point: that 'if the Irish question was going to provoke a split in the Liberal party simply along "class" lines, it would have happened in 1881' (Jenkins, *Gladstone*, p. 172).

21. Hunter, J., 'The Politics of Highland Land Reform, 1873–1895', *Scottish Historical Review*, 53 (1974), pp. 45–68.

22. Dissenters particularly resented Clause 25 of the Education Act, which provided that children from the workhouses should be sent, at the ratepayers' expense, to a local school, which in practice was often an Anglican school. A Conservative government later repealed this clause in 1876.

23. For the view that Chamberlain was willing to make an accommodation with Hartington and was not primarily concerned with drivng him out of the party, see Jenkins, *Gladstone*, p. 195. But that is not to say that Chamberlain, in his eagerness to impose his will on the Liberal Party, might not have been quite willing to run the risk of a Whig secession.

24. Hamer, D. A. (ed.), *The Radical Programme, with a Preface by J. Chamberlain, 1885* (Hassocks, 1971).

25. The most famous work in the genre was Andrew Mearns' *The Bitter Cry of Outcast London* of 1883.

26. See Jones, G. S., *Outcast London* (Oxford, 1971).

27. Armytage, W. H. G., *A. J. Mundella 1825–1897: The Liberal Background to the Labour Movement* (London, 1951).

28. Spinner, T. J., *George Joachim Goschen: The Transformation of a Victorian Liberal* (Cambridge, 1973). There were many other 'conservative' businessmen who by the 1880s were beginning to lose confidence in Gladstone and the Liberal Party, like Nathan de Rothschild, Liberal MP for Aylesbury. On the political perspectives of the 'railway interest', see Chapter 4.

29. Roach, J., 'Liberalism and the Victorian Intelligentsia', *Cambridge Historical Journal*, 13 (1957), pp. 58–81; Harvie, C., *The Lights of Liberalism: University Liberals and the Challenge of Democracy, 1860–86* (London, 1976); Dunne, T., '*La trahison des clercs*: British intellectuals and the first home-rule crisis', *Irish Historical Studies*, 23 (1982–3), pp. 134–73.

30. Perkin, H. J., 'Land Reform and Class Conflict in Victorian Britain', in Butt, J. and Clarke, I. F. (eds), *The Victorians and Social Protest* (Newton Abbot, 1973), pp. 177–217.

31. Southgate, *Whigs*, p. 389.

32. See Roach, 'Liberalism and the Victorian Intelligentsia'; Harvie, *Lights of Liberalism*; Dunne, '*La trahison des clercs*'. Among the defectors were A. V. and Edward Dicey, W. E. H. Lecky, James Fitzjames Stephen and Henry Sidgwick. But others, notably James Bryce, stayed loyal to official Liberalism.

33. There are numerous accounts of the Irish Crisis and the party realignment. A good starting point might be Hamer, D. A., *Liberal Politics in the Age of Gladstone and Rosebery* (Oxford, 1972), Chs. 5–6. Aspects of the subject are examined in greater length in the following two chapters.

3 THE ASSAULT ON FEUDALISM, 1886–1905

1. But on mainland Britain the realignment led to some odd alliances being formed. In Scotland, for example, the Liberal Unionists comprised both the most cautious of Whigs and the most fiery of Radicals. The 'crofters', for example, can be found on both sides of the divide. See Savage, D. C., 'Scottish Politics, 1885–6', *Scottish Historical Review*, 40 (1961), pp. 118–35 and Hutchison, I. G. C., *A Political History of Scotland 1832–1924* (Edinburgh, 1986), pp. 162–8, 171.

2. Labouchere to Chamberlain, 15 April 1886, in Thorold, A. L., *The Life of Henry Labouchere* (London, 1913), p. 291.

3. Joseph Chamberlain to Arthur Chamberlain (his brother), 8

March 1886, in Garvin, J. L., *The Life of Joseph Chamberlain*, Vol. 2 (London, 1933), p. 185.

4.   Barker, M., *Gladstone and Radicalism: The Reconstruction of Liberal Policy in Britain 1885–94* (Hassocks, 1975), pp. 173–4.

5.   During the 1885 general election Parnell issued his 'Vote Tory' manifesto, urging the Irish on mainland Britain to vote for Conservative rather than for Liberal candidates – a course of action which many Irishmen were anyhow predisposed to take because of their educational beliefs. It is difficult to estimate how many seats may have changed hands as a result of this appeal, but Liberals thought it responsible for many of their losses. The resulting bitterness did not make it any easier for Gladstone to 'sell' Home Rule to his party a few months later.

6.   Admittedly, Professor Lubenow, in examining the 1885–6 Parliament, concludes that there was already considerable agreement on policy between the Radical-Liberals and the Irish Nationalists, prior to Gladstone's commitment to Home Rule (W. C. Lubenow, *Parliamentary Politics and the Home Rule Crisis: The British House of Commons in 1886* [Oxford, 1988], pp. 157–8).

7.   Bebbington, D. W., *The Nonconformist Conscience: Chapel and Politics 1870–1914* (London, 1982), p. 90.

8.   Hutchison, *Scotland,* pp. 162–3.

9.   Bebbington, *Nonconformist Conscience,* p. 99.

10. Ibid., p. 103; Matthew, H. C. G., *The Liberal Imperialists: The ideas and politics of a Post-Gladstonian élite* (Oxford, 1973), p. 270; Machin, G. I. T., *Politics and the Churches in Great Britain 1869–1921* (Oxford, 1987), pp. 226–7.

11. Hamer, D. A., *Liberal Politics in the Age of Gladstone and Rosebery* (Oxford, 1972), Ch. 6; Hamer, D. A., The Irish Question and Liberal Politics, 1886–1894', *Historical Journal,* 12 (1969), pp. 511–32.

12. Barker, *Gladstone and Radicalism,* p. 235; Stansky, P., *Ambitions and Strategies: The Struggle for the Leadership of the Liberal Party in the 1890s* (Oxford, 1964), pp. 1–2.

13. Howarth, J., 'The Liberal Revival in Northamptonshire, 1880–1895: A Case Study in Late Nineteenth Century Elections', *Historical Journal,* 12 (1969), p. 101. Barker argues that Gladstone came to see a connection between the cause of Irish freedom and the rights of labour, and thereafter felt more sympathy for the principles of trade unionism (*Gladstone and Radicalism,* pp. 89–92).

14. Bebbington, *Nonconformist Conscience,* p. 92. See also Pelling, H., *Social Geography of British Elections 1885–1910* (London, 1967), pp. 220, 163.

15. Matthew, *Liberal Imperialists*, p. 271.
16. The Liberal Imperialists were divided amongst themselves over whether it was best to postpone Home Rule or to abandon it altogether (Matthew, *Liberal Imperialists*, Ch. 8). Their stand did persuade a few former Liberals, like the Duke of Sutherland, to return to the fold (ibid., p. 98). See Gutzke, D. W., 'Rosebery and Ireland, 1898–1903: A Reappraisal', *Bulletin of the Institute of Historical Research*, 53 (1980), pp. 88–98.
17. On Radical protests at Rosebery's assumption of the premiership, see Stansky, *Ambitions*, p. 80. Similarly in Scotland, where the great landowners remaining loyal to official Liberalism included Rosebery, Elgin and Aberdeen (Hutchison, *Scotland*, p. 163).
18. Loughlin, J., *Gladstone, Home Rule and the Ulster Question 1882–93* (Dublin, 1986), esp. pp. 184–91.
19. Professor Lubenow is keen to deny any connection between social class and voting on the Home Rule Bill. But his own statistics suggest that 37 per cent of Liberal landowning MPs opposed Gladstone in 1886, as compared with 29 per cent of all Liberal MPs (*Home Rule Crisis*, p. 200). See also the table on p. 205, showing that peers and Whigs were disproportionately likely to oppose Home Rule.
20. Howarth, 'Liberal Revival', p. 105; Goodman, G. L., 'Liberal Unionism: The Revolt of the Whigs', *Victorian Studies*, 3 (1959–60), pp. 173–89.
21. Barker, *Gladstone and Radicalism*, p. 113. But Gladstone also referred to 'a small minority of wealthy men'.
22. In fact, before the 'Newcastle Programme', the Liberal Unionists in the Lords voted with the Liberals more often than with the Conservatives: only slowly did the Unionist Alliance cohere, partly as a result of changes in Conservative policy (Phillips, G. D., 'The Whig Lords and Liberalism, 1886–93', *Historical Journal*, 28 [1981], pp. 168–72).
23. Lee, J. M., 'Parliament and the Appointment of Magistrates: the Origins of Advisory Committees', *Parliamentary Affairs*, 13 (1959–60), pp. 85–94; Phillips, G. D., *The Diehards: Aristocratic Society and Politics in Edwardian England* (Cambridge, Mass., 1979), pp. 60–8.
24. Barker shows how conservative Gladstone was on the land question, attacking Harcourt's Budget, though he accepted graduated taxation on income derived from ground rents (*Gladstone and Radicalism*, pp. 250–1).
25. Douglas, R., *Land, People and Politics: A History of the Land Question in the United Kingdom, 1878–1952* (London, 1976), pp. 106–7.

26. Russell, A. K., *Liberal Landslide: the General Election of 1906* (Newton Abbot, 1973), p. 65.
27. Phillips, 'Whig Lords', pp. 168–72.
28. Ramsden, J., *The Age of Balfour and Baldwin, 1902–1940* (London, 1978), p. 98.
29. Bebbington, D. W., 'Nonconformity and Electoral Sociology, 1867–1918', *Historical Journal*, 27 (1984), pp. 643–6.
30. Machin, *Politics and Churches*, p. 206; Bernstein, G. L., *Liberalism and Liberal Politics in Edwardian England* (London, 1986), p. 18: over 40 per cent according to Bernstein.
31. Koss, S., *Nonconformity in Modern British Politics* (London, 1975), p. 230.
32. Taking the 1892 election and the two elections of 1910, in which the Liberal Party did well but not spectacularly so, the English regions where the Liberals achieved the highest percentage of possible wins were: the north-east (78 per cent), the West Riding (72 per cent), the East Midlands (63 per cent), eastern Lancastria (59 per cent), the south-west peninsula (57 per cent) and East Anglia (55.5 per cent). All these regions bar eastern Lancastria contained populous Nonconformist communities.
33. Koss, *Nonconformity*, pp. 28–30; Bebbington, *Nonconformist Conscience*, Ch. 4.
34. Chamberlain to Devonshire, 22 Sep. 1902, Amery, J., *Life of Joseph Chamberlain*, Vol. 4 (London, 1951), p. 496.
35. On Lloyd George's early life, see Grigg, J., *The Young Lloyd George* (London, 1973); George, W. R. P., *Lloyd George Backbencher* (Gomer, 1983). See also Machin, G. T. I., 'Lloyd George and Nonconformity', in Loades, J. (ed.), *The Life and Times of David Lloyd George* (Bangor, 1991), pp. 33–47.
36. Morgan, K. O., *Wales in British Politics 1868–1922* (Cardiff, 1970), pp. 217–18; Machin, *Politics and Churches*, p. 269.
37. Morgan, *Wales*, pp. 189–91.
38. Bebbington, *Nonconformist Conscience*, p. 144.
39. The Unionist Ministry had bowed to the insistence of Lord Milner, High Commissioner in South Africa, that indentured Chinese labourers should be brought in to work in the goldmines of the Witwatersrand, to replace the 'Kaffirs' who had disappeared during the course of the reent war. The decision was attacked by the Opposition Parties (Labour as well as the Liberals) on both economic and humanitarian grounds; the Chinese workers, they complained, were to all intents and purposes, living in a condition of 'slavery'.
40. Bebbington, *Nonconformist Conscience*, p. 8.

41. Russell, *Liberal Landslide*, pp. 184–5.
42. Bebbington, *Nonconformist Conscience*, p. 77; Koss, *Nonconformity*, p. 59.
43. Matthew, *Liberal Imperialists*, esp. Ch. 7.
44. Hutchison, *Scotland*, pp. 235–6.
45. Glaser, J. F., 'English Nonconformity and the Decline of Liberalism', *American Historical Review*, 63 (1957–8), p. 359.
46. Waley, S. D., *Edwin Montagu* (London, 1964), p. 30 (where, however, the lady is wrongly called 'Allen').
47. Bebbington, *Nonconformist Conscience*, p. 158; Machin, *Politics and Churches*, p. 12. On the situation in Wales, see Morgan, *Wales*, pp. 172–3, 262.
48. This means that Paul Thompson's account of Liberal weaknesses in London cannot be used as an indicator of what was happening to the party elsewhere. See Thompson, P., *Socialists, Liberals and Labour. The Struggle for London 1885–1914* (London, 1967).
49. Bebbington, 'Nonconformity and Electoral Sociology', pp. 654–5.
50. Koss, *Nonconformity*, p. 115; Bebbington, *Nonconformist Conscience*, p. 80.
51. That is not to say that all Dissenters were middle-class: Primitive Methodism had a strong following amongst farm labourers and miners, and the Baptist Chapels attracted many skilled workers. But sects like the Congregationalists were overwhelmingly middle-class.
52. This is a point particularly emphasised in Tanner, D., *Political Change and the Labour Party 1900–1918* (Cambridge, 1990).
53. Bernstein, *Liberalism*, *passim*.
54. Douglas, *Land, People and Politics*, *passim*. Though it deals with a later period, there is a useful discussion of the different 'schools' amongst land reformers in Emy, H. V., 'The Land Campaign: Lloyd George as a Social Reformer, 1909–14', in Taylor, A. J. P. (ed.), *Lloyd George: Twelve Essays* (London, 1971), pp. 35–68.
55. Howarth, 'Liberal Revival', p. 106.
56. Adonis, A., 'Aristocracy, Agriculture and Liberalism: The Politics, Finances and Estates of the Third Lord Carrington', *Historical Journal*, 31 (1988), pp. 890–5.
57. Gladstone offended many working men when, attempting to sound a class note, he said that the drinking was 'excusable [and] not unnatural' for workers (Barker, *Gladstone and Radicalism*, pp. 210–11).
58. In the two 1910 general elections 41 per cent of Labour candidates were Nonconformists, compared with 35 per cent of Liberal candidates (Blewett, N., *The Peers, the Parties and the*

People; the British General Elections of 1910 [London, 1972], p. 232).

59. 'Faddists' were also keen on abolishing compulsory vaccination and many campaigned for a repeal of the Contagious Diseases Acts (Howarth, 'Liberal Revival', p. 102).

60. Stansky, *Ambitions*, p. 143.

4 THE 'PROBLEM OF LABOUR', 1886–1905

1. Chadwick, M. E. J., 'The Role of Redistribution in the Making of the Third Reform Act', *Historical Journal*, 19 (1976), pp. 665–83. On the way in which the division of Leeds into five separate parliamentary constituencies damaged the Liberal Party in Leeds, see Roberts, A. W., 'Leeds Liberalism and Late Victorian Politics', *Northern History*, 5 (1970), pp. 154–6.

2. Blewett, N., 'The Franchise in the United Kingdom, 1885–1918', *Past and Present*, 32 (1965), pp. 27–56; Matthew, H. C. G., McKibbin, R. I. and Kay, J. A., 'The Franchise Factor in the Rise of the Labour Party', *English Historical Review* (1976), pp. 723–52.

3. Tanner, D., 'The Parliamentary Electoral System, the "Fourth" Reform Act and the Rise of Labour in England and Wales', *Bulletin of the Institute of Historical Research*, 56 (1983), pp. 205–19; Tanner, D., *Political Change and the Labour Party 1900–1918* (Cambridge, 1990). Liberals were keen to abolish plural voting, which they clearly believed to work to the disadvantage of their own party. In 1906 they introduced a Bill on the subject, which was thrown out by the Lords, and made further attempts to end the 'abuse' with the equally abortive Franchise and Registration Bill of 1912. The government were again formulating a Plural Voting Bill when war broke out in 1914.

4. Hamer, D. A., *Liberal Politics in the Age of Gladstone and Rosebery* (Oxford, 1972), pp. 9–18. Though he admits that to treat it as a section and not a class was becoming increasingly difficult.

5. Pelling, H., *Social Geography of British Elections 1885–1910* (London, 1967), pp. 418–20.

6. Jay, R., *Joseph Chamberlain: A Political Study* (Oxford, 1981), especially pp. 175–80.

7. Barker, M., *Gladstone and Radicalism: The Reconstruction of Liberal Policy in Britain 1885–94* (Hassocks, 1975), pp. 175–93; Matthew, H. C. G., *The Liberal Imperialists: The ideas and politics of a post-Gladstonian élite* (Oxford, 1973), pp. 3–14.

8. Mundella was forced to resign: see Armytage, W. H. G., *A. J. Mundella, 1825–1897: the Liberal Background to the Labour Movement* (London, 1951), pp. 300–5. On the reforms of the 1892–5 Liberal Ministry, see Powell, D., 'The New Liberalism and the Rise of Labour, 1886–1906', *Historical Journal*, 29 (1986), pp. 369–93, and D. Powell, 'The Liberal Ministries and Labour, 1892–1895', *History*, 68 (1983), pp. 408–26.

9. Stansky, P., *Ambitions and Strategies: the struggle for the leadership of the Liberal Party in the 1890s* (Oxford, 1964), pp. 130–5.

10. On the wider issues raised by the Budget, see Emy, H. V., *Liberals, Radicals and Social Politics 1892–1914* (Cambridge, 1973), pp. 191–2. But it is not clear whether Harcourt saw the Budget, in traditional Radical terms, as an attack on the privileges of the landowners, or whether he saw it as a device for appealing to the working-class masses.

11. Matthew, *Liberal Imperialists*, Ch. 7.

12. Lubenow, W. C., *Parliamentary Politics and the Home Rule Crisis: The British House of Commons in 1886* (Oxford, 1988), p. 166.

13. Alderman, G., *The Railway Interest* (Leicester, 1973), Ch. 4, esp. p. 80. The railway interest had been offended by the Liberals' Employers Liability Act of 1880. Nevertheless, in 1881 53.6 per cent of railway directors in Parliament were Liberals. Yet a decade later the proportions had dropped to just over 30 per cent and by 1911 it was as low as 15.6 per cent (ibid., pp. 234–50). The defection of Sir Edward Watkin, the great railway magnate, to Liberal Unionism in 1886 is symptomatic of this trend. However, the railways were not typical of the business world. Many manufacturers and merchants saw them as quasi-monopolies, whose privileges needed to be curbed by state action, in the interest of the wider business community. Many of the attacks on the railways, in fact, came from other Liberal businessmen.

14. Lubenow, W. C., 'Irish Home Rule and the Social Basis of the Great Separation in the Liberal Party in 1886', *Historical Journal*, 28 (1985), pp. 125–42. Lubenow, *Parliamentary Politics*, *passim*.

15. Ibid., pp. 320, 144.

16. Blewett, N., *The Peers, the Parties and the People: the General Elections of 1910* (London, 1972), pp. 14–15. The distribution of MPs by region and the social description of the various English constituencies is based upon Blewett's *Peers*. In the 1885 general election the Liberals picked up ten of the forty-eight urban seats which Blewett categorises as 'urban: predominantly middle class', but in the following four elections they won only one, one, none, and two, respectively.

17. Rubinstein, W. D., 'Wealth, Elites and the Class Structure of Modern Britain', *Past & Present*, 76 (1977), pp. 99–126.
18. Blewett, *Peers, Parties and People*, pp. 380–1. This division was one of long-standing. In the 1892 election, for example, the Liberals won sixty-eight seats in the south of England, but 125 in the North.
19. See Chapter 6.
20. Bernstein, G. L., *Liberalism and Liberal Politics in Edwardian England* (London, 1986), p. 24.
21. See Laybourn, K. and Reynolds, J., *Liberalism and the Rise of Labour 1890–1918* (London, 1984), *passim*.
22. Lloyd, T. O., 'The Whip as paymaster: Herbert Gladstone and party organisation', *English Historical Review*, 89 (1974), pp. 785–813.
23. Barker, *Gladstone and Radicalism*, pp. 149–50.
24. See Illingworth's letter to Harcourt of 12 July 1894 declaring his unwillingness to be associated with a party which interfered with the hours of adult labour by legislation, as the Government was currently doing with its Miners Eight Hours Bill (*The Holden-Illingworth Letters* [Bradford, 1927], 597–9). On Illingworth and Bradford Liberalism, see Laybourn and Reynolds, *Liberalism*, esp. pp. 79, 112–13.
25. Powell, 'The New Liberalism', p. 378.
26. Laybourn and Reynolds, *Liberalism*, pp. 51, 80.
27. The concept is used in Clarke, P., 'The End of Laissez Faire and the Politics of Cotton', *Historical Journal*, 15 (1972), pp. 493–512.
28. Hutchison, I. G. C., *A Political History of Scotland 1832–1924* (Edinburgh, 1986), pp. 218–19. In Paisley one of the Vice-Presidents of the Paisley Unionist Association defected to the Liberal camp (ibid., p. 220).
29. Harris, J., *Unemployment and Politics: A Study in English Social Policy 1886–1914* (Oxford, 1972), pp. 222–6.
30. Gilbert, B. B., *The Evolution of National Insurance in Great Britain: the Origins of the Welfare State* (London, 1966), p. 247.
31. Masterman, L., *C.F.G. Masterman* (London, 1939); David, E., 'The New Liberalism of C. F. G. Masterman, 1873–1927', in Brown, K. (ed.), *Essays in Anti-Labour History* (London, 1974), pp. 17–41.
32. Hamer says his creed drew on Benthamism and on America; 'Government of the people by the people' (Escott, T. H. S., *The Radical Programme [1885]* [ed. with introduction by Hamer, D. A., Brighton, 1971], p. xiv). The same was even more obviously the case with some of Chamberlain's collaborators, like T. H. S. Escott and Francis Adams.

33. Matthew, *Liberal Imperialists*, pp. 140–7; Searle, G. R., *The Quest for National Efficiency, 1899–1914* (Oxford, 1971; new ed., London, 1990).

34. Barker, *Gladstone and Radicalism*, p. 174.

35. Bebbington, D. W., *The Nonconformist Conscience: Chapel and Politics 1870–1914* (London, 1982), Ch. 3.

36. Clarke, P. F., 'The Progressive Movement in England', *Transactions of the Royal Historical Society*, 24 (1974), pp. 159–81; Freeden, M., *The New Liberalism: An Ideology of Social Reform* (Oxford, 1978); Clarke, P., *Liberals and Social Democrats* (Cambridge, 1978); Collini, S., *Liberalism and Sociology: L. T. Hobhouse and Political Argument in England, 1880–1914* (Cambridge, 1979); Weiler, P., 'The New Liberalism of L. T. Hobhouse', *Victorian Studies*, 16 (1972), pp. 141–61.

37. H. V. Emy, *Liberals, Radicals and Social Politics*, p. 101. Some of the Liberal MPs returned in 1906 were members of the Fabian Society.

38. Ibid., p. 105; Freeden, M. (ed.), *Minutes of the Rainbow Circle, 1894–1924* (London, 1989).

39. Peter Clarke, 'Liberals and Social Democrats in Historical Perspective', in Bogdanor, V. (ed.), *Liberal Party Politics* (Oxford, 1983), pp. 27–34.

40. Hobhouse, L. T., *Liberalism* (London, 1909; N. York ed., 1964), p. 48.

41. Emy, H. V., 'The Impact of Financial Policy on English Party Politics Before 1914', *Historical Journal*, 15 (1972), *passim*.

42. Powell, 'The New Liberalism', p. 393.

43. H. V. Emy, *Liberals, Radicals and Social Politics*, p. 142.

44. Moreover, by no means all 'advanced' Radical intellectuals subscribed to the New Liberalism. Bertrand Russell, for example, who later accepted the case for Socialism and joined the Labour Party, continued up until 1914 to adhere to a traditionally Radical view of the world (Rempel, R. A., 'Conflicts and Change in Liberal Theory and Practice, 1890–1918: the case of Bertrand Russell', in Waller, P. J. [ed.], *Politics and Social Change in Modern Britain* [Brighton, 1987], pp. 117–39).

45. Clegg, H. A., Fox, A. and Thompson, A. F. (eds), *A History of British Trade Unions Since 1889*, Vol. I (Oxford, 1964), p. 279.

46. Gregory, Roy, *The Miners and British Politics 1906–1914* (Oxford, 1968).

47. Wrigley, C., 'Liberals and the Desire for Working-Class Representatives in Battersea, 1886–1922', in Brown, K. D. (ed.), *Essays in Anti-Labour History* (London, 1974), pp. 126–58.

48. MacDonald's rejection at Southampton is described in Marquand, D., *Ramsay MacDonald* (London, 1977), pp. 34–6.

49. Purdue, A. W., 'The Liberal and Labour Parties in North-East Politics, 1900–14: The Struggle for Supremacy', *International Review of Social History*, 26 (1981), p. 6. Perhaps two-thirds of the delegates who rejected Henderson were manual workers: see Wrigley, C., *Arthur Henderson* (Cardiff, 1990), p. 17. Purdue, A. W., 'Arthur Henderson and Liberal, Liberal-Labour and Labour politics in the North-East of England 1892–1903', *Northern History*, 11 (1976), p. 200; Brown, J., 'Attercliffe, 1894: How One Local Liberal Party Failed to Meet the Challenge of Labour', *Journal of British Studies*, 14 (1975), pp. 48–77.

50. Laybourn and Reynolds, *Liberalism*, p. 30. Even a middle-class Liberal setting out to 'represent' the working-class community, like W. P. Byles in Shipley in 1892, had great difficulty in securing the backing of the local Liberal caucus (ibid., pp. 81–2).

51. Clarke, P. F., *Lancashire and the New Liberalism* (Cambridge, 1971), pp. 198–9, and also pp. 220–1, for the constant stream of financial demands on candidates of both parties from local clubs and associations. Multiply amounts given by at least forty to establish some equivalent in today's money.

52. On the attempts of the Liberals in the North-West to escape dependence on 'Old Liberal' manufacturing interests, see Tanner, *Political Change*, pp. 135–6. On the earlier problems associated with the running of working-class candidates, see Barker, pp. 130–8.

53. This theme is explored, mainly in relation to the Edwardian decade, in Searle, G. R., *Corruption in British Politics, 1895–1930* (Oxford, 1987), Ch. 7. See also Coetzee, F., 'Pressure Groups, Tory Businessmen, and the Aura of Political Corruption Before the First World War', *Historical Journal*, 29 (1986), pp. 833–52.

54. Wrigley, C. J., *David Lloyd George and the British Labour Movement* (Hassocks, 1976), p. 25. Even a tried friend of Labour like Channing can be found bursting out about 'the baser motives . . . grudges and disappointments . . . noxious weeds to choke pure democratic instincts', when unrest in the shoemaking industry produced independent labour candidates in the 1894 local government elections in Northamptonshire (Howarth, J., 'The Liberal Revival in Northamptonshire, 1880–1895: A Case Study in Late Nineteenth Century Elections', *Historical Journal*, 12 [1969], p. 113).

55. Bealey, F., 'Negotiations between the Liberal Party and the Labour Representation Committee before the General Elections

of 1906', *Bulletin of the Institute of Historical Research*, 29 (1956), pp. 261–74; Bealey, F. & Pelling, H., *Labour and Politics, 1900–1906* (London, 1958), Chs. 6, 10.

56. Douglas, R., *History of the Liberal Party, 1895–1970* (London, 1971), p. 73. The remark was made by Samuel Storey, Chairman of the Northern Liberal Federation, in July 1903, while the 'Pact' was still being negotiated.

57. Tanner, *Political Change*, p. 23. The Pact did not apply in Scotland, because Labour was weakened by ethnic divisions and by the popularity of Liberalism. The Liberal Party accordingly had no incentive to give ground (Hutchison, *Scotland*, pp. 259–60).

58. Bealey and Pelling, *Labour and Politics*, p. 50.

59. Ibid., pp. 144–6.

60. Powell, 'New Liberalism', p. 383. But Campbell-Bannerman added that 'if the time ever came when they [i.e. the Liberal and Labour Parties] parted they would deal with that when it arrived'.

61. J. Herbert to H. Gladstone, 6 Mar. 1903, in Bealey, 'Negotiations', p. 266.

62. Herbert believed that the Pact would give the Liberals an extra ten seats. In the event there were thirty-three constituencies where the Liberals stood down for Labour in the 1906 election (either by refusing to put up a candidate at all or by putting up only one candidate in a double-member constituency). But in only two of these cases did the Liberals 'give up' a seat which they had won in 1900. Clitheroe and Barnard Castle, both of which the LRC had captured in recent by-elections. It is also significant that, of the twenty-nine newly-elected Labour MPs, as many as thirteen had been returned for the north-west, where the Liberal Party had been weak since 1886, as against only three from Yorkshire, where Liberalism was very much stronger.

63. Powell, 'New Liberalism', p. 391. Hamer sees the Pact as a way of restoring a class balance which the Liberals themselves had earlier upset (Hamer, *Gladstone and Rosebery*, p. 309).

64. See Chapter 6.

5   THE RADICALS IN OFFICE, 1905–14

1. Stephens, H. W., 'Party Realignment in Britain, 1900–1925', *Social Science History*, 6 (1982), p. 42 and Table 1.

2. See Boyle, T., 'The Formation of Campbell-Bannerman's Government in December 1905: A Memorandum by J. A. Spender', *Bulletin of the Institute of Historical Research*, 45 (1972), pp. 283–302.

3. Russell, A. K., *Liberal Landslide: the General Election of 1906* (Newton Abbot, 1973). The Liberals won as many as eighteen of the forty-eight heavily middle-class constituencies in England identified by Professor Blewett, which had been barren territory for the Liberals since the 1886 schism.

4. H. V. Emy, *Liberals, Radicals and Social Politics, 1892–1914* (Cambridge, 1973), p. 187; Tanner, D., *Political Change and the Labour Party 1900–1918* (Cambridge, 1990), p. 45.

5. Bealey, F. and Pelling, H., *Labour and Politics, 1900–1906* (London, 1958), p. 265.

6. Koss, S., *Nonconformity in Modern British Politics* (London, 1975), p. 74.

7. Richards, N. J., 'The Education Bill of 1906 and the Decline of Political Nonconformity', *Journal of Ecclesiastical History*, 23 (1972), pp. 49–63; Machin, G. T. I., *Politics and the Churches in Great Britain 1869–1921* (Oxford, 1987), pp. 284–9.

8. Koss, *Nonconformity*, pp. 85–9, Ch. 5; Bebbington, D. W., *The Nonconformist Conscience: Chapel and Politics 1870–1914* (London, 1982), pp. 147–52; on the more general process of disillusionment, see ibid., pp. 79–83.

9. Hepburn, A. C., 'The Irish Council Bill and the Fall of Sir Antony MacDonnell', *Irish Historical Studies*, 17 (1970–1), pp. 470–98.

10. Pelling, H., 'Two By-Elections: Jarrow and Colne Valley, 1907', in *Popular Politics and Society in Late Victorian Britain* (London, 1968), pp. 130–46.

11. Blewett, N., *The Peers, the Parties and the People; the British General Elections of 1910* (London, 1972), Ch. 3; Blewett, N., 'Free Fooders, Balfourites, Whole Hoggers. Factionalism Within the Unionist Party, 1906–10', *Historical Journal*, 11 (1968), pp. 95–124; Sykes, A., *Tariff Reform in British Politics 1903–1913* (Oxford, 1979), Chs 6–11.

12. The most useful short account is Pugh, M., *Lloyd George* (London, 1988). Two more detailed studies covering this period are Gilbert, B. B., *David Lloyd George: The Architect of Change 1863–1912* (London, 1987) and Grigg, J., *Lloyd George The People's Champion: 1902–1911* (London, 1978). For a recent collection of essays, see Loades, J. (ed.), *The Life and Times of David Lloyd George* (Bangor, 1991).

13. Koss, *Nonconformity*, p. 106; Machin, G. T. I., 'Lloyd George and Nonconformity', in Loades, J. (ed.), *The Life and Times of David Lloyd George* (Bangor, 1991), pp. 33–47.

14. Koss, *Nonconformity*, p. 102.

15. Murray, B., 'The Politics of the "People's Budget"', *Historical Journal*, 16 (1973), pp. 555–70. The theme is explored in greater detail in Murray, B. K., *The People's Budget 1909–10* (Oxford, 1980).

16. Harris, J., *Unemployment and Politics: A Study in English Social Policy 1886–1914* (Oxford, 1972), pp. 340–6.

17. On land campaign, see Douglas, R., *Land, People and Politics: A History of the Land Question in the United Kingdom, 1878–1952* (London, 1976), pp. 160–6; Emy, H. V., 'The Land Campaign: Lloyd George as a Social Reformer, 1909–14', in Taylor, A. J. P. (ed.), *Lloyd George: Twelve Essays* (London, 1971), pp. 35–68; Douglas, R., ' "God gave the land to the people" ', in Morris, A. J. A. (ed.), *Edwardian Radicalism 1900–1914* (London, 1974), pp. 148–61; Offer, A., *Property and Politics, 1870–1914* (Cambridge, 1981), Ch. 22; Fforde, M., *Conservatism and Collectivism, 1886–1914* (Edinburgh, 1990), Ch. 5, Packer, I., 'Lloyd George and the Land Campaign, 1912–1914', in Loades (ed.), *Lloyd George*, pp. 143–52. On the 1914 Budget, see Gilbert, B. B., 'David Lloyd George: The Reform of British Landholding and the Budget of 1914', *Historical Journal*, 22 (1978), pp. 117–41; Emy, H. V., 'The Impact of Financial Policy on English Party Politics before 1914', *Historical Journal*, 15 (1972), pp. 129–30.

18. Emy, 'Land Campaign', p. 42.

19. The best introduction to this complex subject is still Jenkins, R., *Mr Balfour's Poodle* (London, 1954).

20. In Scotland there was a vigorous campaign for Scottish Home Rule (Hutchison, I. G. C., *A Political History of Scotland 1832–1924* [Edinburgh, 1986], pp. 241–2). The view that Free Trade, land reform and the old sectarian issues made the Liberal Party popular with the Scottish working class right up until the Great War is argued in W. Hamish Fraser, 'The Labour Party in Scotland', in Brown, K. D. (ed.), *The First Labour Party 1906–1914* (London, 1985).

21. Fforde, *Conservatism and Collectivism*, p. 130.

22. Masterman, L., *C. F. G. Masterman* (London, 1939), p. 259.

23. Hutchison, *Scotland*, pp. 243–5; Fforde, *Conservatism and Collectivism*, p. 157. Ian Packer is impressed by the electoral attractions of the Campaign in English rural constituencies. See Packer, I., 'Land Campaign', pp. 150–2.

24. Cannadine, D., *The Decline and Fall of the British Aristocracy* (New Haven, 1990), p. 110; Thompson, F. M. L., *English Landed Society in the Nineteenth Century* (London, 1963), pp. 321–6.

25. Weston, C. C., 'The Liberal Leadership and the Lords' Veto,

1907–1910', *Historical Journal*, 11 (1968), 508–37; Fair, J. D., *British Interparty Conferences* (Oxford, 1980), Ch. 4.

26. Searle, G. R., *The Quest for National Efficiency, 1899–1914* (Oxford, 1971; new ed., London, 1990), Ch. 6; Scally, R. J., *The Origins of the Lloyd George Coalition: The Politics of Social Imperialism, 1900–1918* (Princeton, 1975), Ch. 7.

27. Jalland, P., 'A Liberal Chief Secretary and the Irish Question: Augustine Birrell, 1907–1914', *Historical Journal*, 19 (1976), pp. 421–51; Jalland, P., *The Liberals and Ireland: the Ulster Question in British Politics to 1914* (Brighton, 1980); Jenkins, R., *Asquith* (London, 1964), Chs. 18–19. Perhaps because his heart had gone out of the Home Rule cause after the Irish betrayal over the 1902 Education Act, Lloyd George gave the impression of wishing to extricate Liberalism from the Gladstonian commitment.

28. This is the theme of a now classic book, Dangerfield, G., *The Strange Death of Liberal England* (London, 1935). On the demoralisation of many Liberal Party activists caused by the Asquith government's failure to enfranchise women, as most Liberal MPs wanted, and the reasons for this failure, see Morgan, D., *Suffragists and Liberals: The Politics of Woman Suffrage in Britain* (Oxford, 1975) and Holton, S. S., *Feminism and Democracy: Women's Suffrage and Reform Politics in Britain 1900–1918* (Cambridge, 1986), esp. pp. 73–4, 119–20.

29. The view that landed society adapted surprisingly well to the problems it faced is vigorously argued in Phillips, G. D., *The Diehards: Aristocratic Society and Politics in Edwardian England* (Cambridge, Mass., 1979). The opposing view is put by Cannadine, *Decline and Fall*, passim.

30. Fforde, *Conservatism and Collectivism*, p. 152.

31. Clarke, I. F., *Voices Prophesying War 1763–1984* (Oxford, 1966); Hynes, S., *The Edwardian Turn of Mind* (Princeton, 1968), pp. 35–53.

32. Phillips, *Diehards*, passim.

33. Morris, A. J. A., *Radicalism Against War 1906–1914* (London, 1972); Morris, A. J. A. (ed.), *Edwardian Radicalism 1900–1914* (London, 1974). Weinroth, H. S., 'The British Radicals and the Balance of Power, 1902–1914', *Historical Journal*, 13 (1970), pp. 653–82; Weinroth, H. S., 'Left-Wing Opposition to Naval Armaments in Britain before 1914', *Journal of Contemporary History*, 6 (1971), pp. 93–120.

34. These xenophobic outbursts are graphically described in Koss, S. E., *Lord Haldane: Scapegoat for Liberalism* (N. York, 1969), Ch. 5.

35. Searle, G. R., 'Critics of Edwardian Society: the Case of the Radical Right', in O'Day, A. (ed.), *The Edwardian Age: Conflict and Stability 1900–1914* (London, 1979), pp. 79–96; Searle, G., 'The "Revolt from the Right" in Edwardian Britain', in Kennedy, P. and Nicholls, A. (eds), *Nationalist and Racialist Movements in Britain and Germany Before 1914* (London, 1981), pp. 21–39; Phillips, G. D., 'Lord Willoughby de Broke and the Politics of Radical Toryism, 1909–14', *Journal of British Studies*, 20 (1980), pp. 205–24; A different perspective is offered in Coetzee, F., *For Party or Country: Nationalism and the Dilemmas of Popular Conservatism in Edwardian England* (N. York, 1990) and in Sykes, A., 'The Radical Right and the Crisis of Conservatism Before the First World War', *Historical Journal*, 26 (1983), pp. 661–76.
36. Cannadine, *Decline and Fall*, pp. 516–30.
37. Searle, 'Critics of Edwardian Society', p. 85.

6 LIBERALISM, LABOUR AND SOCIAL REFORM, 1905–14

1. Fforde, M., *Conservatism and Collectivism, 1886–1914* (Edinburgh, 1990), pp. 158–9; Packer, I., 'Lloyd George and the Land Campaign, 1912–14', in Loades, J. (ed.), *The Life and Times of David Lloyd George* (Bangor, 1991), pp. 143–52.
2. For the most convenient general introduction, see Hay, J. R., *The Origins of the Liberal Welfare Reforms 1906–1914* (London, 1975). The best single study of the subject remains Gilbert, Bentley B., *The Evolution of National Insurance in Great Britain: The Origins of the Welfare State* (London, 1966).
3. Emy, H. V., 'The Impact of Financial Policy on English Party Politics Before 1914', *English Historical Review*, 15 (1972), esp. p. 130.
4. Tanner, D., *Political Change and the Labour Party 1900–1918* (Cambridge, 1990), pp. 123, 448–50. The 1906 Plural Voting Bill was rejected by the House of Lords, while the more wide-ranging Franchise and Registration Bill of 1912 became entangled with the divisive issue of women's suffrage and was withdrawn. Incidentally, between 1886 and 1918 the Liberal Party failed to win a single seat in any of the University constituencies, whose electorate consisted of graduates. The 1912 Franchise Bill would have abolished these constituencies.
5. Blewett, N., 'Free Fooders, Balfourites, Whole Hoggers. Factionalism within the Unionist Party, 1906–10', *Historical Journal*, 11 (1968), pp. 95–124.

6. H. V. Emy, *Liberals, Radicals and Social Politics, 1892–1914* (Cambridge, 1973), p. 226. For the circumstances in which this Budget was produced, see Murray, B. K., 'Lloyd George, the Navy Estimates, and the Inclusion of Rating Relief in the 1914 Budget', *Welsh Historical Review*, 15 (1990), pp. 58–78.

7. Emy, 'Financial Policy', pp. 112–16. Indeed, as Emy argues, it was the Liberals' reneging over Retrenchment after 1906 which caused so much anger among Conservatives.

8. Blewett, N., *The Peers, the Parties and the People: the British General Elections of 1910* (London, 1972), Ch. 12.

9. Clarke, P. F., *Lancashire and the New Liberalism* (Cambridge, 1971).

10. Cited in Tanner, *Political Change*, p. 60 fn 46.

11. Emy, *Liberals, Radicals and Social Politics*, pp. 171–3.

12. Blewett, *Peers*, pp. 346–8; Koss, S., *Nonconformity in Modern British Politics* (London, 1975), pp. 117–18, 105.

13. Blewett, *Peers*, pp. 348–9; Koss, *Nonconformity*, Ch. 5.

14. Beveridge, Lord, *Power and Influence* (London, 1953), p. 92.

15. Clarke, P., *Liberals and Social Democrats* (Cambridge, 1978).

16. Lloyd George and Masterman later quarrelled. See Masterman, L., *C. F. G. Masterman* (London, 1939); David, E., 'The New Liberalism of C. F. G. Masterman', in Brown, K. D. (ed.), *Essays in Anti-Labour History* (London, 1974), pp. 17–41.

17. Perkin, H., *The Rise of Professional Society* (London, 1989), pp. 155–70.

18. Hay, R., 'Employers and social policy in Britain: the evolution of welfare legislation, 1905–14', *Social History*, 2 (1977), pp. 435–55.

19. Tanner, *Political Change*, pp. 88–9.

20. Turner, J., 'The Politics of "Organised Business" in the First World War', in Turner, J. (ed.), *Businessmen and Politics* (London, 1984), pp. 34–5.

21. Gilbert, B. B., 'David Lloyd George: The Reform of British Landholding and the Budget of 1914', *Historical Journal*, 22 (1978), pp. 117–41; also Emy, 'Impact of Financial Policy', p. 130, though some were Radicals who disliked the form of the Budget rather than its contents – for example, Molteno (Tanner, *Political Change*, p. 69).

22. Emy, *Liberals, Radicals and Social Policy*, esp. p. 285.

23. Clarke, P., 'The End of Laissez Faire and the Politics of Cotton', *Historical Journal*, 15 (1972), pp. 493–512.

24. Ibid.

25. Blewett, *Peers*, p. 215.

26. Searle, G. R., 'The Edwardian Liberal Party and Business', *English Historical Review*, 98 (1983), pp. 28–60.
27. Bernstein, G. L., *Liberalism and Liberal Politics in Edwardian England* (London, 1986), pp. 22–4; Bernstein, G. L., 'Liberalism and the Progressive Alliance in the Constituencies 1900–1914', *Historical Journal*, 26 (1983), pp. 617–40. On the West Riding 'millocrats', see Laybourn, K. and Reynolds, J., *Liberalism and the Rise of Labour 1890–1918* (London, 1984), esp. pp. 6, 80, 123, 167. For evidence that such old business oligarchies were coming under challenge from within the Liberal organisation during the Edwardian years, see Tanner, *Political Change*, pp. 255–8, 269–73.
28. Searle, 'Edwardian Liberal Party', pp. 44–6.
29. Searle, G. R., *Corruption in British Politics, 1895–1930* (Oxford, 1987), Ch. 6.
30. Ibid., Ch. 8; Gilbert, B. B., 'David Lloyd George and the Great Marconi Scandal', *Historical Research*, 62 (1989), pp. 295–317.
31. Searle, *Corruption*, Ch. 7.
32. Significantly, Lloyd George's Land Inquiry was a largely personal venture, funded by his friends.
33. Bentley, M., *The Climax of Liberal Politics: British Liberalism in Theory and Practice 1868–1918* (London, 1987), citing Ellins, pp. 144–5.
34. Blewett, *Peers*, pp. 317, 326.
35. For example, Pringle in North-West Lanark in Jan. 1910 and MacCallum Scott in Bridgeton in December 1910 (Hutchison, I. G. C., *A Political History of Scotland 1832–1924* [Edinburgh, 1986], p. 239).
36. Tanner, *Political Change*, p. 344.
37. Bernstein, *Liberalism*, p. 123.
38. Morgan, K. O., 'The New Liberalism and the Challenge of Labour: The Welsh Experience, 1885–1929', in Brown, *Essays in Anti-Labour History*, p. 170.
39. Hutchison, *Scotland*, p. 237.
40. The movement among working men and women to establish a school meal service had been strongly resisted by leading Liberals in the West Riding (Laybourn and Reynolds, *Liberalism*, especially pp. 168–9).
41. Bernstein, G. L., 'Liberalism and the Progressive Alliance'.
42. Ibid., pp. 635, 639–40.
43. Tanner, *Political Change*, pp. 127–8.
44. John Howe, 'Liberals, Lib-Labs and Independent Labour in North Gloucestershire, 1890–1914', *Midland History*, 11 (1986), p. 135.

45. Cook, C., 'Labour and the Downfall of the Liberal Party, 1906–14', in Sked, A. and Cook, C. (eds), *Crisis and Controversy* (London, 1976).

46. Sheppard, M. G. and Halstead, J., 'Labour's Municipal Election Performance in Provincial England and Wales, 1901–13', *Bulletin of the Society for the Study of Labour History*, 39 (1979), p. 42. For the working of the anti-Labour pact in Bradford, see Laybourn and Reynolds, *Liberalism*, pp. 150–1.

47. See Appendix, pp. 216–17. Only by treating Labour MPs as surrogate Liberals is it possible to conclude that the Liberals had strengthened their hold over working-class constituencies in England between 1892 and 1910, and even then the improvement is hardly dramatic. The Liberals won 100 seats in English urban working class and mining constituencies in 1892, and eighty-nine in January 1910 (when Labour won thirty-one seats in this type of constituency). Of course, the Liberals did better in 1910 than they had done in 1895 and 1900, when the party as a whole was in the doldrums, but that was to be expected. It seems invalid to demonstrate a realignment in British politics between 1906 and 1910 by comparing the results of the 1910 elections with the highly untypical result of 1900, which is what has been done by Stephens, H. W., 'Party Realignment in Britain, 1900–1925', *Social Science History*, 6 (1982), pp. 35–66.

48. Rowland, P., *The Last Liberal Governments: Unfinished Business, 1911–1914* (London, 1971), p. 80.

49. Ibid., p. 81. But Asquith thought that the class of small employers was the most hostile.

50. Clegg, H. A., Fox, A. and Thompson, A. F., *A History of British Trade Unions Since 1889: Vol. I 1889–1910* (Oxford, 1964), pp. 402–3. See also Thane, P., 'The Working Class and State "Welfare" in Britain, 1880–1914', *Historical Journal*, 27 (1984), pp. 898–9.

51. Lloyd George to brother, 6 May 1908, in George, W., *My Brother and I* (London, 1958), p. 220. Churchill to Asquith, 29 December 1908, Churchill, R. S., *Winston Churchill, Vol. 2 Young Statesman 1901–1914* (London, 1967), pp. 307–8.

52. Thane, 'Working Class and "Welfare"', pp. 877–900. The article is a response to an earlier claim that the 'Welfare State' initially encountered heavy working-class and Labour resistance (Pelling, H., 'The Working Class and the Origins of the Welfare State', in *Popular Politics and Society in Late Victorian Britain* [London, 1968], pp. 1–18).

53. On the Great Labour Unrest, see Clegg, H. A., *A History of British*

Trade Unions Since 1889: Vol. II 1911–1933 (Oxford, 1985), Ch. 2; Tanner, *Political Change*, pp. 62–3.

54. Gregory, R., *The Miners and British Politics 1906–1914* (Oxford, 1968), passim.

55. Cited in Richter, M., *The Politics of Conscience: T. H. Green and His Age* (London, 1964), pp. 374–5.

56. See Phelps Brown, E. H., *The Growth of British Industrial Relations: A study from the standpoint of 1906–14* (London, 1959), Ch. 6. But the government was sometimes accused of not being sufficiently willing to employ the police to maintain order during industrial disturbances; see Morgan, J., *Conflict and Order: The Police and Labour Disputes in England and Wales 1900–1939* (Oxford, 1987), pp. 43–4.

57. In May 1910, with industrial tension mounting in the valleys, the Welsh journal, *Llais Llafur* pointed out that the Liberal MPs representing South Wales included seven major industrialists, as well as five ministers and many lawyers (Peter Stead, 'Establishing a Heartland – The Labour Party in Wales', in Brown, K. D. [ed.], *The First Labour Party 1906–1914* [London, 1985], p. 67).

58. McKibbin, R., *The Evolution of the Labour Party 1910–1924* (Oxford, 1974), Chs. 3–4. For a very different view, see Douglas, R., 'Labour in Decline, 1910–14', in Brown, *Essays in Anti-Labour History*, pp. 105–25.

59. McKibbin, *Evolution*, p. 76.

60. Tanner, *Political Change*, pp. 319–20.

61. Ibid., pp. 336–7.

62. Ibid., passim.

63. By 1914 Labour was holding 171 seats on municipal councils in England (outside London). True, there were cities where the Labour Party succeeded in significantly increasing its representation on the eve of the war, such as Bradford and Leeds (Laybourn and Reynolds, p. 152). In Birmingham, Sheffield, and the East End of London, on the other hand, Labour was very slow to make any impact at all (Michael Cahill, 'Labour in the Municipalities', Brown [ed.], *First Labour Party*, p. 99; Adams, T., 'Labour and the First World War: Economy, Politics and the Erosion of Local Peculiarity?', *Journal of Regional and Local Studies*, 10 [1990], pp. 24–5), while in Scotland Labour could only claim sixty-nine town councillors and thirteen county councillors even as late as 1915 (W. Hamish Fraser, 'The Labour Party in Scotland', Brown [ed.], *First Labour Party*, p. 57).

64. McKibbin, R. I., 'James Ramsay MacDonald and the Problem of

the Independence of the Labour Party, 1910–1914', *Journal of Modern History*, 42 (1970), pp. 216–35. The Osborne Judgment, a legal ruling upheld by the House of Lords in 1909, restricted the use of trade union funds for political purposes and thus struck a serious blow against the Labour Party.

65. Marquand, D., *Ramsay MacDonald* (London, 1977), pp. 150–1, 159–62.
66. Clarke, P. F., 'The electoral position of the Liberal and Labour parties, 1910–14', *English Historical Review*, 90 (1975), pp. 828–36.
67. Tanner, *Political Change*, pp. 22, 317, 422.
68. For a statistical analysis of elections in five English boroughs which suggests that class realignment was not taking place on a significant scale, see Wald, K. D., 'Class and the Vote Before the First World War', *British Journal of Political Science*, 8 (1978), pp. 441–57.
69. McKibbin, *Evolution*, p. 54. 'What even the closest friends of Labour in the Liberal party often failed to understand was that the demand for greater representation was itself the greatest single issue for the Labour party during any election' (Petter, M., 'The Progressive Alliance', *History*, 58 [1973], p. 58).

7   LIBERALISM AND THE GREAT WAR

1. This is the conclusion of Cook, C., 'Labour and the Downfall of the Liberal Party, 1906–14', in Sked, A. and Cook, C. (eds), *Crisis and Controversy* (London, 1976).
2. Many examples are given in Tanner, D., *Political Change and the Labour Party 1900–1918* (Cambridge, 1990). See also Hutchison, I. G. C., *A Political History of Scotland 1832–1924* (Edinburgh, 1986), pp. 231–2.
3. Ball, S. R., 'Asquith's Decline and the General Election of 1918', *Scottish Historical Review*, 61 (1982), pp. 44–61.
4. Winter, J. M., *Socialism and the Challenge of War: ideas and politics in Britain 1912–18* (London, 1974).
5. Wilson, T., *The Downfall of the Liberal Party, 1914–35* (London, 1966), p. 40.
6. Howard, C., 'Expectations born to death: local Labour party expansion in the 1920s', in Winter, J. (ed.), *The Working Class in Modern British History* (Cambridge, 1983), p. 68.
7. Henderson was kept waiting on the door mat outside the Cabinet Room while his colleagues discussed his 'delinquency' in publicly backing Labour participation in an international conference of

socialists at Stockholm, where the British delegates would have met their German and Austrian counterparts. This was the incident which prompted Henderson's resignation.

8. McEwen, J. M., 'Lloyd George's Liberal Supporters in December 1916: A Note', *Bulletin of the Institute of Historical Research*, 53 (1980), pp. 265–72.

9. The literature on the Crisis of December 1916 is voluminous. Here are a few short accounts which provide a good introduction to the subject: Lowe, P., 'The Rise to the Premiership', in Taylor, A. J. P. (ed.), *Lloyd George: Twelve Essays* (London, 1971), pp. 95–133; Fry, M., 'Political Change in Britain, August 1914 to December 1915: Lloyd George Replaces Asquith: The Issues Underlying the Drama', *Historical Journal*, 31 (1988), pp. 609–27; McEwen, J. M., 'The Struggle for Mastery in Britain: Lloyd George versus Asquith, December 1916', *Journal of British Studies*, 18 (1978), pp. 131–56; Fair, J., *British Interparty Conferences* (Oxford, 1980), Ch. 7.

10. On the problems which this presented to Asquith, see Scott's diary, 9–11 Aug. 1917, Wilson, T. (ed.), *The Political Diaries of C. P. Scott 1911–1928* (London, 1970), p. 298.

11. Christopher Addison's diary, 11 January 1917, Addison, C., *Four And A Half Years* (London, 1934), Vol. 2, p. 315.

12. David, E., 'The Liberal Party Divided, 1916–1918', *Historical Journal*, 13 (1970), pp. 509–33; Hosking, G. and King, A., 'Radicals and Whigs in the British Liberal Party, 1906–1914', in Aydelotte, W. O. (ed.), *The History of Parliamentary Behaviour* (Princeton, 1977)), pp. 154–5.

13. Gooch, J., 'The Maurice Debate 1918', *Journal of Contemporary History*, 3 (1968), pp. 211–28.

14. Wilson attempts to show that the Maurice Debate was less influential in determining who received a coupon than is commonly supposed, but he exaggerates his case: Wilson, T., 'The Coupon and the British General Election of 1918', *Journal of Modern History*, 36 (1964), pp. 28–42. See also Douglas, R., 'The Background to the "Coupon" Election Agreements', *English Historical Review*, 86 (1971); McGill, B., 'Lloyd George's Timing of the 1918 Election', *Journal of British Studies*, 14 (1974), pp. 109–24.

15. Scott's diary, 11–12 Dec. 1917, Wilson, (ed.), *C. P. Scott*, pp. 316–17.

16. McKibbin, R., *The Evolution of the Labour Party 1910–1924* (Oxford, 1974), Ch. 50; Winter, *Challenge of Socialism*, Ch. 8.

17. Wilson, *Downfall*, pp. 18–19. But the book contains two other theses: the 'diabolism' of Lloyd George and the tragic absence of a

Notes

continued alliance between the two progressive parties. A similar
account of the Liberal dilemma, concentrating on the progressive
intelligentsia, is provided in Clarke, P., *Liberals and Social Democrats* (Cambridge, 1978), Ch. 6.

18. The best single study of the UDC is Swartz, M., *The Union of
Democratic Control in British Politics During the First World War*
(Oxford, 1971). There is also a useful discussion in Hanak, H.,
'The Union of Democratic Control During the First World War',
Bulletin of the Institute of Historical Research, 36 (1963), pp. 168–
80, and Robbins, K., *The Abolition of War: The 'Peace Movement'*
in Britain 1914–1919 (Cardiff, 1976). See also Rempel, R. A.,
'Conflicts and Change in Liberal Theory and Practice, 1890–
1918: the case of Bertrand Russell', in Waller, P. J. (ed.), *Politics
and Social Change in Modern Britain* (Brighton, 1987), esp.
pp. 127–37.

19. McGill, B., 'Asquith's Predicament 1914–1918', *Journal of Modern
History*, 39 (1967), pp. 283–303. The respect which most activists
in the country continued to have for Asquith is emphasised in
Bernstein, G. L., 'Yorkshire Liberalism during the First World
War', *Historical Journal*, 32 (1989), pp. 107–29.

20. Robbins, K. G., 'Lord Bryce and the First World War', *Historical
Journal*, 10 (1967), p. 268.

21. Clarke, *Liberals and Social Democrats*, p. 185.

22. Bernstein, 'Yorkshire Liberalism', p. 126.

23. Stubbs, J., 'The Impact of the Great War on the Conservative
Party', in Peele, G. and Cooke, C. (eds), *The Politics of Reappraisal
1918–1939* (London, 1975), pp. 14–38.

24. Pugh, M. D., 'Asquith, Bonar Law and the First Coalition',
Historical Journal, 17 (1974), pp. 813–36. On Bonar Law's problems in December 1916, see Blake, R., *The Unknown Prime Minister: Life and Times of Andrew Bonar Law 1858–1923* (London,
1955), Ch. 19.

25. Ramsden, J., *The Age of Balfour and Baldwin 1902–1940* (London, 1978), pp. 119–21.

26. Tanner, *Political Change*, Ch. 12.

27. Wilson, *Downfall*, p. 29.

28. Ibid., p. 390.

29. Waites, B., *A Class Society at War: England 1914–1918*
(Leamington Spa, 1987), esp. Ch. 4. But for a contrary view, see
Reid, A., 'The impact of the First World War on British workers',
in Wall, R. and Winter, J. (eds), *The Upheaval of War: Family,
Work and Welfare in Europe, 1914–1918* (Cambridge, 1988),
pp. 224–5.

200

30. Roberts, R., *The Classic Slum: Salford Life in the First Quarter of the Century* (Manchester, 1971; Pelican ed., 1973), Ch. 9, esp. p. 200.
31. Adams, T., 'Labour and the First World War: Economy, Politics and the Erosion of Local Peculiarity?', *Journal of Regional and Local Studies*, 10 (1990), esp. pp. 27–32.
32. Harrison, R., 'The War Emergency Workers' National Committee, 1914–1920', in Briggs, A. and Saville, J. (eds), *Essays in Labour History 1886–1923* (London, 1971), pp. 211–59.
33. Tanner, *Political Change*, pp. 375–6.
34. However, some Labour historians do not accept the view that war-time developments made working people view the role of an interventionist state in a positive light. For example, see Adams, T., 'Labour and the First World War: Economy, Politics and the Erosion of Local Peculiarity?', *Journal of Regional and Local Studies*, 10 (1990), pp. 29–30.
35. Bernstein, 'Yorkshire Liberalism', p. 124.
36. Waites, *Class Society*, pp. 48–9.
37. Tanner, *Political Change*, Ch. 12.
38. Ibid., pp. 369–70.

8 THE 1920s

1. Thompson, F. M. L., *English Landed Society in the Nineteenth Century* (London, 1963), Ch. 12; Cannadine, D., *The Decline and Fall of the British Aristocracy* (New Haven, 1990), pp. 110–12; Hutchison, I. G. C., *A Political History of Scotland 1832–1924* (Edinburgh, 1986), p. 320.
2. Douglas, R., *Land, People and Politics: A History of the Land Question in the United Kingdom, 1878–1952* (London, 1976), pp. 189–94; Campbell, J., *Lloyd George: the Goat in the Wilderness 1922–1931* (London, 1977), pp. 119–28.
3. Koss, S., *Nonconformity in Modern British Politics* (London, 1975), Chs 6–7. Machin, G. I. T., *Politics and the Churches in Great Britain 1869–1921* (Oxford, 1987), pp. 310–26. But during the war temperance briefly acquired a new importance as a factor in increasing national efficiency (Koss, *Nonconformity*, pp. 135–8).
4. Hutchison, *Scotland*, p. 327.
5. Cook, C., *The Age of Alignment: Electoral Politics in Britain 1922–1929* (London, 1975), pp. 80–1. But the same situation existed during the Edwardian decade.
6. Cook, C., 'Liberals, Labour and Local Elections', in Peele, G. and

Cook, C., (eds), *The Politics of Reappraisal 1918–1939* (London, 1975), p. 170. But in Huddersfield the Liberals' strength on the Council owed a great deal to the existence of a Liberal-Conservative Pact in municipal elections (Reynolds, J. and Laybourn, K., *Labour Heartland: The History of the Labour Party in West Yorkshire during the inter-war years 1918–1939* [Bradford, 1987], pp. 48–9).

7. Hutchison, *Scotland*, p. 310.

8. On the Coalition, see Morgan, K. O., *Consensus and Disunity: the Lloyd George Coalition Government 1918–1922* (Oxford, 1979). Morgan, K. O., 'Lloyd George's Stage Army: the Coalition Liberals, 1918–1922', in Taylor, A. J. P. (ed.), *Lloyd George: Twelve Essays* (London, 1971), pp. 225–54; Morgan, K. O. and J., *Portrait of a Progressive: The Political Career of Christopher, Viscount Addison* (Oxford, 1980); Kinnear, M., *The Fall of Lloyd George: The Political Crisis of 1922* (London, 1973).

9. Bentley, M., 'Liberal Politics and the Grey Conspiracy of 1921', *Historical Journal*, 20 (1977), pp. 461–78; Morgan, *Consensus and Disunity*, Ch. 8.

10. Campbell, *Goat in the Wilderness*, Ch. 3; Cook, *Age of Alignment*, esp. Chs 13, 15, 17; Wilson, *Downfall*, Ch. 15.

11. Cregier, D. M., 'Lloyd George's Lucre: The National Liberal Fund', in *Chiefs Without Indians* (Washington, D.C., 1982); Searle, G. R., *Corruption in British Politics, 1895–1930* (Oxford, 1987), pp. 379–86; Campbell, *Goat in the Wilderness*, pp. 172–7; McGill, B., 'Glittering Prizes and Party Funds in Perspective, 1882–1931', *Bulletin of the Institute of Historical Research*, 55 (1982), pp. 88–93; Pinto-Duschinsky, M., *British Political Finance 1830–1980* (Washington, D.C., 1981), pp. 116–19.

12. Campbell, *Goat in the Wilderness*, pp. 158–61. The Liberal Council enjoyed considerable support amongst the Liberal MPs from Devon and Cornwall: see Wrigley, C., 'Lloyd George and the Labour Movement after 1922', in Loades, J. (ed.), *The Life and Times of David Lloyd George* (Bangor, 1991), p. 63. On the bitter rivalry between Lloyd George and Simon, who had once seen himself as Asquith's natural successor: see Dutton, D., 'Lloyd George, John Simon and the politics of the Liberal Party, 1919–1931', ibid., pp. 71–86.

13. Bentley, M., *The Liberal Mind 1914–1929* (Cambridge, 1977), p. 213.

14. Koss, S., *The Rise and Fall of the Political Press in Britain, Vol. 2: The Twentieth Century Test* (London, 1984), esp. pp. 448–9.

15. Searle, *Corruption*, pp. 401–6.

16. Bentley, *Liberal Mind*, p. 176.

17. Ibid., passim. But was this 'frame of mind' a cause or a consequence of the declining fortunes of the Party?
18. Wilson, *Downfall*, p. 197.
19. Matthew, H. C. G., McKibbin, R. I. and Kay, J. A., 'The Franchise Factor in the Rise of the Labour Party', *English Historical Review*, 91 (1976), pp. 723–52.
20. One historian argues that Labour's advance was *more* rapid at municipal than at parliamentary level (Hart, M., 'The Liberals, the War and the Franchise', *English Historical Review*, 97 [1982], p. 824). In parts of West Yorkshire, on the other hand, Labour was winning seats in parliamentary contests but performing weakly at local government level. This disparity, however, seems to be explicable by reference to the existence of a Liberal-Conservative Alliance in local politics (Reynolds and Laybourn, *Labour Heartland*, pp. 46–50).
21. Turner, J., 'The Labour Vote and the Franchise after 1918: an Investigation of the English Evidence', in Denley, P. and Hopkin, D. (eds), *History and Computing* (Manchester, 1987), pp. 139–40. However, as McKibbin notes, Turner seems to be admitting that most of the new voters in 1918 *were* working class, which suggests that the critics of his article are divided amongst themselves (McKibbin, R., *The Ideologies of Class* [Oxford, 1990], pp. 66–7, fn).
22. Tanner, D., 'The Parliamentary Electoral System, the 'Fourth' Reform Act and the Rise of Labour in England and Wales', *Bulletin of the Institute of Historical Research*, 56 (1983), pp. 205–19; Tanner, D., *Political Change and the Labour Party 1900–1918* (Cambridge, 1990), Ch. 4 and pp. 385–92. See also Hart, 'The Liberals, the War and the Franchise', pp. 820–32.
23. Asquith to 'Friend' (Mrs Harrison), 30 January 1920, in MacCarthy, D. (ed.), *H.H.A.: Letters of the Earl of Oxford and Asquith to a Friend: First Series* (London, 1934), pp. 124–5. Colin Matthew returns to a discussion of the importance of the 'political cultural explanation' of the Liberal decline in 'Rhetoric and Politics in Britain, 1860–1950', in Waller, P. J. (ed.), *Politics and Social Change in Modern Britain* (Brighton, 1987), pp. 53–6.
24. Bentley, M., 'The Liberal Response to Socialism, 1918–29', in Brown, K. D. (ed.), *Essays in Anti-Labour History* (London, 1974), p. 54; Campbell, *Goat in the Wilderness*, p. 74. However, Gladstone on this occasion felt that, on balance, Lloyd George's style of campaigning probably won votes.
25. The dilemma is brilliantly explored in Bentley, 'Liberal Response', pp. 42–73.

26. Hobhouse to Scott, 7 November 1924, in Wilson, T. (ed.), *The Political Diaries of C. P. Scott 1911–1928* (London, 1970), p. 468.
27. Wilson, *Downfall*, Ch. 14. Hart thinks that Labour's mistaken decision to put Labour in was made 'under a "progressive" delusion' (Hart, 'The Liberals, the War and the Franchise', p. 821). Labour also damaged the Liberals through its interventions in the 1924 general election: of the 104 Conservative gains from the Liberal Party, fifty-one involved Labour interventions (plus one Communist intervention).
28. J. R. Campbell, a prominent Communist, had made a 'Don't Shoot' appeal to soldiers in the *Daily Worker*, as a result of which he found himself charged with incitement to mutiny. But the Labour Attorney-General dropped the prosecution after representations had been made on Campbell's behalf by Labour leftwing backbenchers. It was the Opposition attack on the way in which this case had been handled which led to the fall of MacDonald's government and to the dissolution of Parliament in October 1924.
29. Wrigley, C., *Lloyd George and the Challenge of Labour: The Post War Coalition 1918–1922* (Hemel Hempstead, 1990).
30. • Asquith to 'Friend', 20 October 1920, MacCarthy (ed.), *H.H.A.*, p. 159. Given the weak leadership of Willie Adamson and, to a lesser extent, of Clynes, this contemptuous attitude towards the PLP was understandable.
31. Masterman, L., *C. F. G. Masterman* (London, 1939), pp. 336–44. Keynes, for example, even while calling for co-operation between Labour and Liberals, could at the same time say that the 'progressive Liberal' could 'work out his policies without having to do lip-service to Trade-Unionist tyrannies, to the beauties of the class war, or to doctrinaire State Socialism – in none of which he believes' (Keynes, 'Liberalism and Labour' [1926], in *Essays in Persuasion* [London, 1933], p. 342). Characteristically, he dismissed Marxism with the words: 'How can I adopt a creed which, preferring the mud to the fish, exalts the boorish proletariat above the bourgeois and the intelligentsia who, with whatever faults, are the quality in life and surely carry the seeds of all human advancement?' ('A Short View of Russia' [1925], ibid., p. 300). In fairness, Keynes was also consistently rude about the Conservatives.
32. Dowse, R. E., 'The Entry of the Liberals into the Labour Party, 1910–1920', *Yorkshire Bulletin of Economic and Social Research*, 13 (1961), pp. 78–87; Cline, C. A., *Recruits to Labour: The British Labour Party, 1914 to 1931* (Syracuse, N. York, 1963).
33. Freeden, M., *Liberalism Divided: A Study in British Political Thought 1914–1939* (Oxford, 1986). Also important was the

discrediting of Hegelianism and the new distrust of State intervention caused by the War. One Liberal newspaper wrote in 1918 that 'those who hate and detest the cramping, blundering activities of the State will look to Liberalism alone for escape' (Bernstein, G. L., 'Yorkshire Liberalism During the First World War', *Historical Journal*, 32 [1989], pp. 123–4). But compare Peter Clarke, who stresses the *continuity* between the Edwardian 'New Liberals' and Keynes ('Liberals and Social Democrats in Historical Perspective', in Bogdanor, V. [ed.], *Liberal Party Politics* [Oxford, 1983], pp. 34–5).

34. On Labour's breakthrough in the 1919 municipal elections and the reaction to this among Liberals, see Wrigley, *Lloyd George and Challenge of Labour*, pp. 245–6. In Bethnal Green Labour had no councillors at all on the eve of the war; in 1919 it won eighteen out of the twenty-four seats (Julia Bush, *Behind the Lines: East London Labour 1914–1919* [London, 1984], pp. 222–3, 239). Examples of many of these anti-Labour arrangements are to be found in Cook, *Age of Alignment*, pp. 56–63.

35. In Blackburn, for example, 82 per cent of the Liberal vote in 1923 was shared with the Conservative candidate, as against only 12.5 per cent shared with one of the two Labour candidates (5.5 per cent were 'plumpers'). In 1924 the proportion of votes shared with the Conservatives had gone up to 90.5 per cent. A similar situation prevailed in Oldham and Norwich. A retrospective poll, carried out in the 1960s, also suggested that former Liberal voters had switched to the Conservatives in somewhat larger proportions than to the Labour Party (Butler, D. and Stokes, D., *Political Change in Britain* [London, 1969, 1971 ed.], pp. 306–11).

36. The figure is wrongly given in Cook, *The Age of Alignment*, p. 316.

37. Savage, M., *The Dynamics of Working-Class Politics: the Labour Movement in Preston, 1880–1940* (Cambridge, 1987), pp. 175–6.

38. McKibbin, *Ideologies of Class*, p. 278.

39. Ibid., p. 276.

40. Kinnear, M., *The British Voter: An Atlas and Survey Since 1885* (London, 1968), p. 84.

41. Cook, *Age of Alignment*, pp. 85–6.

42. McKibbin, *Ideologies of Class*, p. 276.

43. Ibid., pp. 195–6. However, ten Liberal MPs who had won in straight fights against Labour actually voted for the Labour amendment!

44. Hutchison, *Scotland*, p. 326.

45. Reynolds and Laybourn, *Labour Heartland*, p. 48.

46. In October 1924 Asquith himself called the Liberal Party 'a dying

party set between the upper and nether millstones' (MacCarthy, D. [ed.], *H.H.A: Letters of the Earl of Oxford and Asquith to a Friend: Second Series 1922–1927* [London, 1934], p. 107). The phrase was also one much liked by Masterman. He wrote to his wife in August 1920, during the coal strike, 'Liberalism is dumb and crushed between truculent Labour and equally truculent wealth' (Masterman, *Masterman*, p. 317). Increasingly, Masterman defined the 'middle class' as an unfortunate group trapped between the profiteers, on one side, and the proletariat on the other. See Waites, B., *A Class Society at War: England 1914–1918* (Leamington Spa, 1987), pp. 48–50, and Searle, *Corruption*, pp. 292–5.

47. In fact, the Liberals enjoyed mixed fortunes in these early 1928 by-elections (Campbell, *Goat in the Wilderness*, pp. 206–16).

48. Masterman, *Masterman*, p. 346.

49. Freeden, *Liberalism Divided*, Ch. 4. Campbell, *Goat in the Wilderness*, pp. 187–201.

50. Skidelsky, R., *Politicians and the Slump* (London, 1967), pp. 51–6, esp. p. 51.

51. E.g. Thomas, T., 'Aggregate demand in the United Kingdom, 1918–45', in Floud, R. and McCloskey, D. (eds), *The Economic History of Britain Since 1700*, Vol. 2 (Cambridge, 1981), pp. 337–8.

52. In the 1929 election campaign, Lloyd George's critics tried, not very successfully, to explain away their earlier dismissals of the 'Yellow Book' programme (Campbell, *Goat in the Wilderness*, pp. 229–30).

53. *Britain's Industrial Future* (1928), p. xx and passim.

54. See also M. Keynes, 'The End of Laissez-Faire' (1926), in *Essays in Persuasion*, pp. 312–22.

55. *Britain's Industrial Future*, pp. 464–5.

56. Cowling, M., *The Impact of Labour 1920–1924* (Cambridge, 1971), pp. 350–1. But, as Cowling says, Asquith seemed largely unaware of the great dangers he was running.

57. Bentley calls this decision 'the greatest political mistake Asquith ever made' (Bentley, 'Liberal Response', p. 55). See also Cowling, *Impact of Labour*, Ch. 18. But other historians argue that he really had no choice in the matter (Wilson, *Downfall*, pp. 265–6).

58. For a short overview of the subject, see Butler, D. E., *The Electoral System in Britain Since 1918* (Oxford, 1963), pp. 10–11, 38–48. A detailed account is provided by Pugh, M., *Electoral Reform in War and Peace 1906–18* (London, 1978).

59. Grigg, J., 'Lloyd George and Electoral Reform', in Bean, J. M. W.

(ed.), *The Political Culture of Modern Britain* (London, 1987), pp. 165–77.

60. Butler, *Electoral System*, pp. 189–94.

61. At the Carlton Club meeting, of the Scottish MPs seventeen voted with Chamberlain, only six (including Bonar Law and the party chairman, George Younger) against. In the ensuing election a pact operated in nearly two-thirds of all constituencies, compared with under one-fifth in England (Hutchison, *Scotland*, p. 314).

62. Perhaps the best brief account of the 'fusion' episode is provided by Morgan, *Consensus and Disunity*, pp. 180–90. See also Wrigley, *Lloyd George and Challenge of Labour*, pp. 201–2, 242–4.

9 CONCLUSION

1. Cited in J. A. Thompson, 'Historians and the Decline of the Liberal Party', *Albion*, 22 (1990), p. 82. When Duncan Tanner claims to be demonstrating the 'viability' of the Edwardian Liberal Party in the face of Labour's 'challenge', he is sometimes doing nothing more than explaining why the Labour Party was never to be as effective a party as the Liberals whom it was supplanting (Tanner, D., *Political Change and the Labour Party 1900–1918* [Cambridge, 1990]).

2. Cited in Glaser, J. F., 'English Nonconformity and the Decline of Liberalism', *American Historical Review*, 63 (1957–8), p. 361.

3. Mackail, J. W. and Wyndham, G., *Life and Letters of George Wyndham*, Vol. II (London, n.d.), p. 539.

4. Cowling, M. *The Impact of Labour 1920–1924* (Cambridge, 1971), Chs 18–20.

5. Cited in Cook, C., *The Age of Alignment: Electoral Politics in Britain, 1922–1929* (London, 1975), p. 183.

6. Samuel Storey, *Newcastle Daily Chronicle*, 12 January 1906, cited Purdue, A. W., 'The Liberal and Labour Parties in North-East Politics, 1900–14: The Struggle for Supremacy', *International Review of Social History*, 26 (1981), pp. 12–13.

7. Matthew, H. C. G., *The Liberal Imperialists: the ideas and politics of a post-Gladstonian élite* (Oxford, 1973), p. 128.

8. A highly sympathetic article by Carolyn W. White describes the author and the circumstances in which the book was written, showing how indebted it is to Strachey and also to Jung ('*The Strange Death of Liberal England* in Its Time', *Albion*, 17 [1985], pp. 425–47).

9. Bentley, M., 'The Liberal Response to Socialism, 1918–29', in

Brown, K. D. (ed.), *Essays in Anti-Labour History* (London, 1974), p. 72.

10. Spender, S., *Forward From Liberalism* (London, 1937), esp. Chs 2–3 and p. 89.

11. Peter Clarke, 'Liberals and Social Democrats in Historical Perspective', in Bogdanor, V. (ed.), *Liberal Party Politics* (Oxford, 1983), pp. 39–42. Clarke's thesis in 1983 was that, with the Labour Party apparently disintegrating, its 'social democratic' wing would finally abandon it and, within the ambit of the 'Alliance', reunite with the more ideologically compatible Liberals.

12. Balfour, M., *Britain and Joseph Chamberlain* (London, 1985), pp. 149–50.

13. Clarke, P. F., *Lancashire and the New Liberalism* (Cambridge, 1971), p. 394.

14. Hutchison, I. G. C., *A Political History of Scotland 1832–1924* (Edinburgh, 1986), p. 312.

15. On this subject, see Hannah, L., *The Rise of the Corporate Economy: The British Experience* (London, 1976).

·16. James, R. R. (ed.), *Memoirs of a Conservative: J. C. C. Davidson's Memoirs and Papers 1910–37* (London, 1969), pp. 289–90. Pinto-Duschinsky, M., *British Political Finance 1830–1980* (Washington, D.C., 1981), pp. 111–13.

17. *National Liberal Federation Report*, 1921.

18. Savage, M., *The Dynamics of Working-Class Politics: the Labour Movement in Preston, 1880–1940* (Cambridge, 1987), p. 144.

19. See for example, MacDonald's remarks at Southampton in 1894, on accepting the invitation to contest the borough as an independent Labour representative: 'Our movement is neither a party nor a class movement, but a national one...', in Marquand, D., *Ramsay MacDonald* (London, 1977), p. 37; this was a claim which he also liked to make in his later 'theoretical' defences of socialism.

20. McKibbin, R., *The Ideologies of Class* (Oxford, 1990), p. 281.

APPENDIX

Liberal Party Leaders, 1885–1931

William Ewart Gladstone	to Mar. 1894
Lord Rosebery	Mar. 1894 to Oct. 1896
William Vernon Harcourt	Oct. 1896 to Feb. 1899
Sir Henry Campbell-Bannerman	Feb. 1899 to Apr. 1908
H. H. Asquith (Lord Oxford & Asquith)	Apr. 1908 to Oct. 1926
David Lloyd George	Oct. 1926 to Nov. 1931
Herbert Samuel	from Nov. 1931

Liberal Cabinets, 1886–1915

GLADSTONE'S CABINET, FEB. TO AUG. 1886

Prime Minister	W. E. Gladstone
Lord Chancellor	Lord Herschell
Foreign Secretary	Lord Rosebery
Home Secretary	H. C. E. Childers
Chancellor of the Exchequer	W. V. Harcourt
Colonial Secretary	Earl Granville
Indian Secretary	Earl of Kimberley
First Lord of Admiralty	Marquess of Ripon
War Secretary	H. Campbell-Bannerman
Sec. of State for Ireland	J. Morley
Scottish Secretary	G. O. Trevelyan (to April)

209

Pres. of Local Govt Board   J. Chamberlain
                                   J. Stansfeld (from April)
Pres. of Board of Trade   A. J. Mundella
Lord President of the Council   Earl Spencer

GLADSTONE'S AND ROSEBERY'S CABINETS, AUG. 1892 TO JUNE 1895

Prime Minister   W. E. Gladstone (to Mar. 1894)
                                   Earl of Rosebery (from Mar.
                                   1894)
Lord Chancellor   Lord Herschell
Foreign Secretary   Earl of Rosebery (to Mar. 1894)
                                   Earl of Kimberley (from Mar.
                                   1894)
Home Secretary   H. H. Asquith
Chancellor of the Exchequer   W. V. Harcourt
Colonial Secretary   Marquess of Ripon
Indian Secretary   Earl of Kimberley (to Mar.
                                   1894)
                                   H. Fowler (from Mar. 1894)
First Lord of Admiralty   Earl Spencer
War Secretary   H. Campbell-Bannerman
Sec. of State for Ireland   J. Morley
Scottish Secretary   G. O. Trevelyan
Pres. of Local Govt Board   H. Fowler (to Mar. 1894)
                                   G. J. Shaw-Lefevre (from Mar.
                                   1894)
Pres. of Board of Trade   A. J. Mundella (to Mar.
                                   1894)
                                   J. Bryce (from Mar. 1894)
V-Pres. of Bd. of Education   A. H. D. Acland
Lord President of the Council   Earl of Kimberley
Lord Privy Seal   W. E. Gladstone (to Mar.
                                   1894)
                                   Lord Tweedmouth (from Mar.
                                   1894)
Ch. of Duchy of Lancaster   J. Bryce (to Mar. 1894)
                                   Lord Tweedmouth (from Mar.
                                   1894)
Postmaster-General   A. Morley
First Commissioner of Works   G. J. Shaw-Lefevre (to Mar.
                                   1894)

CAMPBELL-BANNERMAN'S CABINET, DEC. 1905 TO APR. 1908

Prime Minister	Sir H. Campbell-Bannerman
Lord Chancellor	Lord Loreburn (Sir R. Reid)
Foreign Secretary	Edward Grey
Home Secretary	H. Gladstone
Chancellor of the Exchequer	H. H. Asquith
Colonial Secretary	Earl of Elgin
Indian Secretary	J. Morley
First Lord of Admiralty	Lord Tweedmouth
War Secretary	R. B. Haldane
Sec. of State for Ireland	J. Bryce (to Jan. 1907)
	A. Birrell (from Jan. 1907)
Scottish Secretary	J. Sinclair
Pres. of Local Govt Board	J. Burns
Pres. of Board of Trade	D. Lloyd George
Pres. of Board of Agriculture	Earl Carrington
Pres. of Board of Education	A. Birrell (to Jan. 1907)
	R. McKenna (from Jan. 1907)
Lord President of the Council	Earl of Crewe
Lord Privy Seal	Marquess of Ripon
Ch. of Duchy of Lancaster	Sir H. Fowler
Postmaster-General	S. Buxton
First Commissioner of Works	L. Harcourt (from Mar. 1907)

ASQUITH'S CABINET, APRIL 1908 TO MAY 1915

Prime Minister	H. H. Asquith
Lord Chancellor	Lord Loreburn (to June 1912)
	Lord Haldane (from June 1912)
Foreign Secretary	Edward Grey
Home Secretary	H. Gladstone (to Feb. 1910)
	W. Churchill (Feb. 1910 to Oct. 1911)
	R. McKenna (from Oct. 1911)
Chancellor of the Exchequer	D. Lloyd George
Colonial Secretary	Earl of Crewe (to Nov. 1910)
	L. Harcourt (from Nov. 1910)
Indian Secretary	J. Morley (to Nov. 1910)
	Earl of Crewe (Nov. 1910 to Mar. 1911)

211

Indian Secretary (*contd.*)	Viscount Morley (Mar. to May 1911)
	Earl of Crewe (from May 1911)
First Lord of Admiralty	R. McKenna (to Oct. 1911)
	W. Churchill (from Oct. 1911)
War Secretary	R. B. Haldane (to June 1912)
	J. Seely (June 1912 to Mar. 1914)
	H. H. Asquith (Mar. to Aug. 1914)
	Lord Kitchener (from Aug. 1914)
Sec. of State for Ireland	A. Birrell
Scottish Secretary	J. Sinclair (Ld. Pentland) (to Feb. 1912)
	T. McKinnon Wood (from Feb. 1912)
Pres. of Local Govt Boad	J. Burns (to Feb. 1914)
	H. Samuel (from Feb. 1914)
Pres. of Board of Trade	W. Churchill (to Feb. 1910)
	S. Buxton (Feb. 1910 to Feb. 1914)
	J. Burns (Feb. to Aug. 1914)
	W. Runciman (from Aug. 1914)
Pres. of Board of Agriculture	Earl Carrington (to Oct. 1911)
	W. Runciman (Oct. 1911 to Aug. 1914)
	Lord Lucas (from Aug. 1914)
Pres. of Board of Education	W. Runciman (to Oct. 1911)
	J. Pease (from Oct. 1911)
Lord President of the Council	Lord Tweedmouth (Apr. to Oct. 1908)
	Viscount Wolverhampton (Oct. 1908 to June 1910)
	Earl Beauchamp (June to Nov. 1910)
	Viscount Morley (Nov. 1910 to Aug. 1914)
	Earl Beauchamp (from Aug. 1914)
Lord Privy Seal	Marquess of Ripon (to Oct. 1908)
	Earl of Crewe (Oct. 1908 to Oct. 1911)

	Earl Carrington (Oct. 1911 to Feb. 1912)
	Marquess of Crewe (from Feb. 1912)
Ch. of Duchy of Lancaster	H. Fowler (to Apr. 1908)
	Lord Fitzmaurice (Apr. 1908 to June 1909)
	H. Samuel (June 1909 to Feb. 1910)
	J. Pease (Feb. 1910 to Oct. 1911)
	C. Hobhouse (Oct. 1911 to Feb. 1914)
	C. Masterman (Feb. 1914 to Feb. 1915)
	E. Montagu (from Feb. 1915)
Postmaster-General	S. Buxton (to Feb. 1910)
	H. Samuel (Feb. 1910 to Feb. 1914)
	C. Hobhouse (from Feb. 1914)
First Commissioner of Works	L. Harcourt (to Nov. 1910)
	Earl Beauchamp (Nov. 1910 to Aug. 1914)
	Lord Emmott (from Aug. 1914)
Attorney-General	R. Isaacs (June 1912 to Oct. 1913)
	Sir J. Simon (from Oct. 1913)

Liberal Cabinet Ministers in Coalition Governments, 1915–22

ASQUITH'S MINISTRY, MAY 1915 TO DEC. 1916

Lord Buckmaster	Lord Chancellor
W. Churchill	Chancellor of Duchy of Lancaster (to Nov. 1915)
Marquess of Crewe	Lord President of Council
	Pres. of Board of Education (from Aug. 1916)
A. Birrell	Irish Secretary (to July 1916)
E. Grey	Foreign Secretary
L. Harcourt	First Commissioner of Works

D. Lloyd George	Minister of Munitions (to July 1916)
	War Secretary (from July 1916)
R. McKenna	Chancellor of the Exchequer
E. Montagu	Chancellor of D. of Lancaster (Jan. to July 1916)
	Minister of Munitions (from July 1916)
W. Runciman	President of Board of Trade
H. Samuel	Chancellor of D. of Lancaster (Nov. 1915 to Jan. 1916)
	Home Secretary (from Jan. 1916)
J. Simon	Home Secretary (to Jan. 1916)
H. Tennant	Scottish Secretary (from July 1916)
T. McKinnon Wood	Scottish Secretary (to July 1916)
	Chancellor of D. of Lancaster (from July 1916)

LLOYD GEORGE'S MINISTRY, DEC. 1916 TO OCT. 1922

C. Addison	Minister of Munitions (to July 1917)
	Minister of Reconstruction (July 1917 to Jan. 1919 (not Cabinet post)
	Pres. of Local Govt. Bd. (Jan. to June 1919)
	Minister of Health (June 1919 to Apr. 1921)
	Minister Without Porfolio (Apr. to July 1921)
Sir F. Cawley	Chancellor of D. of Lancaster (to Feb. 1918)
W. Churchill	Minister of Munitions (July 1917 to Jan. 1919)
	War Secretary (Jan. 1919 to Feb. 1921)
	Colonial Secretary (from Feb. 1921)

H. A. L. Fisher	President of Board of Education
Sir H. Greenwood	Irish Secretary (from Apr. 1920)
Sir G. Hewart	Attorney-General (Nov. 1921 to March 1922)
T. Macnamara	Minister of Labour (from Mar. 1920)
I. Macpherson	Irish Secretary (Jan. 1919 to Apr. 1920)
A. Mond	Minister of Health (from Apr. 1921)
E. Montagu	Indian Secretary (July 1917 to Mar. 1922)
R. Munro	Scottish Secretary
Lord Rhondda	Pres. of Local Govt Bd. (to June 1917)
E. Shortt	Irish Secretary (May 1918 to Jan. 1919)
A. Stanley	Pres. of Board of Trade (to May 1919)

General Election Results, 1885–1931

1885	Conservatives 251	Liberals 333
		Irish Nationalists 86
1886	Conservatives 316	Liberals 191
	Liberal Unionists 78	Irish Nats 85
1892	Liberals 273	Conservatives 269
	Irish Nats 81	Lib. Unionists 46
	Ind. Labour 1	
1895	Conservatives 340	Liberals 177
	Lib. Unionists 71	Irish Nats 82
1900	Cons & Lib. Unionists 402	Liberals 184
		Irish Nats 82
	Labour 2	
1906	Liberals 400	Unionists 157
	Irish Nats 83	Labour 30
Jan. 1910	Liberals 275	Unionists 273
	Irish Nats 82	Labour 40
Dec. 1910	Liberals 272	Unionists 272
	Irish Nats 84	Labour 42

1918	Coalition Cons 335	Ind. Liberals, 28
	Coalition Liberals 133	Labour 63
	Coalition Labour 10	Sinn Fein 73
	Independent Cons 23	Irish Nationalists 7
	Irish Unionists 25	Others 10
1922	Conservatives 345	Labour 142
	Liberals 54	National Liberals 62
	Others 12	
1923	Labour 191	Conservatives 258
	Liberals 159	Others 7
1924	Conservatives 419	Labour 151
	Communist 1	Liberals 40
	Others 4	
1929	Labour 288	Conservatives 260
	Liberals 59	Others 8
1931	Conservatives 473	Labour 52
	National Labour 13	Ind. Labour 4
	Liberal Nationals 35	Others 5
	Liberals 33	

Regional Strength of the Liberal Party

GENERAL ELECTIONS

The percentages refer to the proportion of seats in each region won by the Liberals in general elections during these years. The regions are listed in rank order. An equals sign (=) indicates that the Liberals achieved identical ratios of success in these regions. For 1886–1910 the regions are those demarcated in Neal Blewett, *The Peers, the Parties and the People: the General Elections of 1910* (London, 1972); and for 1922–9 those demarcated in Tom Stannage, *Baldwin Thwarts the Opposition* (London, 1980).

1886–1910

1. Forth Valley (87%)
2. North East Scotland (86%) = Rural Wales (86%)
3. Industrial Wales (76.5%)
4. North-East England (74%)
5. West Riding, Yorkshire (71%)
6. Scottish Highlands (67%)
7. East Midlands (62%)
8. Clyde Valley (58%)
9. Southern Scotland (57%) = South-West Peninsula (57%)

10. East Anglia (49.5%)
11. Eastern Lancastria (46%)
12. Lincolnshire (43%)
13. Severn (38%)
14. North and East Ridings, Yorkshire (36%) = Cumbria (36%)
15. Inner London (33%)
16. Western Midlands (28.5%)
17. Wessex (19.5%) = Thames Valley (19.5%)
18. Outer London (17%)
19. Western Marches (14%)
20. Western Lancastria (10.5%)
21. South-East England (6.5%)

1922–9

1. Rural Wales (79%)
2. Scottish Highlands (75%)
3. Western Peninsula (46%)
4. North-East Scotland (36%)
5. Forth Valley (23%)
6. East Anglia (22%) = Southern Scotland (22%)
7. Severn (20%)
8. Lincolnshire etc. (19%) = Eastern Lancastria (19%)
9. East Midlands (16%)
10. North-East England (12%)
11. West Riding, Yorkshire (13%)
12. South-Central England (12%) = Wessex (12%) = Western Lancastria (12%)
13. Rest of Yorkshire (11.5%)
14. North-West Midlands (11%)
15. Inner London (10%)
16. South-West Midlands (7.5%)
17. Clyde Valley (7%)
18. Salop (5%)
19. Cumbria (3.5%)
20. Outer London (3%) = South-East England (3%) = Industrial Wales (3%)

A SELECT BIBLIOGRAPHY

Books

Adelman, P., *The Decline of the Liberal Party 1910–1931* (London, 1981).

Adelman, P., *Victorian Radicalism: the Middle-Class Experience 1830–1914* (London, 1984).

Alderman, G., *The Railway Interest* (Leicester, 1973).

Aydelotte, W. O. (ed.), *The History of Parliamentary Behaviour* (Princeton, 1977).

Barker, M., *Gladstone and Radicalism: The Reconstruction of Liberal Policy in Britain 1885–94* (Hassocks, 1975).

Bealey, F. and Pelling, H., *Labour and Politics, 1900–1906* (London, 1958).

Bean, J. M. W. (ed.), *The Political Culture of Modern Britain: Studies in Memory of Stephen Koss* (London, 1987).

Bebbington, D. W., *The Nonconformist Conscience: Chapel and Politics 1870–1914* (London, 1982).

Bentley, M., *The Liberal Mind 1914–1929* (Cambridge, 1977).

Bentley, M., *The Climax of Liberal Politics: British Liberalism in Theory and Practice 1868–1918* (London, 1987).

Bernstein, G. L., *Liberalism and Liberal Politics in Edwardian England* (London, 1986).

Blewett, N., *The Peers, the Parties and the People; the British General Elections of 1910* (London, 1972).

Bogdanor, V. (ed.), *Liberal Party Politics* (Oxford, 1983).

Briggs, A. and Saville, J. (eds), *Essays in Labour History 1886–1923* (London, 1971).

Brown, K. D. (ed.), *Essays in Anti-Labour History* (London, 1974).

Brown, K. D. (ed.), *The First Labour Party 1906–1914* (London, 1985).

Bush, J., *Behind the Lines: East London Labour 1914–1919* (London, 1984).

Butt, J. and Clarke, I. F. (eds), *The Victorians and Social Protest* (Newton Abbot, 1973).

Campbell, J., *Lloyd George: the Goat in the Wilderness 1922–1931* (London, 1977).

Cannadine, D., *The Decline and Fall of the British Aristocracy* (New Haven, 1990).

Clarke, I. F., *Voices Prophesying War 1763–1984* (Oxford, 1966).

Clarke, P., *Liberals and Social Democrats* (Cambridge, 1978).

Clarke, P. F., *Lancashire and the New Liberalism* (Cambridge, 1971).

Clegg, H. A., Fox, A., and Thompson, A. F. (eds), *A History of British Trade Unions Since 1889, Vol. I* (Oxford, 1964).

Cline, C. A., *Recruits to Labour: The British Labour Party, 1914 to 1931* (Syracuse, N. York, 1963).

Coetzee, F., *For Party or Country: Nationalism and the Dilemmas of Popular Conservatism in Edwardian England* (N. York, 1990).

Collini, S., *Liberalism and Sociology: L. T. Hobhouse and Political Argument in England, 1880–1914* (Cambridge, 1979).

Cook, C., *The Age of Alignment: Electoral Politics in Britain 1922–1929* (London, 1975).

Cook, C., *A Short History of the Liberal Party, 1900–1976* (London, 1976).

Cowling, M., *The Impact of Labour 1920–1924* (Cambridge, 1971).

Cregier, D. M., *Bounder from Wales: Lloyd George's Career Before the First World War* (Columbia, Missouri, 1976).

Cregier, D. M., *Chiefs Without Indians* (Washington, D.C., 1982).

Cross, C., *The Liberals in Power, 1905–1915* (London, 1963).

Dangerfield, G., *The Strange Death of Liberal England* (London, 1935).

Denley, P. and Hopkin, D. (eds), *History and Computing* (Manchester, 1987).

Douglas, R., *The History of the Liberal Party, 1895–1970* (London, 1971).

Douglas, R., *Land, People and Politics: A History of the Land Question in the United Kingdom, 1878–1952* (London, 1976).

Emy, H. V., *Liberals, Radicals and Social Politics, 1892–1914* (Cambridge, 1973).

Fair, J. D., *British Interparty Conferences* (Oxford, 1980).

Fforde, M., *Conservatism and Collectivism, 1886–1914* (Edinburgh, 1990).

Freeden, M., *The New Liberalism: An Ideology of Social Reform* (Oxford, 1978).

Freeden, M., *Liberalism Divided: A Study in British Political Thought 1914–1939* (Oxford, 1986).

219

Freeden, M. (ed.), *Minutes of the Rainbow Circle, 1894–1924* (London, 1989).

Gilbert, B. B., *The Evolution of National Insurance in Great Britain* (London, 1966).

Gilbert, B. B., *David Lloyd George: The Architect of Change 1863–1912* (London, 1987).

Gregory, R., *The Miners and British Politics 1906–1914* (Oxford, 1968).

Grigg, J., *Lloyd George: The People's Champion: 1902–1911* (London, 1978).

Grigg, J., *Lloyd George: From Peace to War: 1912–1916* (London, 1985).

Hamer, D. A., *Liberal Politics in the Age of Gladstone and Rosebery* (Oxford, 1972).

Harris, J., *Unemployment and Politics: A Study in English Social Policy 1886–1914* (Oxford, 1972).

Harvie, C., *The Lights of Liberalism: University Liberals and the Challenge of Democracy 1860–86* (London, 1976).

Hay, J. R., *The Origins of the Liberal Welfare Reforms 1906–1914* (London, 1975).

Hazlehurst, C., *Politicians at War: July 1914 to May 1915* (London, 1971).

Holton, S. S., *Feminism and Democracy: Women's Suffrage and Reform Politics in Britain 1900–1918* (Cambridge, 1986).

Hutchison, I. G. C., *A Political History of Scotland 1832–1924* (Edinburgh, 1986).

Jalland, P., *The Liberals and Ireland: the Ulster Question in British Politics to 1914* (Brighton, 1980).

Jay, R., *Joseph Chamberlain: A Political Study* (Oxford, 1981).

Jenkins, R., *Mr Balfour's Poodle* (London, 1954).

Jenkins, R., *Asquith* (London, 1964).

Jenkins, T. A., *Gladstone, Whiggery and the Liberal Party 1874–1886* (Oxford, 1988).

Jones, G. W., *Borough Politics: Wolverhampton Town Council, 1888–1964* (London, 1969).

Kennedy, P. and Nicholls, A. (eds), *Nationalist and Racialist Movements in Britain and Germany Before 1914* (London, 1981).

Kinnear, M., *The British Voter: An Atlas and Survey Since 1885* (London, 1968).

Kinnear, M., *The Fall of Lloyd George: The Political Crisis of 1922* (London, 1973).

Koss, S., *Lord Haldane: Scapegoat for Liberalism* (N. York, 1969).

Koss, S., *Nonconformity in Modern British Politics* (London, 1975).

Koss, S., *Asquith* (London, 1976).

Koss, S., *The Rise and Fall of the Political Press in Britain, Vol. 2: The Twentieth Century Test* (London, 1984).

Langan, M. and Schwarz, B. (eds), *Crises in the British State 1880–1930* (London, 1985).

Laybourn, K. and Reynolds, J., *Liberalism and the Rise of Labour 1890–1918* (London, 1984).

Loades, J. (ed.), *The Life and Times of David Lloyd George* (Bangor, 1991).

Loughlin, J., *Gladstone, Home Rule and the Ulster Question 1882–93* (Dublin, 1986).

Lubenow, W. C., *Parliamentary Politics and the Home Rule Crisis: The British House of Commons in 1886* (Oxford, 1988).

Machin, G. I. T., *Politics and the Churches in Great Britain 1869–1921* (Oxford, 1987).

McKibbin, R., *The Evolution of the Labour Party 1910–1924* (Oxford, 1974).

McKibbin, R., *The Ideologies of Class* (Oxford, 1990).

Marquand, D., *Ramsay MacDonald* (London, 1977).

Masterman, L., *C. F. G. Masterman* (London, 1939).

Matthew, H. C. G., *The Liberal Imperialists: The ideas and politics of a Post-Gladstonian élite* (Oxford, 1973).

Maurice, N., *The Maurice Case* (London, 1972).

Morgan, D., *Suffragists and Liberals: The Politics of Woman Suffrage in Britain* (Oxford, 1975).

Morgan, J., *Conflict and Order: The Police and Labour Disputes in England and Wales 1900–1939* (Oxford, 1987).

Morgan, K. O., *Wales in British Politics 1868–1922* (Cardiff, 1970).

Morgan, K. O., *The Age of Lloyd George: The Liberal Party and British Politics, 1890–1929* (London, 1971).

Morgan, K. O., *Consensus and Disunity: the Lloyd George Coalition Government 1918–1922* (Oxford, 1979).

Morgan, K. O. and Morgan, J., *Portrait of a Progressive: The Political Career of Christopher, Viscount Addison* (Oxford, 1980).

Morris, A. J. A., *Radicalism Against War 1906–1914* (London, 1972).

Morris, A. J. A. (ed.), *Edwardian Radicalism 1900–1914* (London, 1974).

Murray, B. K., *The People's Budget 1909–10* (Oxford, 1980).

O'Day, A. (ed.), *The Edwardian Age: Conflict and Stability 1900–1914* (London, 1979).

Offer, A., *Property and Politics, 1870–1914* (Cambridge, 1981).

Peele, G. and Cook, C. (eds), *The Politics of Reappraisal 1918–1939* (London, 1975).

Pelling, H., *Social Geography of British Elections 1885–1910* (London, 1967).

Pelling, H., *Popular Politics and Society in Late Victorian Britain* (London, 1968).

Phillips, G. D., *The Diehards: Aristocratic Society and Politics in Edwardian England* (Cambridge, Mass., 1979).

Pinto-Duschinsky, M., *British Political Finance 1830–1980* (Washington, D.C., 1981).

Pugh, M., *Electoral Reform in War and Peace 1906–18* (London, 1978).

Pugh, M., *The Making of Modern British Politics, 1867–1939* (Oxford, 1982).

Pugh, M., *Lloyd George* (London, 1988).

Ramsden, J., *The Age of Balfour and Baldwin 1902–1940* (London, 1978).

Rempel, R. A., *Unionists Divided: Arthur Balfour, Joseph Chamberlain and the Unionist Free Traders* (Newton Abbot, 1972).

Reynolds, J. and Laybourn, K., *Labour Heartland: The History of the Labour Party in West Yorkshire during the Inter-War Years 1918–1939* (Bradford, 1987).

Rowland, P., *The Last Liberal Governments: The Promised Land, 1905–1910* (London, 1968).

Rowland, P., *The Last Liberal Governments: Unfinished Business, 1911–1914* (London, 1971).

Russell, A. K., *Liberal Landslide: the General Election of 1906* (Newton Abbot, 1973).

Savage, M., *The Dynamics of Working-Class Politics: the Labour Movement in Preston, 1880–1940* (Cambridge, 1987).

Scally, R. J., *The Origins of the Lloyd George Coalition: The Politics of Social Imperialism, 1900–1918* (Princeton, 1975).

Searle, G. R., *Corruption in British Politics, 1895–1930* (Oxford, 1987).

Searle, G. R., *The Quest for National Efficiency, 1899–1914* (Oxford, 1971; new ed., London, 1990).

Sked, A. and Cook, C. (eds), *Crisis and Controversy: Essays in honour of A. J. P. Taylor* (London, 1976).

Skidelsky, R., *Politicians and the Slump* (London, 1967).

Stansky, P., *Ambitions and Strategies: The struggle for the leadership of the Liberal Party in the 1890s* (Oxford, 1964).

Swartz, M., *The Union of Democratic Control in British Politics During the First World War* (Oxford, 1971).

Sykes, A., *Tariff Reform in British Politics 1903–1913* (Oxford, 1979).

Tanner, D., *Political Change and the Labour Party 1900–1918* (Cambridge, 1990).

Taylor, A. J. P., *Politics in Wartime* (London, 1964).

Taylor, A. J. P. (ed.), *Lloyd George: Twelve Essays* (London, 1971).

Thompson, J. A. and Mejia, A. (eds), *Edwardian Conservatism: Five Studies in Adaptation* (London, 1988).

Thompson, F. M. L., *English Landed Society in the Nineteenth Century* (London, 1963).

Thompson, P., *Socialists, Liberals and Labour. The Struggle for London 1885–1914* (London, 1967).

Waites, B., *A Class Society at War: England 1914–1918* (Leamington Spa, 1987).

Wall, R. and Winter, J. (eds), *The Upheaval of War: Family, Work and Welfare in Europe, 1914–1918* (Cambridge, 1988).

Waller, P. J. (ed.), *Politics and Social Change in Modern Britain* (Brighton, 1987).

Wilson, T., *The Downfall of the Liberal Party, 1914–35* (London, 1966).

Wilson, T. (ed.), *The Political Diaries of C. P. Scott 1911–1928* (London, 1970).

Winter, J. (ed.), *The Working Class in Modern British History* (Cambridge, 1983).

Winter, J. M., *Socialism and the Challenge of War* (London, 1974).

Wrigley, C. J., *David Lloyd George and the British Labour Movement* (Hassocks, 1976).

Wrigley, C., *Arthur Henderson* (Cardiff, 1990).

Wrigley, C., *Lloyd George and the Challenge of Labour: The Post War Coalition 1918–1922* (Hemel Hempstead, 1990).

Articles

Adams, R. J. Q., 'Asquith's Choice: the May Coalition and the Coming of Conscription, 1915–1916', *Journal of British Studies*, 25 (1986), pp. 243–63.

Adams, T., 'Labour and the First World War: Economy, Politics and the Erosion of Local Peculiarity?', *Journal of Regional and Local Studies*, 10 (1990), pp. 23–47.

Adonis, A., 'Aristocracy, Agriculture and Liberalism: The Politics, Finances and Estates of the Third Lord Carrington', *Historical Journal*, 31 (1988), pp. 871–97.

Ball, S. R., 'Asquith's Decline and the General Election of 1918', *Scottish Historical Review*, 61 (1982), pp. 44–61.

Bealey, F., 'Negotiations between the Liberal Party and the Labour Representation Committee before the General Election of 1906', *Bulletin of the Institute of Historical Research*, 29 (1956), pp. 261–74.

Bebbington, D. W., 'Nonconformity and Electoral Sociology, 1867–1918', *Historical Journal*, 27 (1984), pp. 633–56.

Bentley, M., 'Liberal Politics and the Grey Conspiracy of 1921', *Historical Journal*, 20 (1977), pp. 461–78.

Bernstein, G. L., 'Liberalism and the Progressive Alliance in the Constituencies 1900–1914', *Historical Journal*, 26 (1983), pp. 617–40.

Bernstein, G. L., 'Yorkshire Liberalism during the First World War', *Historical Journal*, 32 (1989), pp. 107–29.

Blewett, N., 'The Franchise in the United Kingdom, 1885–1918', *Past and Present*, 32 (1965), pp. 27–56.

Blewett, N., 'Free Fooders, Balfourites, Whole Hoggers. Factionalism Within the Unionist Party, 1906–10', *Historical Journal*, 11 (1968), pp. 95–124.

Boyle, T., 'The Formation of Campbell-Bannerman's Government in December 1905: A Memorandum by J. A. Spender', *Bulletin of the Institute of Historical Research*, 45 (1972), pp. 283–302.

Brooks, D., 'Lloyd George, For and Against', *Historical Journal*, 24 (1981), pp. 74–86.

Brown, J., 'Attercliffe, 1894: How One Local Liberal Party Failed to Meet the Challenge of Labour', *Journal of British Studies*, 14 (1975), pp. 48–77.

Chadwick, M. E. J., 'The Role of Redistribution in the Making of the Third Reform Act', *Historical Journal*, 19 (1976), pp. 665–83.

Clarke, P., 'The End of Laissez Faire and the Politics of Cotton', *Historical Journal*, 15 (1972), pp. 493–512.

Clarke, P., 'The electoral position of the Liberal and Labour parties, 1910–1914', *English Historical Review*, 90 (1975), pp. 828–36.

Clarke, P., 'Liberals, Labour and the Franchise', *English Historical Review*, 92 (1977), pp. 582–90.

Clarke, P. F., 'The Progressive Movement in England', *Transactions of the Royal Historical Society*, 24 (1974), pp. 159–81.

Coetzee, F., 'Pressure Groups, Tory Businessmen, and the Aura of Political Corruption Before the First World War', *Historical Journal*, 29 (1986), pp. 833–52.

David, E., 'The Liberal Party Divided, 1916–1918', *Historical Journal*, 13 (1970), pp. 509–33.

Douglas, R., 'The background to the "Coupon" election agreements', *English Historical Review*, 86 (1971), pp. 318–36.

Dowse, R. E., 'The Entry of the Liberals into the Labour Party, 1910–1920', *Yorkshire Bulletin of Economic and Social Research*, 13 (1961), pp. 77–87.

Dunne, T., '*La trahison des clercs*: British intellectuals and the first home-rule crisis', *Irish Historical Studies*, 23 (1982–3), pp. 134–73.

Emy, H. V., 'The Impact of Financial Policy on English Party Politics Before 1914', *English Historical Review*, 15 (1972), pp. 103–31.

Fair, J. D., 'The Second Labour Government and the Politics of Electoral Reform 1929–31', *Albion*, 13 (1981), pp. 276–301.

Fraser, P., 'The Liberal Unionist Alliance: Chamberlain, Hartington, and the Conservatives 1886–1904', *English Historical Review*, 77 (1962), pp. 53–78.

Fraser, P., 'British War Policy and the Crisis of Liberalism in May 1915', *Journal of Modern History*, 54 (1982), pp. 1–26.

Fry, M., 'Political Change in Britain, August 1914 to December 1916: Lloyd George Replaces Asquith: The Issues Underlying the Drama', *Historical Journal*, 31 (1988), pp. 609–27.

Gilbert, B. B., 'David Lloyd George and the Great Marconi Scandal', *Historical Research*, 62 (1989), pp. 295–317.

Gilbert, B. B., 'David Lloyd George: The Reform of British Landholding and the Budget of 1914', *Historical Journal*, 21 (1978), pp. 117–41.

Gilbert, B. B., 'Lloyd George and the Historians', *Albion*, 2 (1979), pp. 74–86.

Glaser, J. F., 'English Nonconformity and the decline of Liberalism', *American Historical Review*, 63 (1957–8), pp. 352–63.

Gooch, J., 'The Maurice Debate 1918', *Journal of Contemporary History*, 3 (1968), pp. 211–28.

Goodman, G. L., 'Liberal Unionism: The Revolt of the Whigs', *Victorian Studies*, 3 (1959–60), pp. 173–89.

Green, E. H. H., 'The Strange Death of Tory England', *Twentieth Century British History*, 2 (1991), pp. 67–87.

Griffiths, P. C., 'The Caucus and the Liberal Party in 1886', *History*, 61 (1976), pp. 183–97.

Gutzke, D. W., 'Rosebery and Ireland, 1898–1903: A Reappraisal', *Bulletin of the Institute of Historical Research*, 53 (1980), pp. 88–98.

Hamer, D. A., 'The Irish Question and Liberal Politics, 1886–1894', *Historical Journal*, 12 (1969), pp. 511–32.

Hanak, H., 'The Union of Democratic Control During the First World War', *Bulletin of the Institute of Historical Research*, 36 (1963), pp. 168–80.

Hart, M., 'The Liberals, the War and the Franchise', *English Historical Review*, 97 (1982), pp. 820–32.

Hay, R., 'Employers and social policy in Britain: the evolution of welfare legislation, 1905–14', *Social History*, 2 (1977), pp. 435–55.

Hazlehurst, C., 'Asquith as Prime Minister, 1908–16', *English Historical Review*, 85 (1970), pp. 502–31.

Hepburn, A. C., 'The Irish Council Bill and the Fall of Sir Antony MacDonnell', *Irish Historical Studies*, 17 (1970–1), pp. 470–98.

Heyck, T. W., 'Home Rule, Radicalism and the Liberal Party, 1886–1895', *Journal of British Studies*, 13 (1974), pp. 66–91.

Howarth, J., 'The Liberal Revival in Northamptonshire, 1880–1895: A Case Study in Late Nineteenth Century Elections', *Historical Journal*, 12 (1969), pp. 78–118.

Howe, J., 'Liberals, Lib-Labs and Independent Labour in North Gloucestershire, 1890–1914', *Midland History*, 11 (1986), pp. 117–37.

Howkins, A., 'Edwardian Liberalism and Industrial Unrest: A Class View of the Decline of Liberalism', *History Workshop*, 4 (1977), pp. 143–61.

Hunter, J., 'The Politics of Highland Land Reform, 1873–1895', *Scottish Historical Review*, 53 (1974), pp. 45–68.

Jalland, P., 'A Liberal Chief Secretary and the Irish Question: Augustine Birrell, 1907–1914', *Historical Journal*, 19 (1976), pp. 421–51.

Lloyd, T. O., 'The Whip as paymaster: Herbert Gladstone and party organisation', *English Historical Review*, 89 (1974), pp. 785–813.

Lubenow, W. C., 'Irish Home Rule and the Social Basis of the Great Separation in the Liberal Party in 1886', *Historical Journal*, 28 (1985), pp. 125–42.

McEwen, J. M., 'The Coupon Election of 1918 and Unionist Members of Parliament', *Journal of Modern History*, 34 (1962), pp. 294–306.

McEwen, J. M., 'The Liberal Party and the Irish Question During the First World War', *Journal of British Studies*, 12 (1972), pp. 109–31.

McEwen, J. M., 'The Press and the Fall of Asquith', *Historical Journal*, 21 (1978), pp. 863–83.

McEwen, J. M., 'The Struggle for Mastery in Britain: Lloyd George Versus Asquith, December 1916', *Journal of British Studies*, 18 (1978), pp. 131–56.

McEwen, J. M., 'Lloyd George's Liberal Supporters in December 1916: A Note', *Bulletin of the Institute of Historical Research*, 53 (1980), pp. 265–72.

McGill, B., 'Asquith's Predicament, 1914–1918', *Journal of Modern History*, 39 (1967), pp. 283–303.

McGill, B., 'Lloyd George's Timing of the 1918 Election', *Journal of British Studies*, 14 (1974), pp. 109–24.

McGill, B., 'Glittering Prizes and Party Funds in Perspective, 1882–1931', *Bulletin of the Institute of Historical Research*, 55 (1982), pp. 88–93.

McKibbin, R. I., 'James Ramsay MacDonald and the Problem of the Independence of the Labour Party, 1910–1914', *Journal of Modern History*, 90 (1970), pp. 216–35.

Marrison, A. J., 'Businessmen, Industries and Tariff Reform in Great Britain, 1903–1930', *Business History*, 25 (1983), pp. 148–78.

Matthew, H. C. G., McKibbin, R. I. and Kay, J. A., 'The Franchise Factor in the Rise of the Labour Party', *English Historical Review*, 91 (1976), pp. 723–52.

Morgan, K. O., 'Lloyd George's Premiership: a study in "Prime Ministerial Government" ', *Historical Journal*, 13 (1970), pp. 130–57.

Murray, B., 'The Politics of the "People's Budget" ', *Historical Journal*, 16 (1973), pp. 555–70.

Murray, B. K., 'Lloyd George, the Navy Estimates, and the Inclusion of Rating Relief in the 1914 Budget', *Welsh Historical Review*, 15 (1990), pp. 58–78.

Petter, M., 'The Progressive Alliance', *History*, 58 (1973), pp. 45–59.

Phillips, G. D., 'Lord Willoughby de Broke and the Politics of Radical Toryism, 1909–14', *Journal of British Studies*, 20 (1980), pp. 205–24.

Phillips, G. D., 'The Whig Lords and Liberalism, 1886–1893', *Historical Journalism*, 24 (1981), pp. 167–73.

Powell, D., 'The Liberal Ministries and Labour, 1892–1895', *History*, 68 (1983), pp. 408–26.

Powell, D., 'The New Liberalism and the Rise of Labour, 1886–1906', *Historical Journal*, 29 (1986), pp. 369–93.

Pugh, M., 'Asquith, Bonar Law and the First Coalition', *Historical Journal*, 17 (1974), pp. 813–36.

Pugh, M., 'Yorkshire and the New Liberalism', *Journal of Modern History*, 50 (1978), D 1139–D1155.

Purdue, A. W., 'Arthur Henderson and Liberal, Liberal-Labour and Labour Politics in North-East England 1892–1903', *Northern History*, 11 (1976), pp. 195–217.

Purdue, A. W., 'The Liberal and Labour Parties in North-East Politics, 1900–14: The Struggle for Supremacy', *International Review of Social History*, 26 (1981), pp. 1–24.

Richards, N. J., 'The Education Bill of 1906 and the Decline of Political Nonconformity', *Journal of Ecclesiastical History*, 23 (1972), pp. 49–63.

Roach, J., 'Liberalism and the Victorian Intelligentsia', *Cambridge Historical Journal*, 13 (1957), pp. 58–81.

Roberts, A. W., 'Leeds Liberalism and Late Victorian Politics', *Northern History*, 5 (1970), pp. 131–56.

Robbins, K. G., 'Lord Bryce and the First World War', *Historical Journal*, 10 (1967), pp. 255–77.

Rubinstein, W. D., 'Wealth, Elites and the Class Structure of Modern Britain', *Past & Present*, 76 (1977), pp. 99–126.

Savage, D. C., 'Scottish Politics, 1885–6', *Scottish Historical Review*, 40 (1961), pp. 118–35.

Searle, G. R., 'The Edwardian Liberal Party and Business', *English Historical Review*, 98 (1983), pp. 28–60.

Sheppard, M. G. and Halstead, J., 'Labour's Municipal Election Performance in Provincial England and Wales, 1901–13', *Bulletin of the Society for the Study of Labour History*, 39 (1979), pp. 39–62.

Steele, E. D., 'Gladstone and Ireland', *Irish Historical Studies*, 17 (1970–1), pp. 58–88.

Stephens, H. W., 'Party Realignment in Britain, 1900–1925', *Social Science History*, 6 (1982), pp. 35–66.

Sykes, A., 'The Radical Right and the Crisis of Conservatism Before the First World War', *Historical Journal*, 26 (1983), pp. 661–76.

Tanner, D., 'The Parliamentary Electoral System, the "Fourth" Reform Act and the Rise of Labour in England and Wales', *Bulletin of the Institute of Historical Research*, 56 (1983), pp. 205–19.

Thane, P., 'The Working Class and State "Welfare" in Britain, 1880–1914', *Historical Journal*, 27 (1984), pp. 877–900.

Thompson, J. A., 'The Historians and the Decline of the Liberal Party', *Albion*, 22 (1990), pp. 65–83.

Weiler, P., 'The New Liberalism of L. T. Hobhouse', *Victorian Studies*, 16 (1972–3), pp. 141–61.

Wald, K. D., 'Class and the Vote Before the First World War', *British Journal of Political Science*, 8 (1978), pp. 441–57.

Weinroth, H. S., 'The British Radicals and the Balance of Power, 1902–1914', *Historical Journal*, 13 (1970), pp. 653–82.

Weinroth, H. S., 'Left-Wing Opposition to Naval Armaments in Britain before 1914', *Journal of Contemporary History*, 6 (1971), pp. 93–120.

Weston, C. C., 'The Liberal Leadership and the Lords' Veto, 1907–1910', *Historical Journal*, 11 (1968), pp. 508–37.

White, C. W., '*The Strange Death of Liberal England* in Its Time', *Albion*, 17 (1985), pp. 425–47.

Wilson, T., 'The Coupon and the British General Election of 1918', *Journal of Modern History*, 36 (1964), pp. 28–42.

INDEX

229

Index

Chamberlain, Joseph: as Radical leader, 16, 20, 21; 'Unauthorised Programme', 23–7, 46, 63, 84; and Irish Crisis, 27–8, 29–30, 31, 33, 36; and social policy, 52–3, 80; tariff reform campaign, 58–60, 78; mentioned, 39, 57

Channing, F. A., 33

Chinese Labour, 41, 45, 79

Christian socialism, 61–2, 64

Churchill, Lord Randolph, 28

Churchill, Winston S., 78, 82, 107, 112, 113, 114, 123, 124, 129, 172

citizenship, 5, 166

Clarke, Peter, 65, 103–4, 170

Clifford, John, 64, 84

Clydeside, 154

Coalition Liberals, *see* National Liberal Party

coalition ministries: of Asquith, 124–5, 127–8, 135; of Lloyd George, 125–6, 135, 143, 144–5, 163

Cobden, Richard, 13, 15, 16, 17, 20, 24, 65, 85

Collings, Jesse, 24, 46

conscription, 127, 132, 135

Conservative Party: the nature of its creed, 7; its survival, 10, 168; Liberal defections to, 17, 156; gains from Home Rule crisis, 33; class basis of, 38, 56–7, 105; and middle-class electorate, 98–9; its behaviour during Great War, 123, 126–8, 135; and working-class voters, 155; and 'fusion' with National Liberals, 163–4; its fund-raising methods, 173; views on class, 174–5; attitude towards Liberal Party, 167–8; draws upon Liberal ideas, 170; also mentioned, 3, 78

Constitutional Crisis (1909–11), 86–7, 88–90, 91

Corn Laws, repeal of, 14, 18, 19–20

Cowdray, Lord, 147

Crewe, Earl of, 37

Crooks, Will, 73

Dangerfield, George, 91, 169

Davidson, J. C. C., 173

Davies, David, 128

Davitt, Michael, 22

December 1916 Crisis, 9, 125–6, 128–9

Derby, Lord, 113

Devonshire, 8th Duke of, 23, 24, 25–6, 29

'Diehards', 94–5, 150

diplomatic service, 14–15

Disestablishment, 13, 20, 30

Dissenters, *see* nonconformists

'doormat incident' (August 1917), 126, 151; *see also* Henderson, Arthur

Easter Rising (1916), 124

Edge, Sir William, 161

education: as political question, 23, 25, 31–2; Education Act (1870), 23; Education Bill (1896), 32; Education Act (1902), 39–40, 60, 79, 81; Education Bill (1906), 81

Edward VII, 86

eight-hour day, 53–4

'electoral reform', 9, 131, 150, 161–3, 166, 174

Elibank, Master of, 106

employers liability, 37, 58

Employers' Parliamentary Association, 103

Fabian Society, 53, 54, 63, 65

factory legislation, 24, 25–6

'feudalism', 15, 38, 141, 166

First World War, 99–100, 104, Ch. 7, 166, 171–2

Fisher, Admiral John, 123

foreign policy, 14–15, 48, 93–5

Forster, W. E., 20, 21, 23, 26

Free Trade, 10, 105, 118, 132, 142, 143, 155, 157, 158, 169–70

'fusion' (1920), 163–4, 174

general elections: (1885), 24, 51; (1886), 51; (1892), 34, 51, 111; (1895), 51, 52, 77; (1900) ('Khaki'), 32, 51, 52, 77; (1906), 72, 74–5, 77–80, 167; (January 1910), 2–3, 75, 86, 92, 98, 104, 105, 108, 109, 111, 119; (December 1910), 75, 87, 92, 98, 99, 104, 108, 109, 117; (1918) ('Coupon'), 121–2, 130, 135, 172; (1922), 144, 154; (1923), 143, 146, 152, 155, 157; (1924), 146, 153, 156, 157; (1929), 147, 157, 158, 173

General Strike (1926), 147, 156–7, 159, 160, 171

George V, 87, 160

George, Henry, 46

Germany, 6, 25, 52, 93–4, 102, 130, 132, 163, 168, 169

Gibson, Milner, 21

Gladstone, Herbert, 34, 41, 60, 71, 118, 145, 149

Gladstone, William Ewart: as Liberal Leader, 21–2, 48; and Home Rule crisis of 1885–6, 23–4, 27, 29, 30, 36,

Index

55, 171; and nonconformity, 31, 43, 84; his views on Ireland, 32, 35; heads fourth ministry, 33, 35, 53–4; and Radicalism, 36–7; his economic views, 62, 66; mentioned, 9, 26, 34, 51, 133, 165

Glasier, Bruce, 72

Glasgow, 52, 60, 110, 125, 156

Goschen, George Joachim, 26, 27, 28

Great Depression (1873–96), 5

Great Labour Unrest (1911–14), 2, 112–15, 171

Green, T. H., 13, 65

Greenwood, Hamar, 144

Grey, Earl, 19

Grey, Edward, 34, 37, 78, 88, 94, 129, 133, 145, 147

Guest, Captain Freddie, 161

Haldane, R. B., 34, 53, 78, 92, 123, 124

Hammond, Barbara, 134

Harcourt, William Vernon, 3, 21, 33, 42, 45, 47, 48, 54, 146, 171

Hardie, Keir, 47, 69, 72, 73, 117, 165

Harris, Percy, 155

Hartington, Lord, *see* Devonshire, 8th Duke of

Hayek, F. A., 173

Henderson, Arthur, 47, 69, 125–6, 131, 135, 137, 150, 151

Henderson, Hubert, 158

Herbert, Jesse, 71, 74

Hobhouse, L. T., 65, 66, 67, 101, 114, 150, 152

Hobson, J. A., 65, 66, 67, 153

Holland, Canon Scott, 61

Holt, Richard, 102

'Home Rule All Round', 89–90

honours trafficking, 106–7, 173

Horne, Silvester, 44

House of Lords reform, 33, 36, 47, 96, 108; *see also* Constitutional Crisis

Hughes, Hugh Price, 31, 32, 64

Illingworth, Alfred, 58

imperialism, 7, 169

Independent Labour Party (ILP), 51, 65, 72, 116–17, 135, 152

Independent Liberals, 143

industrial relations, 53, 58

Ireland: its importance in British politics before 1885, 20, 22–3; disestablishment of Church in, 13, 31; coercion in, 142, 144; *see also* Irish Home Rule, Irish Nationalist Party

Irish Home Rule: consequences for Liberal Party of its commitment to, 27–8, 29–37, 38–9, 55–6, 111, 165, 171; First Home Rule Bill, 27, 35–6; Second Home Rule Bill, 33, 36; Liberal reservations over in 1906, 78, 79; during Constitutional Crisis, 88–9; Third Home Rule Bill, 2, 90–1, 94, 95, 96, 123, 124

Irish Nationalist Party, 1, 30–2, 51, 81, 86, 88–90, 91, 92, 119, 124–5; influence over Irish voters on mainland Britain, 30, 34, 125

Isaacs, Rufus (Lord Reading), 106

Kellaway, Frederick, 128

Kemp, George, 105

Kenworthy, Commander, 157

Kenyon, Barnet, 155

Keynes, John Maynard, 152, 153, 158

Kitchener, Lord, 123, 127, 128

Kitson, James, 57

Labouchere, Henry, 29–30, 64

labour exchanges, 97, 109, 112

labour legislation, 53–4

Labour Party: electoral pact with Liberal Party, 3, 71–6; attacks 'feudalism', 46–7, 96; its desire for class representation, 68; and social policy, 80, 99; keeps Liberals in office in 1910, 86, 92; its respectability, 96–7; and nonconformity, 101; relations with Liberals on eve of war, 113–20; and 1918 general election, 121, 130–1; improves its position during war, 125–6, 135–40; its position in the 1920s, 148–52, 153, 157; forms government in 1924, 155–6, 160, 167; and electoral reform, 162; its debt to liberalism, 164, 170; and class, 174

Labour Representation Committee (LRC), *see* Labour Party

Lancashire, 70, 74, 103

Land Campaign (1912–14), 46, 85, 87–8, 90, 97, 108, 167; (1925–6), 141–2, 156

land reform, 12, 13–14, 20, 23, 24–5, 26, 30, 37, 44, 45–7, 85–6, 87–8

land sales, 92, 141

Lansdowne, Lord, 23, 135

Law, Thomas, 39, 45

Lawson, Wilfrid, 20

League of Nations, 157–8

Leeds, 52, 57, 110, 156

Leicester, 57, 110, 155

Lib-Lab Pact (1903), 71–6, 80, 107, 109, 116, 118, 154

Lib-Labs, 69

Liberal Council, 147

231